TEN TEXAS FEUDS

Historians of the Frontier and American West
Richard W. Etulain, Series Editor

10 TEXAS FEUDS

C. L. SONNICHSEN

with a Foreword by Dale L. Walker

Published in Cooperation with the University of New Mexico
Center for the American West

UNIVERSITY OF NEW MEXICO PRESS   ALBUQUERQUE

Library of Congress Cataloging-in-Publication Data

Sonnichsen, C. L. (Charles Leland), 1901–
Ten Texas feuds / C. L. Sonnichsen ; with a foreword by Dale L.
    Walker.—2nd rev.ed.
p. cm.—(Historians of the frontier and American West)
Originally published: 1957. With new introd.
Includes bibliographical references and index.
ISBN 0-8263-0225-4 (pbk. : alk. paper)
1. Vendetta—Texas—History. 2. Violence—Texas—History.
    3. Crime—Texas—History.
4. Texas—History. I. Title. II. Series.

HV6452.T4 S66 2000
976.4—dc21   00-028632

For Mary Augusta
with her Father's Love

Contents

Foreword

> It was so long ago—and there is so little
> we can really know about such things!
> —*C. L. Sonnichsen, "Feud at Mitchell's Bend"*

The story behind *Ten Texas Feuds* began twenty-six years before its publication, on the first day of June, 1931, while the Golden State Limited coasted south out of Tucumcari toward El Paso. Among the passengers peering out of their coach car windows at the scrubby scenery was a handsome, urbane, thirty-year-old Iowa gentleman, more recently a resident of Cambridge, Massachusetts, and what he saw racing past his eyes was a landscape as foreign to him, and as barren, as the craters of the moon. He had a summer teaching job at the Texas College of Mines and Metallurgy in El Paso, had a letter of introduction in his luggage certifying that Charles Leland Sonnichsen had been newly awarded a doctorate in English Philology at Harvard University, and had a dream of returning east, as quickly as possible, to teach "in some ivy-colored college with a minor version of the Potomac flowing nearby."

But except for brief visits, he never went back. He stayed at the College of Mines (subsequently Texas Western College and the University of Texas at El Paso) forty-one years. He rose from associate professor to chairman of the English Department, which post he held an astonishing twenty-seven years; dean of the Graduate School; H. Y. Benedict Professor, and the most memorable and beloved figure in the University's history—an eminence that remains his possession almost a decade after his death.

Sonnichsen stayed, not because he fell in love with the desert country he found so appalling as his train rolled into Alamogordo and El Paso in '31. The love for it came later. He stayed because college teaching positions were scarce in the Great Depression era and because he was appreciated at the college where doctoral degrees were scarcer than jobs and Harvard doctorates unknown. "I was a big fish in a little pond," he would later say.

From the beginning of his sojourn on the border he wanted to write. He had caught the bug as an undergraduate at the University of Minnesota where he contributed humor pieces to the Sigma Delta Chi magazine *Ski-U-Mah*, the first of them in June, 1922. At Harvard he wrote his dissertation on Thomas Sprat, the 17th century clergyman-philosopher, and developed a passion for Samuel Butler (1612–1680), the English satirical poet. But since El Paso was clearly no place for the research and writing of such esoterica, Sonnichsen made a light-year leap to a study of Texas feuds, the idea presented to him by an insurance salesman in whose home the Harvard man was boarding. The salesman had grown up near Houston and told hair-raising tales of warring families and factions, foul murders, bushwhackings, and lynchings, in Civil War and post-bellum times in east Texas. There was even a feud in El Paso's back yard, he said, the Salt War of 1877.

Sonnichsen loved these stories, almost none of which had been chronicled, and set out, inspired by Eugene Manlove Rhodes's dictum that "A faint heart never filled a spade flush," to gather information on them. On weekends and holidays, and times when he served as visiting professor at the University of Texas in Austin (substituting for the redoubtable J. Frank Dobie), he roamed the back country of east and south Texas, bumping over country roads, knocking on doors, interviewing cautious and suspicious old-timers ("a sort of conversational dentistry, every fact wrenched out by the roots") and reading dusty county record books. He became, he said, of the genus *Historianus herbidus*, a grassroots historian, one who "recognizes that the original researcher was an old plainsman lying in a buffalo wallow standing off a bunch of Comanches—and too busy to write anything down."

Twenty years passed before any of the feud work reached book fruition but Sonnichsen, never idle his entire life, found other subjects for other books. He discovered an old saloon-keeper and lawman named William Aurelius "Billy" King in Arizona, and wrote his life as *Billy King's Tombstone* which Caxton of Idaho issued in 1942. He became intrigued by Judge Roy Bean of Langtry, Texas, and wrote a book on him which Macmillan of New York published in 1943. In 1949, he began a five-month, 15,000-mile trip through thirteen Western states studying the cattle business under a University of Oklahoma grant, and wrote *Cowboys and Cattle Kings*. In 1948, a few months before the cattle investigation, Sonnichsen sent the Oklahoma Press a 700-page manuscript on his Texas feuds, nineteen of them, brightly written, humorously told, vastly documented. The press liked the book but wanted it shorter. He resisted and tried a New York literary agent who found an interested editor at Harper & Brothers. The Harper editor liked the book too but also wanted it cut, drastically.

This time Sonnichsen cut it and the book appeared from Harper's in 1951 as *I'll Die Before I'll Run* (from the Smoky Mountain ballad, "Wake up, wake up, darlin' Cory! / And go get me my gun. / I ain't no hand for trouble, / But I'll die before I'll run.")

In his surgery on the manuscript, he slyly and wisely removed ten stories, some of the best of what he called Texas "broils": the Regulators and Moderators war in Shelby County; Miss Sue Pinckney of Hempstead who wrote Victorian drawing-room novels and lived through a horrendous feud in which two of her beloved brothers were killed; Jim Miller of Pecos who kept a tally of his murders on a notch-stick; Bill Mitchell, alias "Baldy Russell," and the bloody Mitchell-Truitt business in Hood County in 1874–75; the Laredo Election Riot; and the El Paso Salt War, among them.

Ten Texas Feuds went to the University of New Mexico Press which in 1955 had published *Alias Billy the Kid*, Sonnichsen's collaborative effort about the Western Lazarus Ollie L. "Brushy Bill" Roberts of Hico, Texas. This man claimed Billy did not die from a Pat Garrett bullet in 1881, but escaped and lived to be over ninety years old. Roberts said he was Billy and had proof of it. The controversial book has been in print forty-five years.

New Mexico Press originally issued *Ten Texas Feuds* in 1957 and this new printing of one of the most sought after of Sonnichsen's twenty-seven books, attests to the durability of his grassroots research.

Everybody called him "Doc," something he countenanced only because it was bestowed on him by hard-rock mining engineers too early in his career, and became too widespread, to change. He had a legendary conviviality and generosity, a beautiful tenor singing voice, and an unrivaled presence as a public speaker, playing an audience with virtuosity. He made people laugh and think, think and laugh.

He remained handsome, urbane, and witty to the end, the eyes behind his old-fashioned rimless spectacles agleam with new ideas for new books.

His last public appearance was as a panelist at the annual Western Writers of America convention in Oklahoma City in June, 1991, where he spoke eloquently on "The Future of Western Fiction."

A few days after he returned to Tucson from the convention, on June 29, 1991, he died quickly and quietly at age 89.

Dale L. Walker
El Paso, Texas
April 20, 2000

Wake up, wake up, darlin' Cory,
And go get me my gun.
I ain't no hand for trouble,
But I'll die before I'll run.

—Smoky Mountain Ballad

Prologue to Trouble

You are sitting in a comfortable chair with a little reading time on your hands before you have to go about your business. You know where your next meal is coming from, and you are not expecting to be shot at before bedtime. The fields and towns of a prosperous and peaceful America surround you. There may be violence and death in other countries, but not here. If you can get along with your wife and stay off the highways on the Fourth of July, you are pretty safe. So what has a book about Texas feuds to do with you?

Well, with a few changes in the circumstances, you might be in it. The men who fought these battles were mostly pretty good people, not much different from the rest of us. They wanted to make a living and enjoy their families and walk the earth with some dignity. In the words of the old song, they were "no hands for trouble," but sometimes a man has to fight; and when he has to, he will.

You can test this for yourself. Suppose you lived in bad times in a hard country and the law would not or could not help you. What would you do if outlaws (including some of your neighbors) had stolen half your cows and all your best horses, and had "hoorawed" you as you crouched impotently behind your corral fence, dodging their bullets? Would you or wouldn't you join the vigilance committee your friends had organized to eliminate those thieves and murderers? And if the gang was big enough and strong enough to make a stand and shoot it out, would you or wouldn't you stay and fight?

You know the answer.

In "killing times" people have these choices to make, like it or not. For a feud is not necessarily the hillbilly shooting match that many people think it is, beginning in a quarrel about a jug of moonshine and ending in slaughter for slaughter's sake. It can start with intolerable conditions, grievances past bearing, or unforgivable assaults on personal or family dignity. Nobody feuds for fun. Your life or your livelihood is in danger; your county is being exploited by a band of rascals; your brother has been ambushed, and the jury, which knows better, has ruled that the rascal who killed him acted in self-defense. What are you going to do about it?

Your ancestors knew what to do. They laid down the rules, and there hasn't been much change in them for several thousand years. The earliest form of criminal law known to our race was feud law— an eye for an eye and a tooth for a tooth.[1] Revenge was a duty which a kinsman could not shirk. The manslayer must be slain.

Only day before yesterday, as history goes, did it become possible for an Englishman to pay money *(wergild)* to the avenger as a substitute for blood.[2] Only yesterday, with the coming of the Normans, did murder become a crime against the state and not against the kindred of the victim.[3] Even today, many people believe in settling their differences man to man, with a gun, if necessary, when great wrongs have been done them.

Such people hold that if a man runs off with your wife, it is better and more manly to shoot him than to have him indicted. Examine your thoughts as you read these words; you may find yourself agreeing.

If you think that all the feuding blood belongs to the mountaineers and the cowboys, just read the morning paper. Every day the news reminds us that the instinct for getting even hasn't been bred out of us. The law of the cave and the forest has not been repealed, just momentarily set aside. We go back to it, as a man takes a bucket and goes after drinking water when the kitchen tap fails to function. For "Lynch law is merely a reversion to the ways of primeval men."[4]

It can happen again. A disastrous war and a period of painful reconstruction will bring on a rash of feuds. We hope and pray that the bombs may never fall on our country, that the invader may never come. But if the worst happens, if we ever have to dig out from under the rubble, destroy the collaborationists, and patch up a ruined economy, Lynch Law will prevail again. There will be abuses and hatreds and retaliations and counter-retaliations until we can trust the law and the courts once more.

You won't find a better laboratory for the study of feuds than the State of Texas. From the days of settlement, Texans have had more compulsion to fight than most people, more pistols and rifles to fight with, more opportunities and excuses for slaughtering each other.

The mere fact that Texas was a frontier state for so long accounts for a good deal of the trouble. The roughest sort of people found refuge there in the early days, and sometimes the only way the good settlers could deal with them was to resort to "folk justice," otherwise known as Lynch Law.[5] Many of these settlers were Southerners, and they brought their own code of honor with them: a code which taught every man to right his own wrongs, no matter what the teachings of Jesus or the law of the land said about it.[6] Put the Code of the Frontier beside the Code of the Southerner, and you have the groundwork for conflict.

Add to that the almost unbelievable corruption and villainy which had to be rooted out in the bad times both before and after the Civil War, and you can see why these troubles had to be. For many a Texan it was simply a case of kill or be killed. And when the killing got out of hand, there was a feud situation.

If trouble had to come, the people of Texas were well prepared for it. Little boys went armed to school. Preachers sometimes carried pistols into the pulpit with them. Most Texas women could shoot, and shoot straight. Everybody killed game, and many had to kill Indians. The best people sincerely regretted the bloodshed which went on around them, but they had to get used to it.

Thieving and outlawry started the first Texas feud, the War of the Regulators and Moderators, in the 1840's; and the pattern laid down in that terrible outbreak became standard. The typical Texas feud was a Regulator or "mob" feud, but there were vendettas of other types too. After the war, in areas where Yankee soldiers and carpetbaggers were common, hatreds born of the war itself started the shooting. In the cattle-and-cotton country between San Antonio and Houston, the proud old Southern families developed some bitter feuds among kin-folks. The citizens of the Lower Rio Grande Valley have fought for more than a hundred years over politics. West of a line drawn between Austin and Dallas, then on the edge of civilization, outlaws ran rampant and mob feuds were the rule.

Often more than one cause operated to bring angry men together. The killing at Columbus started with cattle trouble but ended in a family-style feud.[7] Two of the broils described in this book pitted one racial group against another: Germans against "Americans" in Mason County in 1875; Mexicans against "Gringos" at El Paso in 1877.

In most cases, if you traced the conflict back to its beginning, you would find that somebody had taken something that did not belong to him. This was particularly true in the sixties, seventies, and eighties, when conditions in Texas were at their worst. The business of stealing and murdering was managed by well organized gangs of desperadoes who carried off their depredations with a high hand. As a result, citizens' committees, minutemen, whitecaps, and mobs sprouted and flourished everywhere.

What made it all so difficult and distressing was the way good people and bad people got mixed up together. At the start, a vigilance committee might enroll only the best citizens; but as time went on, bad men crept into the ranks. Inevitably these tough birds made mistakes and hurt or scared good people, who immediately took the other side. In the end there was complete confusion and hell to pay.

Before the Texas Rangers began to get the upper hand (about 1883), there was much heated discussion in the Texas papers of the question: To Hang or Not To Hang. One editor would react with horror against a multiple killing, declaring that the killers were "as bad as the men who were ushered into eternity by them, and no effort should be spared to bring such butchers to the punishment the law justifies in such cases."[8]

In contrast, another columnist would greet with cheers the news of a dead horse thief and recommend a little hanging in his own community. ". . . if the police are not equal to the task, we hope a vigilance committee will be formed by our citizens."[9]

If you want a sample of the way these arguments went, listen to old Buck Barry, Ranger and Indian fighter, who blew up in the columns of the Austin *Statesman* in 1874:

"In reply to your editorial of July 2, this mob law you say is to be regretted; but who of us is to regret it? Shall it be those composing the mob, *as you call it,* who have stood for four or more years as a lamb before the butcher, tied and gagged (by those who robbed them of their political rights), and saw the last cow that gave their children milk driven off, their women raped and their neighbors killed. . . . I would call you all miscreants and cowards were you to stand by and witness your neighbor robbed, his life taken, his women ravished, and not use your manly strength to avenge his wrongs in the most certain way to expedite justice."[10]

You have to sympathize with a man as earnest as Buck Barry, but you can't escape the fact, either, that it was this philosophy that started the feuds and kept them going.

There must have been thousands of Buck Barrys scattered around to produce the numerous vendettas that Texans have lived through since the 1840's. At least a hundred of them might be totted up if the facts were all known. Probably no one could find out about all the little feuds that happened in out-of-the-way places. The truth about them is surprisingly hard to get at.

A real man-sized feud takes about fifty years to cool off, and by that time almost everybody involved in it is beyond the reach of interviews. The few who remain alive would rather not talk, remembering a day when men paid with their lives for opening their mouths.

In most feuding districts, also, you will run into the theory that if everybody keeps quiet the feud may be "lived down."

All this makes life difficult for a feud collector, and he is further frustrated by the fact that every man with a story to tell insists that his version is the only true one, and that all who disagree should be forcibly corrected.

In spite of all difficulties, however, these stories should be told. They have played an important part in our history. They follow a pattern which is likely to repeat itself in times of great stress. They give a convincing if unflattering demonstration of the power and persistence of our folkways. And they show the working out of primitive tendencies which are latent in all of us.

"Vengeance is Mine!" saith the Lord. But in and out of Texas He has always had plenty of help.

WHEN TEXAS
WAS YOUNG

His heritage had been the young earth, with its skies, its waters, and its winds, its huge primeval forests, and plains throwing out their broad breasts to the sun—and living things that moved and were articulate beneath God's eye—and what cared he for the authority of men.

C. W. Webber, "Jack Long; or the Shot in the Eye," from *Tales of the Southern Border*.

1. The War of the Regulators and Moderators

ROGUE'S
PARADISE

Killing was no novelty to Charley Jackson, and he felt nothing but an eagerness to get on with the job as he came charging with long strides into Shelbyville. In 1840 the place was no more than a frontier log hamlet, and it took only a few steps to bring him to the center of town.

He had timed it right. Joseph Goodbread was sitting on the hitching rack talking to a friend. They were relaxed and comfortable, and the morning sun was warming their backs. They cast only a brief glance at Jackson as he hurried up with his gun over his shoulder and stopped in front of them, feet planted wide, eyes sparkling, teeth showing in what people sometimes mistook too late for a smile.

Jackson swung the rifle down from his shoulder and held it under his arm, the muzzle pointed at Goodbread's stomach. With his left hand he reached into his pocket and pulled out a folded piece of paper.

"Goodbread," he snapped, "here is your letter. I am going to answer it."

Goodbread sat still. He seemed to be struggling to understand what was happening. At last he said mildly, "Jackson, I am unarmed."

"So much the better. Get up on your feet."

"Charley, I was mad when I wrote that letter. I was too hasty."

"Stand up."

"I didn't mean to do any more than scare you a little, Charley. . . ."

"Stand up."

Slowly, as if compelled, Goodbread stood. When he was almost erect, Jackson shot him, and he fell, struggling.

Jackson watched till he was sure that he was dead. Then he looked around at the handful of men who had come into the dusty street at the sound of the shot. "If there are no more of Goodbread's damned rascals in town, bring on your sheriff," he said.[1]

That was the way the first and worst of the great Texas feuds began. History calls it the War of the Regulators and Moderators, and it went on and on until it seemed that nothing could stop it.

Two men emerge from its bloody annals as the progenitors of a long line of ruthless chieftains in the troubles which stained the records of Texas for the next half-century. One was Charles W. Jackson. The other was his successor, Watt Moorman—a man even more dangerous than Jackson.

To understand what made these leaders and gave them their opportunity, we need to look at the great wilderness, the lonely cabins, and the weedy little towns where the feud was hatched.

The country was big and wild. Mile after mile the oaks and hickories, sassafras and sweet gum, crowded together, broken here and there by a belt of pine trees. There were pecan groves in the bottoms, and vast canebrakes. In places the woods clotted into enormous thickets where an army could have disappeared.

Through the midst of this primeval forest ran a broad belt of red clay—the Redlands. It was rich and fertile land, full of centuries of stored sunshine, looking after a sharp rain almost as red as blood.

The scattered clearings of the pioneers were swallowed up in the timber except where the Royal Road of the King of Spain (only an ordinary wagon track, in spite of its name) came out of Louisiana and wound through the woods to Nacogdoches where the Spaniards had set up a *presidio* and mission long before. Along this road were occasional settlements. Near the Sabine River, forty or fifty miles east of Nacogdoches, there were more. A few villages—Teneha, Shelbyville, San Augustine—were beginning the long struggle which makes civilized communities out of frontier outposts.

The people were American pioneers from Kentucky, Louisiana,

Tennessee, Arkansas. They had begun to filter in as early as 1822, when settlement was still unauthorized, and by 1827 enough of them had come to organize the Teneha municipality, which stretched north and south along the eastern border of the district for almost a hundred miles.[2]

The old settlers intermarried and possessed the land, living a primitive life, owning few slaves, raising small crops and large droves of hogs, sharing what they had with strangers, and managing their own affairs. They had little to do with laws, taxes, elections, and other manifestations of formal government, but every man stood up for his own rights and helped his kinfolks when they needed help.

Some of them were very rough customers. Up on McFaddin Creek, in the northern part of Shelby County, was a nest of them. Old Sam McFaddin was the patriarch. He had three tough sons, William, Bailey, and Rufus. Nearby lived the Stricklands—four boys named Jim, Amos, Henry, and Dave, who were notorious even in that time and place. "Tiger Jim" Strickland was probably the worst of the lot. He was bad to look at—yellow cheeked and expressionless. His face did not change even when he gave forth his curious grunting laugh. He lived by stealing and occasional trading, and he did not mind liquidating a man in the course of earning his livelihood.

Some thought that the second brother, Henry, was even worse than Jim. He was certainly worse about fighting. He was always in some sort of trouble, though he seemed to have bad luck when he got down to serious battling. He was a dark, red-faced man with a hard eye and a bullying manner.

Bill McFaddin was of the same stripe as the Stricklands and had earned the nickname of "Buckskin Bill."[3]

The McFaddins and the Stricklands and their friends were old residents. The men who lined up against them were apt to be newcomers, though the lines were not strictly drawn. Hence there is some color for the idea that the feud was a quarrel between the old and the new settlers. It was not as simple as that, of course. In troubles of this sort, after a while, both factions become strangely assorted and it is impossible to disentangle the right from the wrong on either side.

The worst fault of the old residents seems to have been a willingness to put up with desperadoes, and even to protect them; but perhaps they had little choice under the circumstances. Of one thing we may be sure. Few of them were Tiger Jims or Buckskin Bills.

The thing that is hardest for us to grasp now is the extent of the evil which flourished and abounded under those oaks and pines. Hell itself could hardly have promoted a better crop of wickedness. The Sabine River was partly to blame. From 1807 to 1819 this meandering stream was the boundary of the Neutral Ground which the United States and Spain agreed that neither should claim. So the region became a sanctuary for many desperate characters from both countries.

When the boundary was established, the Sabine was still the line between two nations, offering escape in either direction to sinful men, and the land on both side of the river continued to be a refuge for an astonishing assortment of crooks, desperadoes, and assorted fugitives from justice. Good people found it necessary to be very courageous and very cautious if they expected to stay in the country and live.

Fear became a part of every man's daily life, and secrecy came to be as natural—and as necessary—as breathing.

Things grew worse in the thirties after the break-up of the great Murrell Conspiracy. This was an incredible but all-too-real plot to turn the whole southwestern portion of the then United States over to a gang of freed slaves and unscrupulous hoodlums. It was no outlaw's pipe dream either. Murrell had the men and the means to carry out his nefarious plans. His organization was enormous. Before he could organize his big strike, however, his luck ran out. In 1834 he was apprehended and sent to prison, and before the next year was finished, his gang was scattered.[4]

This was a good thing for the rest of the country, but it was hard on Texas. Murrell's men concentrated on the border as soon as their former haunts became unsafe.

About this time, probably as an aftereffect of the shock of the Murrell exposure, a wave of ruthless righteousness struck the South and many communities rose up and expelled the shady characters they had been tolerating. All the exiles headed for Texas—where else could they go?—and the bankrupt law of 1841 brought a few more. The result was a gathering of undesirable citizens which brought the familiar saying, "Hell in Texas," closer to realization than it had ever been before or has ever been since.

Before long the rogues had established a fraternity on the Murrell model. With terrible oaths they swore each other to secrecy and obedience. To betray the brotherhood was certain and sudden death. On the other hand, nonmembers were to be deceived and misled without scruple. What made it all so completely and brutally effective was the fact that the band included some of the most influential and outwardly respectable people in the country.

Business men, planters, cattlemen were members. So were judges and officers of the law. Samuel A. Hammett (whose pen name was Philip Paxton) visited Texas in the early 1850's and found ample evidence that the inhuman fraternity was still alive. He told of a "cordon of robber police" reinforced by *"judges, lawyers, clergymen, militia officers of high rank,* planters, merchants, etc.," who "recognized each other by certain signs and the correspondence between the leaders was conducted in cipher."[5]

Justice was a farce. If the judge happened to be honest, the jury could be tied up, witnesses killed or intimidated, and the whole body of law-abiding men overawed. And there was nothing anybody could do about it. "There is no possibility of improvement," Hammett reported, "for the moment the clan have obtained and exhibited a supremacy in any county, from that instant they will increase in numbers and boldness, until it is certain death to any who may attempt to prosecute them, or even mention their misdeeds."

One shudders to imagine what evil possibilities a good man faced in those terrible times. He could not even tell who his enemies were. His nearest neighbor, likable and friendly and a sympathetic listener, might be a member of the secret band, ready to relay his incautious remarks to headquarters and shoot him from ambush if word came from above to do so. His property was not safe, and might disappear at any time. If he had a few dollars, he kept the fact carefully to himself and pretended to be as poor as the rest of the neighborhood, for there were men about, and not just a few of them, who would cut a throat for pennies.

The crooks had several favorite rackets.[6] They were horse thieves without fear and beyond reproach. They could also boast of a number of gentlemanly counterfeiters like the one mentioned by historian Noah Smithwick. This one was looked on as a public benefactor because he furnished the only currency available and always replated his coins when the silver began to wear thin.[7] And then there was the land-scrip racket.

Nearly everybody was mixed up in land graft.[8] Smithwick says it started as early as 1829 when a Commissioner of the Mexican Land Office came to Nacogdoches, got into trouble, and was put in jail. He left all his papers, including a batch of land titles already stamped and sealed with only the property owner's name lacking, to be taken over by the gang.

The really impressive stealing, however, began in 1838 when the newly established Texas Land Office began granting "headrights" to citizens who had been in Texas before or during the revolution. These headrights, good for a tract of land, could be sold or transferred, and in this fact the "land pirates" found a glittering opportunity. A tremendous traffic in bogus certificates sprang up, in which county officials were apt to be the chief promoters.

Dr. Levi Ashcroft, who came to the Teneha District from North Carolina in 1838 and left an unpublished account of the troubles, declares that fake land certificates were turned out in such quantities that they "were frequently pawned in grog shops for a dozen drinks" —and whiskey was cheap in those days.

Shelby County, in the heart of the Teneha municipality, was the acknowledged focal point of all this underhanded meanness. Not that other parts of Texas were innocent. It was just that Shelby County, haunted by thieves and gangsters from the very earliest times, had a head start over other parts of the Republic in the concoction of villainy.

At long last, in 1840, the odor of these scandals penetrated to the seat of government, and the Texan Congress turned loose a board of Traveling Land Commissioners who were to validate and certify the land titles in each county. In due time this step brought some sort of order out of chaos, but the district paid heavily in trouble and blood, and it was a long, weary process.

The most heartless part of the gang's business was its traffic in Negroes. It worked something like this:

Some of the "boys" would cross the river into Louisiana and pick up a few slaves that they had spotted, running them back into Texas or up into Arkansas. If they had a chance at a couple of "thousand-dollar niggers" in their own neighborhood, they would steal them and run them over into Louisiana. Just before the Regulators and Moderators started killing each other, a notorious incident of this kind took place.

Over toward Nachitoches, across the Louisiana border, lived a family of mixed blood composed of an old Frenchman, his mulatto wife, and their quadroon children, including several grown daughters. Among their neighbors was a group of vicious men named Yoakum —possible survivors of the Murrell gang. It occurred to the Yoakums that here was a good thing going to waste. They assembled a group of friends, killed the old Frenchman, burned his body on a heap of logs, herded his family across the Sabine, and secreted them near the San Augustine road while they celebrated by getting good and drunk.

One of the girls slipped away and luckily reached the house of a brave Texan named David Renfro. He was sympathetic, and with some of his neighbors succeeded in driving the Yoakums off. What happened to the girl and her kinfolks after that, the record does not say, but the Yoakums drifted south and went on to construct a wonderful career of villainy in other parts of the piney woods country.[9]

A little of this sort of thing goes a long way in a pioneer region where the old settlers are in the habit of attending to offenders personally. Before long the time came when the old settlers had had enough.

THE BIRTH
OF THE
REGULATORS

This brings us to the year 1840 and to the emergence of Charles W. Jackson as a leader, a character out of a story-book who happened to be born into real life.[10]

Jackson was a desperate and violent man with a long record of wild encounters and narrow escapes behind him when he came to Texas. Like so many outlaw leaders, however, he had a powerful personality and an engaging way. Eph Daggett, a prominent Regulator who knew him well, says, "He was always sober, had a mouthful of teeth, wore a smiling countenance, and always laughed when he wanted to or had an intention to fight."

Dr. Levi Ashcroft adds that his equipment included "a reckless bearing, and a certain degree of rough eloquence, or rather volubility," and that he was "eminently fitted to become the leader of a lawless mob."

Some facts about his earlier career were notorious in his lifetime. He was a Kentuckian of little education who was able to rise in the world by sheer push. Eventually he became a steamboat captain on the Red River and on the Mississippi. Trouble dogged his steps and he never went out of his way to avoid it.

He was credited with killing one merchant and wounding another after a big disagreement in Alexandria, Louisiana. The whole country was roused to indignation and a price of thirty thousand dollars was placed on his head. Jackson continued to steam up and down the rivers in spite of the wrath of his fellow citizens. Finally, in complete exasperation, the Alexandrians got hold of a cannon and prepared to blast him off the river next time he passed their landing.

Jackson heard of it, however, and got a cannon of his own. On his next trip he stopped below town while he sent word to the cannoneers that he was ready for them and would burn their city about their ears if they bothered him.

They didn't bother him. But his troubles were just beginning. Another attempt to arrest him was made when he returned to New Orleans, but he was surrounded, as usual, by a gang of men as tough as himself who helped him fight his way out.

He sold his steamboat interests and lay low for a while at Shreveport, but he was never safe. That thirty-thousand-dollar reward hung over him like a guillotine blade, and he took every step in peril.

As a result of one well-timed scheme, he was seized at the steamboat landing and hustled aboard a boat headed for Alexandria. Again he escaped (perhaps with the connivance of the captain) by jumping overboard after pretending to undress and go to bed. He came near drowning, but his last desperate efforts brought him to shore and he got back to Shreveport.

A little later he was attacked by another money-hungry character with the suggestive name of Maulheel Johnson. Maulheel came off second best, lost several of his men, and had to swim for his own life, but the episode convinced Jackson that he had better move to Texas. He settled in the Shelbyville neighborhood some time in the late thirties, made friends (Daggett says he "made friends or enemies wherever he went"), and even had the nerve to run for Congress.

It was the frustration of his political hopes that finally made an embittered man out of Jackson. After all these years of fighting off his persecutors and battling for his life, defeat in an election soured him. He grew more and more convinced that the world had wronged him and that he had a long score to settle.

Probably he was beaten because he was a newcomer and had not taken pains to win the confidence of the old settlers, but he preferred to think that he was a victim of a conspiracy. He laid all his new troubles at the door of the ring which had been getting rich off fake land certificates, and in particular he blamed Sam Todd, who was thought to be the boss.[11] There is not much doubt that Jackson would have joined the ring and shared in the graft if he could have muscled in, but the election closed that door.

And that was how Charley Jackson came to be filled with righteous wrath at the swindlers who were having their own way in the county. Shortly after his defeat a fresh batch of fraudulent titles began to circulate, and his resentment rose so far that he began writing letters— to New Orleans, to Houston, to Austin—declaiming against the ring of county officers.

People did not like that. Once, Jackson was shot at as he was coming home through the woods. A little later he got a letter. It was signed by Joseph Goodbread, a prominent member of the "ins," related by marriage to Sam Todd. The letter said that Jackson had better stop minding other people's business or he would get himself killed.

This was in the summer of 1840. Eph Daggett was passing Jackson's house at the time the letter arrived, and Jackson called him in for consultation. What, he wanted to know, was the best thing to do?

"You are a better judge of that than I am," said Daggett with proper caution.

Mrs. Jackson interposed. "You have had to kill rascals all your life, and you might as well kill a few more before they will let you alone."

Daggett remembered long after how "Jackson raised the letter up in both hands and swore he would kill Goodbread on first sight if nothing prevented, and told me to tell Goodbread nothing if I saw him or any of his friends as I went home through Shelbyville. I assured him I should not tell Goodbread, or any other person as it was no business of mine. I told him that I had had a difficulty with Goodbread and had slapped his cheeks with the same knife he fetched to Texas and had succeeded in scaring him into terms and we had then agreed to drop our differences.

" 'When I see him I may scare him, but it will be a damned quick scare. He shan't live, he shan't,' said Jackson."

Even then Jackson's murderous impulse might have burned itself out if a third party had not developed an interest in stirring up trouble. This was Alfred George, later to be known as Sheriff George, a politician who was having slave trouble. In 1839 he had sold a Negro to Goodbread, and had accepted in payment ten headright certificates each worth "a league and a labor" of land (5,605 acres). The certificates were fraudulent.[12] Both men may have expected, as many people did, that such spurious titles would eventually be made good, since it would be easier to validate them than to run a lot of unwilling Texans off the land and start over.

The Board of Land Commissioners put a spoke in their wheel, however, when they met in Shelbyville in July, 1840, and rejected a multitude of fake certificates, including the ones transferred to George in payment for his Negro.

Left with neither acres nor African, George determined to undo his bargain. Somehow he got possession of the Negro and hid him. After a fruitless search, Goodbread got even by making the whole transaction public.

This worried George considerably. It was almost time for elections and, as a candidate for the office of sheriff, any reflections on his character were, to say the least, inconvenient. To put a stop to Goodbread's tale-telling, he hatched up a malicious scheme, and it worked.

He knew that there was bad feeling between Goodbread and Jackson. He therefore went to Jackson and informed him that Goodbread was threatening to shoot him down like a dog the next time they met. Jackson flared up and said he would see about that, and George promised to help him. Next time Goodbread came to Shelbyville, George sent out the word. Jackson came to town with his rifle on his shoulder, and they had their meeting.

George and Jackson worked hand-in-hand after the killing. Jackson was brought before a justice of the peace after his arrest and freed on a bond of two hundred dollars, pledged to appear at the next session of court.

At the proper time he was indicted, probably to his surprise, and preparations were made to try him. These preparations soon became alarmingly energetic, and Jackson told George they were going to have to do something about it. George thought it over and came up with a solution.

He went to the county officials and complained that the jail was insecure—that he could not be responsible for the safety of his prisoner. The officials accommodatingly agreed to change the venue of the case to an adjoining county. Armed with his authorization, George departed with his charge, but as soon as they were out of sight of the courthouse he simply turned his man loose.

From that point on, Jackson needed no help from George or any man. He gathered about him a band who called themselves the Regulators, and prepared to defy any and all opposition.

A word has to be said here about the moral justification, if any, for the organization of such bands as this. Dozens—possibly hundreds—of them came into being before the bad times were over in Texas. They were a standard part of the pattern of frontier feuds.

One might say, and not be far wide of the truth, that Jackson organized his little army in order to escape punishment for his crimes. On the other hand it might be just as true that Jackson was sick and tired of the rascality in the county and decided that he was the man to put a stop to it. The chief argument in favor of this latter view is the fact that rascality was actually heaped up and running over in the region. One cannot ignore, either, the presence of many excellent citizens among the Regulators. Finally, there can be no doubt that their first efforts were directed at killing or running off some very bad citizens.

The mixture of good and evil in these affairs is what makes them so hard to discuss in terms of right and wrong. It is safe to say, however, that the history of these "mob" feuds in Texas proves repeatedly that it takes a strong and willful character like Jackson to organize a vigilante group, and that in the early stages he is likely to get his support from the best men in his community.

In Shelby County it was cattle stealing which gave Jackson his excuse for calling his friends and neighbors together, and that excuse was to become a part of the Texas feud pattern.

A notorious thief named Boatwright was hanging about the country at this time, and he joined forces with one Squire Humphreys to steal some horses belonging to Peter Stockman and others. Humphreys belong to one of the old rough-and-ready families who stood against the "newcomers." "Squire" was a first name and not a title—the man was young and unmarried.[13] The tale of his misfortunes was recollected for the Rusk *Cherokee Standard* fifty years later:

"On Jan. 31, 1840, Boatwright, accompanied by James Turner and Henry Sylvester, entered Stockman's pasture. The night was stormy, and a drizzling rain, which turned into ice as it fell, kept most of the people within doors. Selecting thirty-two of the best horses in the herd, the adventurers speedily drove them into Arkansas, intending to sell them there. The next morning, when Stockman became aware of the theft, he dispatched two of his agents, Louis Henderson and Henry Brown, in pursuit, and they succeeded in recapturing about fifteen head of the stolen horses, which were returned to Stockman's pasture. Much indignation was expressed at the theft, and Charles W. Johnson [obviously Jackson], a prominent citizen of Shelbyville, formed a small company which he called the 'Regulators' and took Squire Umphus [sic] out on the square and publicly whipped him, a proceeding in those days termed 'black jacking.' After this Jackson informed Umphus that if he did not leave the Republic within five days he would have him shot. Three days afterward the squire fled to Panola, and there joined James Strickland and William McFadden, commonly known as 'Tiger Jim' and 'Buckskin Bill.' "[14]

The whipping itself was an extraordinary proceeding, according to Eph Daggett. The Regulators arrested Squire Humphreys and Wade Hampton West, the husband of Humphreys' sister Susan. They took Humphreys out to a tan yard, tied him lengthwise on a tanning log, and whipped him terribly across the back. He took it, and stoutly denied stealing anybody's horses. Finally, an old-time plantation overseer who had learned about handling men on the Red River said, "Turn him over with his back to the log."

They did so, and the ex-overseer started whipping just under the chin, working gradually down. "When I get to his belly," he said, "he'll belch the truth."

Humphreys heard him and broke down. "Let me up. I'm guilty and I'll let the truth come. I'd rather be hung than whipped to death."

He talked freely and they took everything down. The longer he talked, the worse they felt about the unfortunate state of society into which people like Humphreys had to be born.

"I was raised to do these things," he confessed. "I don't think I'm a very bad man by nature, but almost the first thing I can remember is holding stolen horses in the thicket to graze. This is what I got for doing it."

An old overcoat tied to the saddle had been his reward for driving the horse herd across the Red River.

It wasn't over yet. Old Man West, father of Humphreys' brother-in-law, now stepped forward and took the blame for his son. "There never was a more obedient boy," he said. "I told him to go out there and get Squire Humphreys and steal Stockman's horses. He is guilty of nothing but obedience, and whatever you do should be done to me. I am ready to undergo anything, but spare my son."

After much talk the Regulators agreed to let the three men go, provided they would leave the country. They got over such weakness later.

ONE BAD TURN...

One of the great moments of Charley Jackson's life came to him when he went on trial in July, 1841, for the murder of Joseph Goodbread. The case was called in Harrison County and Jackson came swaggering into the little court room at the head of one hundred and fifty belligerent Regulators. They were surrounded by at least an equal number of their enemies, as yet unorganized and therefore impotent.

The presiding judge was a bibulous character named John M. Hansford who could hardly have been more appalled at the situation in which he found himself. Since Hansford was more-or-less typical of the noncombatants who sometimes got caught in the cross-fire, we will let Eph Daggett describe him:

"Judge Hansford was another bird. Educated as a doctor, he went as Sergeant on a U. S. man of war, did some dirt, got discharged, came to Texas and took up the profession of law, and liked a rascal better than an honest man. He got mixed up with Sam Todd and his certificate friends, and moved up in Harrison county. He became judge of the District Court, got drunk and puked on the docket, and General Rusk adjourned court for him. Judge Hansford was on the bench at old Pulaski when Charley Jackson had his trial for killing Goodbread."

The Judge can hardly be blamed for being a little jumpy when he saw Jackson stalk into his courtroom with the sheriff, a gun in his hand, a grin on his face, and an air of great self possession about him. His followers, similarly armed with rifles and self-assurance, came trooping after. Hansford demanded to know what the sheriff meant by being so careless of the proprieties and put him down for a stiff fine.

At that point, Jackson took over. He jumped up, laid his gun on the Judge's desk, took off his coat and shoes, put his chair directly in front of the seat of justice, looked the Judge defiantly in the eye, and demanded his trial.[15]

It was enough. Hansford collapsed inwardly, fiddled with his papers, mumbled a few words, and adjourned court until nine o'clock next day. Then he retired to a friend's house in the country, there being no tavern in the town at the time. Next morning he sent the sheriff a letter:

At Judge McHenry's, July 15, 1841

To the Sheriff of Harrison County:

Sir:—Being unwilling to risk my person in the Court House any longer, where I see myself surrounded by bravo's and hired assassins, and no longer left free to preside as an impartial Judge at this special term of the court, called for the trial of C. W. Jackson, I want you to adjourn court tomorrow at 8 o'clock, by proclamation, without delay. From you at the regular term, I shall expect the prisoner. You will secure the prisoner and keep him safely until then, by causing him to be securely ironed, and keeping a strong guard, until delivered by due course of law.

Yours &c.

John M. Hansford
Judge of 7 Judicial
District

There was great indignation among the Regulators when the contents of this letter became known. Their honor, they felt, had been questioned, and one of them named William H. Landrum worked off his indignation by sending Hansford's letter and his own comments to the San Augustine paper, *The Redlander*. The Judge, he reported, had told his friends before the trial that "the d——d rascal Jackson" was on his way and they had better assemble and "hold themselves in readiness for battle." On the bench he appeared to be "two parts intoxicated" and obviously prejudiced against the prisoner. Finally, seeing that "the good citizens had united *en masse* to see that he got a fair and impartial trial, he at once declined sitting on the case."[16]

Sitting around the courthouse after the sheriff had adjourned court, Jackson and his men felt themselves invincible. There was talk of this and that. Tiger Jim Strickland was said to have been seen in a cornfield near by, armed with a good rifle. What was he doing there? Why, he was trying to get a shot at Jackson, of course. Hadn't you heard that Humphreys was staying at the Strickland place ribbing Tiger Jim up to committing murder?

A party went to search the cornfield, hoping Tiger Jim would not be there. He wasn't.

Then Jackson spoke up. "Boys," he said, "there are eight or ten nigger-stealers living around here. They came in yesterday to take a look at me. Now let's take a look at them and carry them over to Nachitoches. There is a two-hundred-dollar reward out for every one of them."

The men looked at each other, surprised and pleased. It was a clear case for regulation, and within the hour a party of volunteers had gone off to round up the villains. They got them, too. Eph Daggett says they all were sentenced to seven years in the penitentiary. Presumably the Regulators collected the reward money.[17]

With their cash and confidence at an all-time high, Jackson and his men now decided that it was time to move on the enemy in his private strongholds. Humphreys and Boatwright, the Stricklands and the McFaddins, were still alive and dangerous. So Jackson and fourteen men rode up to McFaddin Creek in the north end of the county.

Time had gone by in disposing of the "nigger-stealers" and in organizing this new expedition, and it was early winter when they finally took up the trail through the bitter chill under the bare branches of the oaks and hackberries. Jackson led, and beside him rode a tall young man named Watt Moorman who was destined to make a good deal of noise in those parts.

They called first at Tiger Jim Strickland's house. Fortunately for him, Tiger Jim was not at home. They left a guard to keep Mrs. Strickland from getting to their next stop ahead of them, and then went over to the house of Bill and Bailey McFaddin, only a short distance away. The nest was empty there too.

The men talked it over and decided that the best way to let the outlaws know the strength of their purpose was to burn their houses with all the contents. They set about their work at once, to the accompaniment of the screams and sobs of the McFaddin women who begged them not to carry out their cruel purpose. "Don't you realize that it is winter," they cried. "We haven't brought out so much as a blanket. The children will suffer—maybe freeze."

Captain Jackson showed all his teeth in a smile and told his men to "light her up."

The houses began to burn briskly, and one of the McFaddin women, almost hysterical, begged again to be allowed to go in before it was too late after some bedding. Jackson, pleasant but implacable, again said no.

The women thereupon picked up her child and tried to run into the flames, shrieking that she would rather go that way than freeze or starve to death. One of the Regulators held her back, and no doubt took credit afterward for saving her life.

When there was nothing left but a heap of ashes, the house burners rode away and left the women to shift for themselves.[18]

There is no record of what passed when the husbands and fathers of these miserable creatures came home, but they were men, and not the kind to put up with wanton injury. It was their turn now to feel that the time had come to take the law into their own hands. And that was the beginning of the Moderators.

It does not take much imagination to picture them, fearful but determined, getting together at out-of-the-way places—in darkened log cabins or by lonely springs in the woods somewhere. Eph Daggett heard that Squire Humphreys joined them down in the Sulphur Bottoms, and probably the McFaddins and the Stricklands were there too.

The old pattern was working itself out again, as relentless as Nemesis. The vigilantes, organized to combat the rule of the lawless, had become lawless themselves, and now the counter-vigilantes were in the saddle, burning for revenge.

The names they went by were traditional also. There was Regulation in the Carolinas in the 1760's. The term "Lynch Law," which began to be used in Revolutionary times, was another phrase which meant the same thing, though "lynching" usually meant whipping in those days. For the first hundred years of our existence as a nation, frontier Americans often resorted to Regulation as a means of making their democracy work.[19]

It was, of course, a case of fighting fire with fire; but it is hard to find a historian who does not have to admit that there was a *little* something to be said for the practice—at least in its early stages. Of course after it went too far—well, that was something else.

Moderators, as their names implies, pretend to work by milder methods. They wish to help the officers of the law and see to it that the courts can function. In Shelby County, the Moderators came into being to moderate the Regulators; but, from the beginning, it was hard to see much difference. The new group, with fresher grievances, began a campaign of extermination which put all previous examples in the shade.

The men the Moderators wanted were Jackson's house-burners, and they ranged the country far and wide looking for them. Watt Moorman nearly got his at a wedding. Forty Moderators tried to waylay him, but he was tipped off and got away by dressing himself in women's clothes and riding boldly past them.[20]

Harmless people, as usual, got in the way of some of the lead. There was, for instance, a quiet young surveyor named McClure who was working over on the Sabine and boarding at the house of a Mrs. Kelly. Tiger Jim and Buckskin Bill caught him arranging his field notes.

"We've found the damned rascal," said one of them, and they dismounted and leveled their weapons.

"I am not the man you are mad at," McClure protested. "You know I never injured you."

"You're a damned liar," Strickland growled.

Mrs. Kelly ran up and told them they were bad men and that they ought to go home and get together something to feed their starving children. They paid her no attention but went ahead and shot McClure until he was dead. John Middleton, a Regulator leader, heard that they were hired to do it by a man who thought McClure's surveys would cut him out of some property.[21]

The episode illustrates how easily the righteous indignation of either Regulators or Moderators could be perverted to bad ends.

Charley Jackson was the man most in demand during this manhunt, but it took the Moderators some time to find a way to get at him and it was through the efforts of a special committee that they finally succeeded. About thirty men devoted themselves to the pursuit of Jackson, and they chose as their chief a determined but cautious character named Edward Merchant. He and his band were convinced that "the law was totally inadequate to the ends of justice," and that it was time men should "fall back upon their natural rights and seek satisfaction by their own hands."

Jackson did his best to help them. Naturally reckless and hot headed, success had made him careless. Like a character in Greek tragedy, he assumed his own invincibility and thereby lost the support of whatever gods he had. The word came to Merchant and his men that Jackson had gone on business to Logansport, across the Sabine in Louisiana. It was the break they had been waiting for.

Again an innocent man got hurt. A Shelbyville storekeeper named Sidney Lauer, agreeable and liked by everybody, rode with Jackson as he passed through the McFaddin Creek district on the way to Logansport. He was still by Jackson's side as they rode back over the same road and crossed the sights of half a dozen guns in the hands of men hidden beside the road. All at once the guns spoke together and Jackson and Lauer fell from their horses, sieved by buckshot. Lauer died instantly, but tough Charley Jackson survived for twenty-four hours.[22]

With his death, the trouble in Shelby County became a full-fledged feud.

WATT MOORMAN TAKES CHARGE

Assassinations have occurred frequently in Texas, but they have never been approved of. After the Jackson murder the whole country was aroused and indignant. President Lamar, of Texas, offered five hundred dollars each for the capture of the Stricklands.[23] Good men who had kept out of it up to now declared for the Regulators, saying that amushing and waylaying had to stop. The Regulators themselves, of course, were up in arms.

For a few days they were left without a leader, but a mass meeting soon took care of that. The new chief was Watt Moorman, who assumed the imposing title of Colonel Commandant of the Shelby Guards.

Moorman is the most prominent, puzzling and fascinating figure
in the whole tangled pattern. At this time, in 1841, he was twenty-six
years old, a vigorous and dangerous man. Son of a Mississippi farmer,
he had a good opportunity to make something of himself, but he was
a mischief-maker from the start. He quit school when he was fifteen,
preferring an idle and adventurous life to a productive one, and continued to add to his reputation for recklessness after he got a job in a
store in Columbus, Mississippi.

In this new environment, however, he found that his pleasures and
escapades cost money which no one else was willing to provide. Eventually he forged a draft (Ashcroft says it was for $250), and thence-
forward made his home in Shelby County, Texas.[24]

Almost at once he became a marked man. He was a six-footer and
an athlete to begin with, not an ounce of anything on his bones but
muscle, with natural coordination that made him a famous shot.
"Watt never missed," they said of him.

He was a dark man with black hair and black eyebrows usually
knit into a menacing frown, and beneath those brows were a pair
of eyes that a man never forgot, particularly if they were fixed on him
in anger. Usually they roved restlessly from one object to another.
His dress had a military cut, without quite being a uniform, and he
always carried two pistols and a Bowie knife in his belt.

Nobody ever knew him to do any work. He seemed to expect that
his friends should share what they had with him, and to do him justice he had no hesitation in sharing with them anything that came his
way. To complete his equipment he had a persuasive tongue, and for
several years he was able to make his cause appear just to many honest
men.

With Moorman in charge, the Regulators concentrated on the murderers of Jackson. Who had done it? By one means or another they
added name after name to the list of the men they wanted. Jim Strickland's name was there; so were those of Bill, John and Bailey McFaddin, Squire Humphreys, Boatwright, and a man named Bledsoe.

These men helped to accuse themselves by gathering up their families and leaving the country ahead of the wrath they had stirred up.
Sheriff George had long since departed, "fearing danger to his life,"

and John W. Middleton was appointed to take his place. He organized a posse, which included "Colonel" Watt Moorman, and the pursuit began.[25]

They had a long ride before they came up with the rear guard of the fugitives. On the outskirts of Crockett, a hundred miles to the southwest, they flushed Tiger Jim Strickland out of his camp near the house of "One-eyed Williams." He got away, but later tried to creep up on them at night and had to run for it again, this time with a bullet in his shoulder.

Still another hundred miles from home, near the town of Montgomery, the Regulators located the McFaddins. After nightfall they surrounded the house where they had taken refuge. The McFaddins and Humphreys came out rather than have the place burned down over their heads, agreeing that they would not try to escape and that they would submit to the judgment of the citizens of Shelby County. Bledsoe was more fortunate than his friends. He blundered into the posse as he was coming unsuspectingly back to the house, put up a magnificent fight, and was shot to death. That made it simpler for him.

Bill McFaddin was the only other casualty. He tried to run when the rest of the family gave up, and was brought down by Watt Moorman with a long shot which struck him in the heel.

And now the tables were almost turned on the Regulators. Friends of the McFaddins talked about attempting a rescue, and Tiger Jim built the tension higher by going to Crockett and demanding the arrest of Middleton, Moorman, and three others. They got around that when they reached Crockett by swearing out a warrant for him. He did not come in to press the case, and nothing was done on either side.

The people of Crockett, be it added, were definitely hostile—"only about one-fourth being in our favor," says Middleton. The possemen felt lucky to get back to Shelby County with their lives and their prisoners.

At twelve o'clock on the Saturday following their arrival, the people of the county, at least the ones who were in sympathy with the Regulators, assembled in Shelbyville to pass judgment. This was on October 9, 1841. The old frontier mass meeting was resorted to, as if courts of law had never been heard of in Shelby County. Watt Moorman used to laugh and say that the McFaddins got a fair trial, all right—with three hundred people trying them.

They were voted guilty and condemned to death. The youngest McFaddin, Rufus, was spared on account of his years, but the two older ones were hanged on a gallows set up for the occasion a mile east of town beside the highway.

Before they died they said they regretted the death of Lauer, but had no qualms about the killing of Jackson. Humphreys admitted that he deserved to die. He had promised to leave the country and had broken his word because he wanted to help kill Moorman and Jackson.

"I was after you too, Watt," he said just before he was swung up. "You thrashed me with a hickory stick [this was over a horse Moorman had borrowed from him],[26] and now instead of killing you, you are going to hang me, so be at it. Let the thing be over and done with."

Then Bill McFaddin started in to curse the Regulators, calling them liars and thieves who were worse than he was. "You have stolen my life," he said, "and you'll wade through blood for it. You fellows that are grinning now will bleed and die to pay for this murder."

"Do you think we'll die as you are dying to pay for murdering Lauer, McClure, and Jackson?" a voice from the crowd asked derisively.

"Oh, damn you, you ain't worth killing," answered McFaddin. "Here, help me up on this horse." (He couldn't climb on alone because of his injured heel.) A minute later the horse was led out from under him.[27]

The Stricklands and Boatwright were the only ones on the list who were still at large. They hid out in the Louisiana canebrakes for months, hoping for a chance to get even. Henry Strickland got cut to pieces in a fight, however, and moved to Hunt County. He was eventually killed when he went on a spree one night and picked a fight with the wrong man.[28]

Tiger Jim was more cautious and kept his head above water for a while longer,[29] but Boatwright was caught. They found him in Louisiana not long after the hanging, picking cotton on the plantation of a Mr. Ferguson and earning the money he needed to replace the hat and shoes he had lost in making his escape.

A party of Regulators went over and captured him and brought him to the Texas side of the Sabine. They did not have the courage to shoot him in cold blood, as Dr. Ashcroft tells the story,[30] so a lawyer named Charles L. Mann approached him with friendly words, advised him to make a break, and shot him when he did. It was reported in the Texas and Louisiana papers that they "cut him in pieces and hung the fragments of his body on the surrounding trees." This account caused indignant comment in the United States press and Texas editors made what defense they could.

The *Redlander* for October 28, 1841, summarized Boatwright's character as "notorious," described him as a *"horsethief, counterfeiter and highway robber,"* and said he was suspected of murdering his wife. The implication was that anybody who would put such a monster out of the way deserved the world's thanks.

Eventually the law took notice of these bloody doings. It is said that Moorman was tried for the Boatwright murder but proved that the killing took place in Panola County, out of the jurisdiction of the authorities of Shelby County where the indictment originated.[31] The Grand Jury likewise failed to bring in any indictments for the McFaddin hangings. Too many of the jurors had helped with the arrangements.

By this time, fear was rife in the land and many frightened people were thinking of leaving their homes. The *Redlander* for October 27 was sorry and polite about it: "We regret to learn that there are a few citizens who recently emigrated to Texas, who have expressed their determination to leave the country; we are inclined to think their resolution has been prematurely formed. . . ."

To people who received one of Watt Moorman's letters of dismissal, there was nothing "premature" about a sudden departure. One such letter found its way into the Houston *Telegraph:*[32]

Shelby County, January 4th, 1842

Mr. WEST:

Sir: Not finding you at home, this means of notifying you to leave our country by the 14th inst., has necessarily been adopted. If, sir, after the prescribed time, you are found within the limits of our county, you will be dealt with according to Lynch: this certainly cannot be comfortable; nevertheless you must and shall go, as the undersigned and others will convince you on a failure to comply with the requisitions.

By order of the Shelby Guards
C. W. MOORMAN,
Col. Commandant
B. F. HOOPER,
W. COOK,
CHAS. B. DAGGETT.

To show that there was still some life in the other side, Tiger Jim and some of his friends came back to the Texas side of the river and almost got John Middleton.[33] Early on the morning of March 26, 1842, they tied his mare in thick brush, made themselves a blind close by, rigged a fish line to the mare's bell, and decoyed Middleton into gun range. He stopped four bullets but walked to the house "without falling or giving way to weakness." Five days later he was in the saddle, scouring the country for the would-be killers.

Six weeks afterward he heard that Tiger Jim had been killed in Louisiana for stealing slaves, but rumors continued to circulate for some time that Jim was alive and back in his old neighborhood.

There seemed to be no way to fight this whirlwind. Repeatedly, citizens of Shelby County had gone to Austin and begged President Sam Houston to do something. "Old Sam" didn't see how he could do much.

"I have no money or troops to send," he told them. "The treasury is empty and without credit, and on account of just such situations as the one you are talking about we have lost the respect of other people. I think it advisable to declare Shelby County, Tenaha and Terrapin Neck free and independent governments, and let them fight it out."[34] The President often spoke ironically of "The Free State of Tenaha" in this connection.

On January 31, 1842, he did issue a proclamation calling on local authorities to "prosecute all offenders" and authorizing them to call on the military for help if necessary.[35] But proclamations are poor weapons for stopping a feud.

HEAVY
SKIRMISHING

The year 1842 was deceptively quiet. The Regulators, with headquarters at Shelbyville, had the upper hand and it was likely to go hard with any Moderator who set foot on those sacred streets. He was certain to be insulted and stood in some danger of a good caning.

Moorman kept only fifteen or twenty men under arms, but he had a huge reservoir of manpower to draw on. By this time it was hard for anyone to remain neutral and something like two hundred men were enrolled in Moorman's organization.

Moorman's bodyguard was composed of the toughest men the Regulators could muster, and stories are still told of their overbearing conduct.[36] The Colonel particularly enjoyed meeting preachers on unfrequented roads and making them dance while he urged them on with pistol or knife. Other inoffensive citizens had to dance to his tune in one way or another.

Not many men would go up against Moorman in those days, even from ambush, and the result was a temporary lull in the Regulating business. Articles in the *Redlander* took the place of hot lead. John M. Bradley of the Moderators blasted the other side, and was answered by H. W. K. Myrick with great bitterness three months later, on November 10.

Myrick signed himself "Commander" and mentioned a meeting held on July 9 which elected him "in place of Col. Moorman, resigned." Probably Watt had become bored with inaction and had decided to step out for a while. He was doing business again as usual, however, when, in early 1843, trouble began to pile up again. At first the new difficulties looked particularly insignificant, but little by little they added up to something catastrophic.

It started with hog stealing. Henry Runnels, a Regulator, accused Samuel N. Hall of poaching in his pig pen. Hall said he was no thief and went home after his pistol. Runnels did the same, but before he could act, a man named Stanfield, who lived at the Runnels home, met Hall and killed him. Stanfield escaped from jail before he could be brought to trial, but some of Hall's relatives pursued and hanged him. The Halls, Deals, and Hickses, who were related by marriage, stuck together against the Runnels sympathizers and for a while carried on an old-style family feud within the larger difficulty.

To follow the activities of both these factions, hunting each other like wild beasts and ambushing each other without scruple, does not make cheerful reading but it does show how feuding operates.

The Hall party went to work by drawing up a list of the people they wanted and added an estimate of how much the blood of each man was worth to them. The Regulators heard that Moorman's price was $1000, his lieutenant John E. Myrick's was $700, and so on down the line. Runnels, who started it all by accusing Hall of mishandling his hogs, was worth only $500. Several professional killers were brought in from outside and given a chance to earn the money.[37]

Runnels went first. Two of the killers stopped by his place, pretending to be in pursuit of horse thieves and in need of directions. Old man Runnels was preparing to leave for Shreveport the next day with a load of cotton. At his invitation they stayed all night and got off ahead of him in the morning. When he camped the following evening, they came in and shot him down just as he was extending another invitation to light and share what he had.

This revolting crime brought the Regulators out in an angry swarm. Moorman and his men took the trail of the killers and caught up with one of them in Louisiana. The other reached the Texas bank of the river and escaped, supposedly on a horse belonging to John M. Bradley. Williams, the one they caught, confessed under pressure that he was guilty, but placed most of the blame on Bradley and some of his friends. Having squeezed out of him all the information they were likely to get, the Regulators hanged him.[38]

Through this confession, Bradley suddenly became the object of intense dislike on the part of the Regulators. Their efforts to do away with him brought to light some startling bits of information about his activities. Probably he was a prime example of the outwardly respectable citizen who was secretly tied up with the thieves' underground organization.

Alexander Horton, who knew him, says he kept a tavern midway between Shelbyville and San Augustine "for the accommodation of thieves and dealers in bogus money." Ashcroft, another acquaintance, calls him a "strange medley of contradictions. As a citizen of his own county he had but seldom offended against the law; he was a kind parent, a good husband and an obliging man; yet he was known to be connected with men banded together to swindle and defraud the public in various ways."[39]

He had some good connections, for he was a brother-in-law of the Governor of Arkansas,[40] but how he used them is shown in a remarkable piece of evidence published in the Austin *Bulletin* on December 23, 1841—a letter supposed to have been picked up on the street of a Louisiana town.[41]

Col. JOHN DAVIDSON
of the alphebit
Claiborn
La

By Litefoot
  of the same

Texas October 25th 1941

Dear sir it is with much pleasure that I acknowledg the receit of your favor of the 10th inst from which I learn that you and the old Doctor are locating on the Bodcaw which will grately facilitate our opperations I send you by Litefoot a part of the proceeds of the two mules that you hooked on the river—In Arkansas paper as there is no other kind except Texas to be had here . . . after considerable reflection I concluded it best for you and Vincent Walker to abandon the progect of killing old Jones—as I have learned that he is in det and has no money about him and christmas is an unfavorable time as the owners of slaves are generaly watching them at such times . . . I am just from Opelousas where I have left $20,000 of the new tipe to distribute among the blacks. There is some fellows there that is worth fleecing . . . if you should get into difficulties and want a safe counselor apply to old Fleetwood Herndon, of long prarie, who has made half his fortune by the alphabit without the slitest suspision, he has saved my life five times and my liberty at least a dozen. Litefoot will give you all important information, I shold not have written at all but Litefoot having so much on his mind he could not retain all that was necessary you should know. Here I will take the liberty to Reprimand you for the imprudent act of sending me a letter by a man that dose not Belong to the alphabit. There is great risk in Riting on this subjecte and I think at our meeting I will try to have it intirely dispenced with. . . . Burn this letter amediately after reading. be Faithful and I will be with you in six troubles and in the 7th I will not forsake you I am with greatest respect yours

JOHN M. BRADLEY.

This document was given to the *Bulletin* by a member of Congress from Shelby County and its authenticity was vouched for by thirty-six prominent citizens. If it is authentic, it makes very clear what Bradley was, and takes some of the stigma from the Regulators for determining that such a man had to go.

Before Moorman made a serious effort to put Bradley out of the way, he attended to some of the smaller fry, the first being Joseph Hall, a brother of the hog stealer. Joseph was brought in, but talked so convincingly that he was let out on bond and soon left the country.[42]

It might be pointed out here that the Hall brothers were Regulators when all this trouble started, but now the Regulators were regulating them, and there was nothing for it but to line up with the Moderators, which they did. As time went on, the Regulators lost other citizens, some of great influence in the county—for instances the Truitts. Moorman tried to regulate one of Uncle Jimmy Truitt's sons-in-law. When Uncle Jimmy protested, Watt attacked him, and they had a fight. It was all Eph Daggett could do to keep them from hurting each other. After that the Truitts became Moderators.[43]

And now the Regulators let it be known that they were ready to go after John M. Bradley and two of his supposed lieutenants.[44] One of these was William Todd, a "peaceful and industrious citizen" whose chief offense lay in his being a brother of Sam Todd of the land-certificate ring. The Todds had a large circle of kinfolks. Joseph Goodbread had married into the family, and when he was dead a Truitt had married the widow. The other proscribed Moderator was Amos Hall. When they heard that they were accused of complicity in the Runnels murder, they got their guns and went to Bradley's house, determined to make a stand if necessary.

They waited. And no attack came. They appealed to their brother Moderators to get their guns and put an end to the suspense, but these friends, while sincerely regretting their predicament, hated to bring on open hostilities. At last, in order to break the deadlock, Bradley swore out warrants against several men for hanging Williams over in Louisiana after the Runnels murder. Moorman was one of these men, and when Sheriff Llewellyn came for him he said coolly that he wanted two or three days to decide whether or not he wished to be arrested. Llewellyn gave him the time desired.

This was the signal for the final gathering of the clans. Moorman put fifty of his henchmen under arms and kept them on the alert in Shelbyville. Llewellyn countered by gathering a posse of about the same number of Moderators.

There could not have been a dozen neutrals in the county, and the mobilization included practically the entire male population. Immediately all the hysteria that goes with war making began to operate. Women were terrified and ran about pleading with the men to lay down their arms or go away. Everybody knew it would take just one shot—just one—to start a war of extermination.

In the midst of these palpitations came word from Moorman to Sheriff Llewellyn that he would give up. Llewellyn soon found that there were complications, however. Moorman and his friends refused to appear before Judge Lister, who had issued the warrants, and insisted on being tried by John Ingram, who had Regulator sympathies. That was the way it had to be, and that was the way it was. Ingram took only a few minutes to find that the indictments were defective and illegally issued.

Then came the riposte. About the time Llewellyn rejoined his men, who were camped two miles out of town near Captain Todd's place, an officer appeared bearing Justice Ingram's writs for John M. Bradley, Amos Hall, and Samuel Todd as accessories in the Runnels killing. There was also a note for Sheriff Llewellyn which Ashcroft quotes in full:

Shelbyville, Texas

A. LLEWELLYN, You have been so damned energetic in attempting to enforce the laws of the county, I herewith forward you writs against your particular friends, Bradley, Todd and Hall. We will now see if you are as persevering in the discharge of your duty as you have recently been, but we will see that you do your duty. If you do not, by God I'll make you.

C. W. MOORMAN

The Moderators found it easy to turn Moorman's trick against him. They went before their own justice to be tried, and since the alleged offense had been committed in Louisiana, the judge had a reasonable excuse for turning them loose.[45]

Moorman is said to have had no illusions about the possibility of obtaining a conviction. What he wanted was a chance to bushwhack the prisoners as they left for home. They were too wary for him, it turned out, and he gave up for the time being, remarking that he would wait until they "got tame."

Meanwhile another of the Hall brothers—James Hall—came up for attention. They got him as he was plowing by hiding near the fence and shooting him as he turned his plow at the furrow's end. His brother John was with him and recognized three of the assassins, but the poor fellow was a half-wit and fell an easy prey to the lawyers when the case was called a year or two later. He became confused on the witness stand during the trial of Stephen Runnels, a son of the dead Henry Runnels, and the prisoner was not held.[46]

Even some of the Regulators were shocked by the Hall murder, but the Moderators in their fury were beyond making distinctions between good Regulators and bad ones. They talked of exterminating them all, and their resentment culminated in a meeting at Belle Springs, six miles from Shelbyville, attended by about fifty of the leaders. An election of officers was held in the accustomed manner of American militia troops, and John F. Cravens was elected colonel of the "regiment."

Cravens was a young man for such a task, only about thirty-five years old. He was a deputy sheriff, but not by any means a fire-eater, or even a leader like Moorman or Jackson. As it turned out, however, he was the man for the place. Next morning he moved on the enemy, marching into Shelbyville and taking possession.

Moorman and most of his men were away at the moment, which made the occupation rather simple. It was a shock to the Regulator chief when he heard of it. "He knit his brow and a dark scowl overspread his features," says Dr. Ashcroft, who wasn't present but heard all about it. "For a time his feelings of indignation checked his utterances, but he soon recovered himself and gave vent to his wrath in a volley of curses so remarkable for vindictiveness and profanity that those who heard him never forgot his language. He prided himself upon having invented more new oaths than any other man in the world. I have never heard of anyone so desirous to dispute the claim with him."[47]

A WEDDING
AND A
MURDER

The year 1844 came along and the tension was still rising. Neutrals and newcomers were pressured to join one side or the other, and bad feeling spread to adjoining counties as friends or relatives of the Shelby County citizens were drawn in.

Dr. Ashcroft points out that the Moderators were now a different group from the one assembled under Merchant three years before while Charley Jackson was still above ground. The new Moderators preferred to call themselves "Reformers," and were mostly people who were less interested in getting even than in getting the county back to normal.

They were even cautious about whom they admitted into their ranks and are supposed to have refused many applications for membership—among them that of John M. Bradley who had gone off to live in San Augustine, where he was not so likely to be shot. He thought he would be in a better position if he renewed his association with the Moderator party, but they would have none of him.

Unfortunately for the Moderators, they were never able to clean up their ranks completely. Remnants of the old "Teneha Gang" of freebooters clung to the organization and gave the Regulators an excuse for cherishing the fierce conviction that they themselves were the law-and-order party.

This conviction may have helped Watt Moorman to acquire a wife in January of 1844. He found a girl who was much too good for him—the high-spirited and handsome daughter of a Shelby farmer on the Regulator side. Helen Mar Daggett was named for the heroine of great-grandmother's favorite romantic novel, *The Scottish Chiefs*. She had the temperament to live up to her namesake, was violently loyal to her cause, and passionately devoted to its leader who became her husband. If there is a heroine in this story of blood and hate, she has no rival for the title.[48]

Her family was distressed over the marriage. Brother Eph, though he stayed with his party, was at outs with the chief for some time. "Watt and myself did not speak for he had stolen my sister and I was very much opposed to the match," he says.[49] It did not take long for Helen herself to see that she had made the wrong choice, for Moorman practically abandoned her after a few months of marriage. She wrote in her diary, as her great-niece quotes it: "Something of a barrier, Something entirely unexplainable, a seeming dignity and cold indifference arose, making a breach which widened as the days passed."

But though her romance was blighted, Helen was still willing to die for her cause. So were many other good people, and when Cravens and his little army moved toward Shelbyville, these earnest Regulators loaded their guns and flocked to put themselves under Moorman's orders. He soon had over a hundred men, which was a little better than what Cravens was able to muster.

The two forces watched each other warily and kept on the move. Cravens soon took his troops into the country where he could find good horse feed and running water. The minute he left, Moorman took over the town, but soon went into camp himself at Graham's Springs, two miles away. With only three miles between them, the two companies worked feverishly preparing for battle. Everybody thought there was bound to be a fight, but once again butchery was postponed when Colonel Ashton, Major Edwards, and other neutrals went between the camps and tried to arrange a truce.

Both sides were willing. Moorman wrote out a long set of articles of agreement, which still exists in his own handwriting, dated July 24, 1844, pledging the Regulators "not to Molest or in any manner disturb, any good and unoffending citizen."[50]

Moorman and Cravens signed this document. The Moderators noted the loophole which Watt had left for himself—he had merely promised not to molest anyone he approved of—but they decided to accept it and go home. As soon as they were over the hill and out of sight, Moorman seized the opportunity to get rid of some of the people he did not class among the "unoffending citizens," and he began with John M. Bradley.

To trap Bradley was no small feat, for he was fearless and determined, and had many times threatened to kill Moorman on sight, just as Moorman had threatened to do to him.[51] Careful planning was needed, and Moorman sent John Farrar to look the set-up over.

Farrar prowled about San Augustine and found out where Bradley was boarding. He learned also that a great Baptist revival was to begin on the following Saturday evening, and that a large crowd would be there. He started home, laden with this information, and by ill luck ran into Bradley himself on the road. He had to pretend to be his own brother, just in from Arkansas, before he could quiet Bradley's suspicions and get past. He went home through the woods, breathing hard.

On Saturday night Moorman and five of his followers, bristling with weapons, were lurking in the outskirts of San Augustine. As soon as the revival meeting got under way, they drifted toward it by the back streets.

The assembly was held in the Masonic Hall, the first floor of which was used for public meetings. The preacher was a powerful exhorter, known far and wide for his command of religious audiences, and the place was packed. There was even a crowd on the roofed porch in front of the building. Many Negroes had found a place there where they could see what went on without intruding on the white folks' meeting. Inside the hall the singing and praying and preaching went forward while creeping wickedness closed in outside.

Moorman spotted Bradley on one of the benches within. One story says that Bradley spotted Moorman too, and went home after his gun. If he did, he might as well have stayed in the building and listened to the exhortation which he so badly needed. Moorman was waiting for him outside as the congregation poured out onto the dark gallery after the services. He reached around or over some of the brethren and shot Bradley in the stomach with a pistol.

A dreadful scene followed. Women became hysterical, half a dozen people shrieked that they had been hit and were dying, and everybody wanted to know, at the top of his voice, who was hurt and who did it.

It happened that Justice of the Peace Anthony Patton was at Moorman's elbow when the shot was fired, and he immediately said, "Watt, I will have to arrest you."

"Certainly," Moorman replied, "Hadn't we better go to your office?"

Before they had gone a hundred feet through the excited crowd, Patton perceived that he was surrounded by heavily armed men. Moorman had his hand in his pocket, and the Justice thought he heard an ominous click.

"I am your friend, Mr. Moorman," he said, knowing he had more trouble than he could handle. And the Regulators walked off through the darkness to where they had left their horses.[52]

Back in Shelbyville they staged a great celebration, believing that the death of Bradley portended the breaking up of the Moderators. Among other edibles they served up a huge pound cake baked in a ten-gallon wash kettle, and 250 men were there to help eat it.

Bradley was taken to his house and every effort was made to save him, but it was no use. He died hard, crying out that he had had no chance, and begging that his family be assured he had not died a coward's death.

THE STORM BREAKS

Old Man Lindsey watched the posse ride grimly up to his door. He knew what they were there for. Bradley was six feet under, and Moorman was starting to clean out the rest of the Moderator leaders. "They're going to hang me," Lindsey thought, "but they'll have trouble doing it."

He was an old man, past seventy, and they had caught him off-guard, in his bare feet.

There were five or six men in the group. He knew them all, and they seemed embarrassed as he looked them over with his burning, indomitable old eyes.

Nobody said anything for a minute. Then the leader of the posse spoke: "Get your horse, Lindsey. You're coming with us."

Lindsey said nothing—just kept looking at them.

"We're taking you with us. Will you get your horse?"

"No," said Old Man Lindsey.

"All right, we'll get your horse. You go get your shoes on."

"I won't do that, either." And he opened up and told them why. "You damned cutthroats can't cheat me out of many days, anyway," he sneered. "I don't intend you shall rob me of anything more than enough to pay for the rope, and if you get me, you can come here and take me."

The posse backed down and assured the old man that they just wanted to ask him and Captain Todd some questions, and he finally came along. At the Regulator rendezvous, he and Captain Todd were quizzed about Cravens and the Moderator organization, then turned loose. It looks as if the Regulators used the time to arrange for getting rid of Lindsey the easy way. He was shot at from ambush on his way home, but his luck held and he got through.[53]

The alarm spread like a prairie fire. Todd's daughter got on a horse as soon as her father was taken away, and indignation rose as the word went round. So this was Watt Moorman's truce! They had been easy marks once, but they wouldn't be again. If they hanged Sam Todd, they would pay in blood! So once again the guns were cleaned and terrified families "forted up" in somebody's house, expecting every minute to hear the rifles talking in the surrounding woods.

And now it was Moorman's turn to hear voices and see visions. Like Jackson before him, he began to believe that all things were possible to him except defeat. He meant to wipe out his enemies to the last man, and then go on to realize a more Satanic ambition. Ashcroft says his ultimate aim was no less than the domination of the country and the replacement of the Texas government by his own Regulator organization. Fantastic as this sounds, Ashcroft takes it seriously and gives a very circumstantial account of the scheme.[54]

One thing is certain: a meeting of the Provisional Committee of the Regulators was held at the home of Matthew Brinson on July 28, 1844. It resulted in a proclamation that twenty-five of the Moderators would have to leave the country within fifteen days. Moorman made out the list. Sheriff Llewellyn's name came first, followed by those of John F. Cravens, five Haleys, two Todds, two Stricklands, and such men as Isaac Hall, John Anderson, and Laurel Lang.

Some of these men, like John Anderson, bore the reputation of excellent citizens. Some, like William Todd, were related to the wrong people. Some, like Laurel Lang, a wild man of the woods who had stolen hogs and killed a few men, needed a dose of Regulation.[55]

The older and wiser heads among the Regulators were uneasy about such indiscriminate blacklisting,[56] but the young men stood with Moorman and voted their elders down.

"All right," said Colonel M. T. Johnson, "you have them to fight, so lick your flints, keep your powder dry, and don't deceive yourselves —it's a bad move."

"It has to be a fight!" the young men shouted, and the skeptics said no more.

The committee sent out to notify the blacklisted men made only one stop. They approached the home of Thomas Haley stealthily from the rear, but Mrs. Haley saw them in time to tell her husband to get his gun. He opened up from the barn with a rifle charged with two balls and succeeded with a single shot in killing one horse and breaking the arm of one committee member. The notifications after that were confined to an announcement nailed to the courthouse door.[57]

After this one-shot battle, Moorman decided that he had better get ready for a finish fight. He sent part of his command into the country west of Shelbyville to find a good place for a fort, while he himself went off to recruit his forces in the northern part of the county. He made a rather pointless attempt to cover his tracks by giving it out that he was going on a fishing trip.

The Moderators got busy too. The surprise party at Haley's occurred on July 29, 1844. That evening Cravens began assembling his troops. By morning he had fifty men around him, all resolved that the only course left to them was to kill every member of the Regulators' Provisional Committee. They pledged themselves to fight until the last Moderator went down.

To wipe out the Regulators, it was first necessary to find them, and a party of fifteen men went on scout. While they were gone, a gang attacked old Lewis Watkins on the Shelbyville road, shot him in the neck, and left him for dead. Watkins was a Regulator, and consequently the Moderator scouts were blamed for this assault, though it was said that Tiger Jim was back and had done the deed.[58]

Moorman's force located in an improvised fortification on Beauchamp's farm three miles west of Shelbyville. They were in a log house surrounded by an old-time zigzag split-rail fence against which they had laid several thicknesses of new lumber which Mr. Beauchamp happened to have on hand.[59] The spy company rode up, looked things over, exchanged a few futile shots, and went back to report. Cravens' immediately moved to attack.

The armies were approaching full strength now, but estimates of their numbers reflect the hysteria of the moment. Eph Daggett, who got to the Regulator fort just ahead of the Moderator scouts, says there were sixty-five men inside against two hundred twenty-five Moderators outside. Ashcroft simply turns the figures around, pitting sixty-five Moderators against a much greater number of holed-up Regulators. Probably the forces were about even.

Half of Cravens' men attacked from the front and half from the rear. Almost immediately they perceived that the plank barricades were thick enough to turn bullets while they themselves offered perfect targets for the barricaded men. There was nothing for it but a retreat to the woods just out of rifle range, and from this shelter the Moderators took an occasional long pot-shot and wished for water, it being a warm day.

Meanwhile a rumor had gone back to Shelbyville that the Regulators were being massacred and that it would soon be all over. Immediately a swarm of mothers, wives and sweethearts headed for the fort, straight through the ranks of the Moderators, expecting to bind up the wounded and carry off the slain. Finding a few wounded and no slain, they marched back the way they had come.

"Will you take a message back to your men?" a Moderator asked Mrs. George.

"What is it?"

"Tell them we are going to keep them here and take all recruits prisoner until they surrender, or we will pile them up in a heap."

"I can tell you the answer to that now."

"Then tell them we are going to charge in and finish them, and we are going to start pretty soon."

"They have already said that the hotter the fight the sooner the peace. They are able to fight all the rascals in the state and will make Texas too hot to hold you before they are done. Why don't you go out where they can see you? You fight like cowards."[60]

The hours went by. One young Regulator got tired of waiting and began to make fun of the whole business. He got up on the fence, flapped his arms, and crowed like a rooster.

"Get down, and don't act like a fool," his friends advised him. "Do you want to get shot?"

He kept on anyhow until a bullet struck him in the side of the head, cut his hatband, and ran around his skull, taking off the hair but not cutting very deep. He landed on his back like a chimney falling as he came off the fence, and that was the last of his crowing.

Then the Regulators won a round when one of them knocked a Moderator out of a tree at 480 paces—a shot so improbable that the man who made it christened his gun "Tremendous."[61]

Three times the Moderators gathered as if preparing for a charge, and three times they changed their minds. Finally, parched with thirst, they drew off to a creek two miles away, where they made camp. This concluded what came to be known from the rail fence around Beauchamp's house as "The Battle of the Cowpens."

That night the Regulators drew off too, and marched to Hilliard's Spring fifteen miles north on the Marshall road. Moorman had brought in thirty or forty new men, and the next morning Colonel Boulware arrived with a force of Regulator sympathizers from Harrison County. Ashcroft says there were a hundred of them. Daggett raises the estimate to "nearly three hundred." At once they started felling trees and building a fort.

The Moderators were right behind. They concentrated at Strickland's Church, an old log building two miles or so from the enemy. A few recruits had come their way too, and they had about a hundred sixty-five men under arms. They occupied the church about ten o'clock on the morning of August 8, posted sentries, and began laying plans for an attack the following day.

On the morning of the ninth, however, a woman rode into their camp and created a situation which gave the story tellers a field day for many years after.

It was Helen Moorman herself who had come to spy on the Moderator position. Asking for Colonel Cravens, she complained that some of his men had fired on her as she was riding down the road near camp, and asked him to do something about it. Cravens was most apologetic—he would try to find out who did it—the man would certainly be punished. Helen rode away with her head in the air, and not long afterward the rifles opened up from the woods around the old church. Of course nobody had fired a shot at her.[62]

The battle raged for about two hours. The Moderators succeeded in killing Colonel Davidson and two of his men when they tried to take position under a bluff along the creek bank behind the church. Other Regulators were shot by their own allies. They had no uniforms or other means of identification and there were many strangers fighting on the same side. Eph Daggett says:

"We had three killed I am sure by our own men. I was shot at twice by a Harrison county man by mistake."

Moorman finally used his little hunting horn to call his men back to camp. He never thought of this skirmish as a disaster, but the Moderators claimed a victory and the battle has been known ever since as "Helen's Defeat." Ashcroft computes that the Regulators lost fifteen in killed and wounded, while only six Moderators were wounded, none badly. Middleton, a Regulator, reverses the arithmetic and figures that there were sixteen dead and twenty-five wounded among the Moderators to two killed and one wounded for the Regulators.

Next day the Moderator scouts found no Regulators left in camp. They had dispersed with orders to reassemble south of Shelbyville where it would be easier to obtain supplies.

Men on both sides now began to want to go home, and some of them did. The life of a feudist was no picnic. They had to hide in the woods like animals and eat cornbread and beef—if they ate at all. Water was scarce. The weather was hot. There were ticks and flies and other annoyances. And larger evils loomed in the background, for many had been unable to plant crops and more had been too busy to tend what they had planted. There was actual hunger in some families.[63]

Young men without families did not feel the pinch so much, but as Alexander Horton says in his reminiscences of this period, "Nearly all the men engaged in this deadly feud were small farmers, recent emigrants to Texas; most of them had been dragged into this thing by unscrupulous men. A very large majority of them were good men, honest and true, but they had fallen on evil times."

The ones who refused to give up encamped near each other in the vicinity of Shelbyville—waiting. For a few days there was skirmishing between small patrol parties. Mark Haley was shot through the thigh in one such engagement. Whetstone and Castleberry, Moderators, were also wounded and nearly captured, but Castleberry saved himself by running and Whetstone, who couldn't run, was hidden under Mrs. Choat's kitchen floor.

Colonel Cravens now tried a little strategy. He moved his camp secretly to a dry creek bed with ten-foot banks not far from the Regulator position, hoping to get in a surprise attack. Moorman sensed that something was going on. He stopped Old Man Bowles on his way back from the grist mill and tried to make him tell where Cravens was.

"If you mix it with those boys," chirped the old man, "you'll likely eat supper in hell tonight with your friend the devil."

Moorman grinned. "Show me where they are," he said, "and I'll send some of your friends there in my place."

"Just you go on down the creek a few hundred yards more," retorted Bowles, "and you can make the experiment."

"How many men have they got?"

"About a hundred; the rest are on scout."

"If you lie to me I'll hang you to the first limb I come to after I find you, you old rogue."

"If you hang all the rogues in your company, you'll have no ropes to spare."[64]

After this bit of repartee, Moorman made up his mind to move in on the Moderators who, unknown to him, were watching every motion and fingering their triggers some distance out of rifle range. He called Colonel Boulware of the Harrison County forces and told him to take the lead. Boulware refused, saying that he had taken the lead at the battle of the church and didn't see why he should risk his men up there in front every time.[65]

When Moorman insisted, Boulware threatened to pull out and go home, and the upshot was that both groups went back to their camp, probably saving a good many lives thereby.

THE SHOUTING DIES

In the old melodramas, when the plot was so thoroughly tangled up that it seemed no human agency could unravel it, a rich uncle from Australia arrived unexpectedly to put things right. In our East Texas drama such a character now entered from the wings and stole the show. His name was Sam Houston. Such frantic messages had been coming to him out of the blood-spattered woodlands that he at last determined on personal intervention.

He came up to San Augustine, fifteen miles from the seat of the trouble. Then, instead of riding dramatically in between the battle lines, he went out behind the Huston Hotel and whittled. Judge Ochiltree, Colonel Broocks, O. M. Roberts (later governor of Texas) and others sat on the woodpile with him and watched the clean pine shavings fall while they decided what to do.[66]

Next day a proclamation was carried throughout the region:

"I, Sam Houston, President of the Republic of Texas, to the end that hostilities may cease and good order prevail, command all citizens engaged . . . to lay down their arms, and retire to their respective homes."[67]

To put teeth into his command, Houston called out the militia in the counties of San Augustine, Sabine, Nacogdoches, and Rusk—six hundred men in all. Colonel Travis G. Broocks of San Augustine was placed in command and was forever after known as General Broocks.[68] The President also issued an order to "Sandy" Horton, Marshal of the Republic, to bring in ten of the leaders from each side.

The Regulators first heard of these doings when a woman on horseback came riding through their camp as they lay watching the Moderator position in the creek bed. She asked about some men they knew to be on the Moderator side.

"They are a little farther down the line yonder," they said. "What do you want with them?"

"I want them to get away. Sam Houston's militia is coming down the Shelby road."

When Watt Moorman heard of this new turn, he blew a few blasts on his hunting horn to call his men in.

"We will have to disband for a while," he told them. "Every man take the best care of himself he can."

"Such a stampede I never saw before," reminisced Eph Daggett many years later. "The pine knots flew ten feet high, knocked by the horses' feet as the rowels entered their sides. The woods were the nearest way home. Some did not go home for a long time, and some left the country, I for one. . . . Moorman and a few men went up in the northern part of the country. He was indifferent and careless for he supposed that the militia would return when they learned that both armies had disbanded.[69]

The Moderators did not disband. When the militia arrived, the day after the proclamation reached Shelbyville, they pitched their tents a stone's throw from Cravens' men. In the morning General Broocks formally demanded a surrender.

The episode of the Three Generals occurred at this time. A green sentry was on duty outside the Moderator camp when three gentlemen came up to the lines. He placed all three under arrest and took them to where Colonel Cravens and his officers were having breakfast. They introduced themselves as General Broocks, General J. G. Berry, and General N. H. Darnell (the last two had been militia generals in their home states). When the sentry heard all three addressed as "General," he expressed an opinion that he had done pretty well to capture three generals "before breakfast."[70]

The Moderators, greatly relieved, surrendered at once. Ten of their leading men were taken to Shelbyville by Marshal Horton, and shortly afterward nine of the top Regulators appeared and gave themselves up. Moorman was not among them.

Broocks and Horton went after him. They left guards with his friends along the way lest somebody break ahead and warn him, and perhaps for that reason they rounded him up without trouble. Watt had gone back to his old camp at Hilliard's Spring, and since he was in a rather low frame of mind he began spending some time at a dram shop about a mile away. By a freak of luck the officers caught him, alone and off guard, as he was coming back from this place, riding with his head down. They surrounded him on the open prairie, and he surrendered at once. Just afterward a small troop of his men rode up, but when they saw him in custody, they turned and fled.[71]

Houston allowed the twenty leaders to go free on bail, but Moorman was re-arrested for the Bradley murder and imprisoned in chains until he was able to give bond for that offense too.

And now "Old Sam" did what very few men could have done. Judge Ochiltree convened the District Court at Shelbyville, and Sam took the floor. He read the twenty leaders a lecture they never forgot. He "talked to them as a father might to a lot of bad boys who had been quarreling among themselves," writes George W. Crocket, the San Augustine historian, and although those twenty leaders were not given to accepting personal criticism, they took what Houston gave them.[72]

Meanwhile both sides were working on a treaty of peace. The finished product was signed by James Truitt and John Dial, Moderators, and M. T. Johnson and John H. McNairy, Regulators. It read:

We the undersigned citizens of the Republic of Texas, in view of the disastrous consequences, anarchy and misrule attendant upon the late attempts in the county of Shelby and elsewhere, to turn the law from its legitimate channels, and to the end that law and order may prevail, peace and quietude restored, do hereby solemnly pledge ourselves to assist the civil [authorities] in carrying out, enforcing and maintaining the law of the country and to that end:

1st. Be it resolved, that we do hereby favor discarding the odious designation of Regulators and Moderators, and will henceforth be hailed and recognized by no other name than that of Texans.

2nd. Resolved, that we will forever forget and forgive and will frown upon and discountenance any and every attempt to revive the unfortunate divisions which have for so long distracted the country; that we will give the hand of fellowship to every worthy citizen, no matter under which party banner he may have rallied.

3rd. Resolved, that a voice has come to us from our firesides, from our wives and little ones, that its pleadings for peace shall not pass unheeded, and we do therefore pledge our sacred honor to the strict observance and faithful performance of the foregoing resolutions.[73]

This declaration was circulated, and was signed by a great many of the citizens, including some who had kept more or less out of the trouble.

So the feud was over, except for minor and scattered outbreaks. On the second day of the court proceedings as Alfred Truitt was mounting his horse to leave town, he saw Regulator Charles A. Luton approaching him with a shotgun. Truitt threw himself over on the opposite side of his horse as Luton pulled the trigger, the buckshot whistling harmlessly over his head. He himself fired under his horse's neck, inflicting a bad wound, but was later acquitted. Luton, out on bond, left the country.[74]

A few days after court adjourned, a Moderator named Duncan picked a fight with a Regulator named Harris and was killed for his pains. Harris gave himself up when he got ready, and was exonerated. Again at a session of the county court soon after the troops had left (they stayed a month), forty men sprang to arms in the courtroom when somebody mentioned gunpowder, but they were stopped in time.

Then followed the Wilkinson poisoning. In the early part of May, 1847, while attending a wedding at the house of the Wilkinson family, sixty guests got a stiff dose of arsenic in the wedding cake. Twenty-three of them, and maybe more, died from the effects. Newspaper gossip said that Wilkinson was a Moderator and wanted to kill off as many ex-Regulators as possible.[75]

It was too late to revive the feud, however, for the Mexican War had begun and all differences were forgotten as the volunteers marched off to fight for Texas. Two companies were raised, one under Moderator Alfred Truitt; the other under Regulator M. T. Johnson. The men joined pretty much according to the old battle lines, but they fought side by side through the war and came home with the breach completely healed.[76]

Moorman tried to join both groups, but neither would have him.

On the return of the soldiers a celebration was given which made history in East Texas. J. Pinckney Henderson, Governor of the State and ex-commander of the Texas contingent in the Mexican War, was one of the speakers, and "the utmost good feeling prevailed."

Moorman, acquitted of murdering Bradley, lived a haunted and unhappy life for the few years that he had left—his enemies say he lived a criminal one—and finally he got himself killed. He fell out with a certain Dr. Burns of Logansport, Louisiana. Burns was convinced that Moorman had tried to ambush him and would renew his attempt. When it was reported to him that Moorman had just got off the ferry and was coming up the street, he took his gun, waited at a window of his house, and killed his enemy with one lucky shot.[77]

Gradually the cloud lifted. Departed residents ventured back. Land was worth something again. Men did not carry guns and start at every shadow. But it was a long time before some people could be free and easy with each other, and legend says that for as much as fifty years it was necessary to be very cautious in discussing the feud.

AFTERMATH   It was amazing what the romancers did with the facts as soon as they began hearing of the Regulators and Moderators. The lying, or perhaps it would be better to say dreaming, started almost as soon as it was over.

In the early fifties C. W. Webber spun a tale called *Jack Long; or the Shot in the Eye* which he included in his *Tales of the Southern Border* in 1855. Eph Daggett identifies Long with Tiger Jim Strickland.[78]

In 1856 Charles Summerfield (the pseudonym of A. W. Arrington) fathered a blood-and-thunder romance called *The Rangers and Regu-*

lators of the Tanaha which is mostly imagination but shows an acquaintance with the background and with some of the facts.

Other articles and stores inflated still further the romantic aspects of the feud, particularly those involving Helen Daggett Moorman who married again and lived out her life in Ft. Worth where she was buried in 1895.[79] "One faction was for years under the complete control of one woman," says a writer in the Dallas *News* for May 13, 1899. "She planned their battles, was in several fights, and was always at the head of her faction. The most notable battleground here still bears her name. It is called 'Helen's defeat,' for there she met her Waterloo. On this occasion she led the charge against a church in which the enemy lay hidden and barricaded.

"She reckoned that she could dislodge them, but she failed in the attempt, losing a number of her men and inflicting no injury upon the enemy. A moment later she was having made a cannon. The next morning it was mounted, loaded, and ready for service. It was simply a sweet gum log bored out to a desired caliber and mounted upon a pair of wagon wheels. In it was a death dealing load . . . several pounds of powder and a bucketful of lead and iron. As her forces were being massed . . . a posse of state rangers rode up . . . formed a line . . . between the two factions . . . by order of General Houston . . . and each faction agreed to cease fighting."

That cannon crops up again and again. There probably was one. Governor Roberts mentions that "some of the old settlers conceived the idea, and, with some help, selected a dark-looking log, hoisted it on wheels, so as to have the appearance of a cannon, and placed it in front of the 'Moderators' camp."[80]

General J. H. Cosgrove, writing in the *Texas Magazine* for May, 1912, lets himself go a little further in speaking of the heroine:

"A woman, beautiful, 'tis said, as a dream, fearless herself and a Diana in horsemanship, became the leading spirit of this strange, eventful period. Withal she must have been superior in intellect, in cunning, and in nerve. Named from her who brought woe to Troy, she planned forays and ambuscades, which denoted superior skill and judgment, and one, the last, which bears till this day her name.

"This Helen was evidently a coquette, whose beauty and wiles played havoc with hearts on both sides of the quarrel. . . . Houston, the President had issued a proclamation denouncing both belligerents as outlaws, calling upon them . . . to disperse, when Helen planned a *coup*—which was hoped and believed would end the Moderators to a man before Houston could reach the scene.

"These were 'forted' in Shelby County near the Augustine border, and Helen went ostensibly to meet her lover who was one of them, but really to entice the garrison out into rifle range of her friends. Superbly mounted, dressed in full, long, flowing velvet riding habit, as was the fashion in those days, with banded beaver on her head, she cantered up to the forted Moderators, the fort being a double log house planked up and surrounded with a fence. She called her lover and at the fence laughed and joked with glee and talked of other things than war.

"Her friends, she said, had 'quit on old Houston's order'; had gone to their homes, or were far away and she was for peace for her family, for which she had come to sue. All the while her friends were creeping up to get within full range of the foe. The men of the fort came one by one to the fence, their fears relieved, and chatted with Helen. And then she made her mistake. She looked towards the nearby woods once too often, and, at last, too anxiously. This her lover noted, but true to his clan he warned them 'to cover and be quick about it,' when the crack of a rifle, which was fired from a nearby thicket, desperately wounded him. Helen, swooping to her horse's mane, turned and fled. The fort responded with a volley, and Helen, falling from her horse, was dragged by her foot, which caught in the stirrup, along a wild country road. When rescued, her head had been pounded to a pulp. This affair was known as 'Helen's Defeat.' "

Such was the lore which the great feud left behind. If the facts were not as romantic, they were at least as painful.

2. *Old Rose and Senator Potter*

The Regulator type of feud is one disease which must be labeled "contagious." When you find vigilantes or "mobs" at work in one community, you can be fairly certain of finding them in another.

In the piney woods country of East Texas in the 1840's Regulators and Moderators, or their equivalents, made local history. "The contagion had spread far and wide," says Dr. Ashcroft. "Companies had been organized in several counties; among the rest Harrison, Panola, Nacogdoches, Sabine, and San Augustine."

The great conflagration in Shelby County has overshadowed most of the lesser blazes and they have mostly been forgotten; but the memory of one lives on. This was the Rose-Potter broil which came to its climax in 1843 on the shores of Caddo Lake in Harrison County, seventy-five miles north of Shelbyville. It is one of the famous scandals of early Texas history.

Among the strange characters who drifted west to Texas in early times, none was stranger than Robert Potter. Born in 1800 in North Carolina, he made an idol of John Paul Jones, spent five years in the United States Navy, came back to practice law in his native state, and set out to "put the bottom rail on top, playing the devil and breaking the meat axe."[1]

Fiery and fearless, he made enemies right and left. The aristocrats wouldn't fight duels with him because he was not a gentleman, but he made them smart anyway. He wrote a mock-heroic poem called

The Head of Medusa in which he disposed of them individually and collectively by boiling them in hot scorn.[2] After two unsuccessful tries, he got himself elected to the State Legislature in 1826 and at once began to run the Carolina bankers crazy by digging into a financial scandal. In his spare time he cooked up a "Political Education Bill" which would have given poor boys a chance at a college education a century before public opinion called for such a step.

Then in 1831 he ran into bad luck. Because he believed his wife to have been unfaithful, he personally emasculated the Rev. Louis Taylor, a Methodist preacher fifty-five years old (said to have been his own uncle), and a seventeen-year-old youth named Louis Wiley. So notorious did this case become that his method of taking revenge became known as "Potterizing," and was a capital offense in North Carolina until 1868.[3]

Instead of destroying Potter's popularity, this episode merely gave him another issue to take to the people. He made speeches through the bars of his cell and went back to the House of Commons for another term.

A gambling scandal finally finished him in his home state, and after being expelled from the Legislature, he found a haven in Texas in the summer of 1835.

He had no trouble in making his way in this new country. Undoubtedly he was one of the most striking figures ever to cross the border—a slender, high-strung, dynamic man with "Restless, rolling black eyes and stern cast iron lips."[4] His bearing was lion-like; his voice moved and excited all who heard him, though he never raised it; his manners were courtly in the extreme. The Texans barely looked at him before making him a delegate to the Constitutional Convention. He signed the Declaration of Independence and became the first Secretary of the Navy in the Republic of Texas.[5]

In 1836 he met a Mrs. Harriet Ames in Austin, the wife of a man named Solomon Ames who didn't stay around much and usually left his wife and children to starve or shift for themselves. Potter was wary about contracting any further marriage ties, though his wife had divorced him and he was free, but he fell in love with Mrs. Ames and persuaded her to live with him. In her memoirs she says that he went through a ceremony with her after convincing her that she was not legally married to Ames.[6]

About the same time he took up a headright grant in a beautiful location on Soda Lake still known as Potter's Point, and there they settled.

In 1839 Captain Pinckney Rose became their neighbor. He was from all accounts a man to be reckoned with, "long and lean, six feet two inches high, with the eye of a hawk and the muscle of a horse."[7] His enemies picture him as a dreadful savage who killed everybody he didn't like and ran things with a high and violent hand. His grandson says, "He could be aroused to a high pitch of anger, but ordinarily was a warm-hearted, companionable man, and of great strength of character."

Whatever his personal shortcomings, Rose was connected with some of the best families in the South and had done good service for his country, having been in command of a company in the Battle of New Orleans in 1815.[8]

Harrison County was overrun by thieves, like the rest of East Texas, and very soon after his arrival Rose formed, or helped to form, a regulating company. In due time a group of Moderators organized in opposition. Harriet Ames tells how they lined up:

"In those days, Texas was ruled by two parties, the Moderators and Regulators; the former believed in administering justice in a legal way and the latter in dealing it out in arbitrary and usually quite sudden fashion. Col. Potter belonged to the Moderator party. . . ."[9]

Potter was elected to serve as a senator in the Fifth and Sixth Congresses, but he had to overcome heavy opposition from Rose and his men.[10] He got even by helping to have his enemy declared an outlaw. Rose was charged with murdering John B. Campbell, Sheriff of Panola County, and two other citizens in January of 1841. On November 15 President Lamar put a price of $500 on his head.

Potter made up his mind that he was going to collect that reward. As soon as Congress adjourned, he hurried home, gathered a posse of seventeen men, and swooped down on the Rose establishment.

It was early in the morning—about daylight—and Rose had, fortunately for him, just stepped outside. He knew what the visit meant as soon as the men rode up, and he knew he had to act quickly. Near him a force of Negroes were clearing some new ground. He made them pile brush over him and set the pile afire. Potter's men made a thorough search of the premises, but it never occurred to them that a man would hide under a burning brush pile, of all places.

Once Rose thought he was done for when an enterprising rooster spied him under the brush and began to peer and squawk and raise an alarm. Rose's Negro Jerry quieted the noise without arousing suspicion, and as soon as Rose came out, he put a permanent end to that rooster's curiosity.[11]

In searching the house, according to accounts of the Rose partisans, Hezekiah George pried open a bureau and "filched from the drawer a gold watch belonging to Mrs. Rose." If George did it, he paid for his crime just a few hours later.

Disappointed, Potter went home and proceeded to relax, being tired after his long ride from Austin and his exertions of the morning. His wife was afraid he might have started something he couldn't finish, but he laughed at the idea.

Rose was terribly angry over the raid and went at once to have warrants sworn out for Potter on a charge of trespassing. In such cases a warrant was usually just a pretext, however, and to show how much importance Rose attached to his, we have the fact that he came in the middle of the night to serve it, surrounded the house with a party of men including his son-in-law John Scott, and prepared to surprise the household at daybreak.

Harriet Ames had a feeling that they were not far away, and she remembered every detail when, as an old lady, she wrote it all down:

"I felt very anxious as the night advanced, and presently the barking of the dogs warned me that some stranger was around our house. I woke my husband up and called his attention to this fact, but he would not believe that the house was being surrounded and said that he was very tired and to let him alone. I was too uneasy to sleep myself. . . . So the night wore on until I felt that I could bear the suspense no longer. We always had our meal ground for breakfast in the steel mill, and it was almost time for the performance of that first morning duty. I arose and woke the boy whose business it was to grind the meal, and told him it was time to get the meal ready for breakfast. The boy was obliged to cross the yard in order to reach the corn crib and get a supply of corn for the mill. In a few moments he went out; he did not return, and as time went on and the gray morning began to break into the dusk of night and shadows became less deep and dark, I roused my brother and told him about the boy's absence. He went out to look for him and he, too, remained. We had an old man living with us who always fed the hogs and when he started out to his work, I said to him, it is very strange that George does not commence to grind the meal for breakfast. I wish you would see what is the matter. I waited a while and unable to stand the anxiety any longer I decided to go myself. I stepped out into the early morning and started toward the kitchen. Just as the man Hezekiah went over the stile some little distance from the left hand side of the house, I was half way to the kitchen. A posse shot him down and tried to take me prisoner. I was very active and I darted away from them and into the house."

This Hezekiah was the one accused of rifling Mrs. Rose's bureau drawer. Old Rose let him have both barrels in the rear as he was trying to get away, and he was ever after known as "Old Rose's lead mine."[12]

Potter was awakened by the shooting, but never quite found his wits. He determined to try to escape by the lake, though Harriet did her best to persuade him that his best course was to stay and fight. "We can defend ourselves," she said. "I will stand by you as long as we both live. If you will just kill old Rose and Scott, the difficulty will be at an end."

Potter wouldn't listen. He ran through the back door, leaped over the fence, dashed down the bank to the lake, leaned his gun against a cypress tree, plunged in and started to swim for it.

Rose's son-in-law Scott picked up the gun and shot him in the back of the head. Harriet found his body along the shore next day.[13]

As she tells the story, she went in fear of her life but was determined to have Rose and Scott brought to justice. She did manage to have them arrested, but they succeeded in evading trial.[14]

Later Harriet married again and enjoyed a few years of peace, though she had to endure the humiliation of learning that she had never been legally married to Potter at all, and could not inherit his property.

Rose moved to another part of Texas, settling near Victoria where some of his descendants still live.

This case came to the attention of none other than Charles Dickens while he was enduring his first trip to America and trying not to make an ungentlemanly display of the repugnance aroused in him by the crudity of American manners. He quoted an interesting version of Potter's death taken from the " 'Caddo Gazette,' of the 12th inst.," in his *American Notes:* [15]

He was beset in his house by an enemy named Rose. He sprang from his couch, seized his gun, and, in his nightclothes, rushed from the house. For about two hundred yards his speed seemed to defy his pursuers; but, getting entangled in a thicket, he was captured. Rose told him *that he intended to act a generous part,* and give him a chance for his life. He then told Potter he might run, and he should not be interrupted till he reached a certain distance. Potter started at the word of command, and before a gun was fired he had reached the lake. His first impulse was to jump in the water and dive for it, which he did. Rose was close behind him, and formed his men on the bank ready to shoot him as he rose. In a few seconds he came up to breathe; and scarce had his head reached the surface of the water when it was completely riddled with the shot of their guns, and he sunk, to rise no more!

BORN of WAR

And so when your ordinary citizen . . . sees that he has placed justice in a dead hand he must take justice back into his own hands where it was once at the beginning of all things. Call this primitive, if you will, but so far from being a defiance of the law, it is an assertion of it.

James G. Leyburn,
Frontier Folkways.

3.

Blood in
Bell County

This is about Sam Hasley, a farmer boy from the brush-and-post-oak country fifty miles north of Austin, who came home after the Civil War to find himself mixed up in a feud.

Sam was not much to look at and even less to listen to. Nobody ever took the trouble to describe for posterity his appearance and personality, but the record shows that he was a patient, self-effacing fellow who let other people do the strutting while he stayed in the background figuring out how to do what had to be done. It happened that the job he felt he must do involved killing quite a lot of people, but a job was a job to Sam and he went at this one with conscientiousness and determination.

Though he came of country stock and wore home-made pants, Sam had deep and tender feelings toward his family—particularly toward his white-bearded old father, Mr. Drew (or Drury) Hasley. Had it not been for this, a number of people might have lived longer.

Sam's unobtrusiveness makes the Bell County affair one of the hardest of Texas feuds to reconstruct. It was amazing how the whole thing was carried on under cover—how tracks were erased, names were concealed, and witnesses were avoided at crucial moments. Some quiet, crafty man did the planning and managing. If it wasn't Sam Hasley, one would like to know who it was.

As you would have expected, Sam felt he had to go to war when Texas joined the Confederacy. His leaving created some family problems, for his father was getting along in years and it would be hard to run the farm with only the younger boys to help. But Mr. Drew raised his head proudly and thrust out his white beard at his son. "You go along," he said. "We'll make out all right." So Sam bade them a quiet goodbye and went off to fight the Yankees.

He left with less regret than he otherwise might have felt because he knew a Home Guard company was being organized to protect the settlers who stayed at home. He could not foresee that the Guards would soon fall into discredit and become more of a menace than a help, or that he himself would soon be battling to the death with some of the guardsmen.

The Home Guard was a good idea, but it was too easily perverted to bad uses. Supposedly its members were old men and boys, too decrepit or too immature for military service, but undesirable characters had little trouble getting in.[1] Some were the sons of rich men whose fathers considered them too important to risk their lives in battle. Some were bullies. Some were sticky-fingered rodents who used the activities of the Guard as a cloak for thieving. Before long the old Texans began calling the organization the "Heel Flies" after a mischievous insect which runs horses crazy in the summertime.

A good deal of trouble after the war, including the Bell County bloodshed, went back to Heel-Fly activities. In his unpublished memoirs[2] one old Confederate named James Hatch shows how it worked out: Furloughed soldiers, he says, often "fell into the hands of this self-constituted home defense army and were rushed to the recruiting officers and started back to Lee's army in Virginia before they had recovered from the effect of gunshot wounds." In their spare time, he adds, they branded cattle that belonged to their absent neighbors. "Owners on returning began counterbranding these stolen cattle and horses; this caused many rows frequently resulting in shootings between former friends. Soon vendettas formed during the late sixties and seventies . . . and hundreds of murders was the consequence."

In Bell County the Heel Flies were very active and very obnoxious. They specialized in routing deserters out of their hideouts in the rough country toward the west. In the early part of 1865 they got on the trail of three unnamed fugitives, brought them out of the brush, and went into camp with them near Reed's Lake in the eastern part of their territory. Old John Reed, who had settled near this lake and become well to do, had three sons in the Guard[3] and they no doubt wanted to camp near home and hot coffee.

During the night the three prisoners were taken out of camp and hanged to a big pecan tree. It happened that two companies of soldiers were quartered at Reed's place to take care of a concentration of horses and supplies belonging to the Southern army.[4] With so many men about it was hard to fix the blame for this revolting act, and consequently nothing much was said at the time. Later on it caused much trouble and bitterness.

The next mistake the Heel Flies made was to call on Mr. Drew Hasley. At the head of the company was one John Early, a shifty character who at this time posed as a passionate secessionist but who a little later went over to the Union invaders. It is hard to imagine what Mr. Hasley had done to deserve this visit. He seems to have had no feeling of guilt about it, whatever it was, and he stood up to Early with the sturdy pride he had passed on to his son. Before it was over, Early had abused and manhandled the old man and had pulled a handful of white hair out of his venerable beard.[5]

Before Early was much more than over the hill, Sam Hasley came home on furlough. He found his father terribly angry and humiliated, almost beyond speech. When he finally got a clear account of what had happened, Sam thought it over for a while. Finally he said, almost casually,

"Well, I guess I won't be going back to the army—anyway not till I've done for John Early."

"You mean you're going to desert, Son?"

"Maybe I can get him before my furlough's up. I can try. But if I don't, I'll stay here till I do."

Drew Hasley had no more to say. Sam's decision seemed right to both of them. It wasn't legal and it wasn't Christian, but for a boy like Sam, living when and where he did, there was no other way out. People spoke softly or not at all on the Texas frontier, and kept their hands off their neighbors. A blow was something one did not put up with unless he happened to be a coward or an outsider. Sam's blood kept up a slow and steady boil as he thought of the indignity which had been placed upon his father, and he began laying plans to wipe out the stain.

Fortunately for him, Lee surrendered before it was time to go back, and he was free to plot his revenge. He was glad when Early went over to the Yankee side, for now he had stronger proof that such a man ought not to be allowed to live.

He spent his spare time watching Early's movements and figuring how he could best get at him. The man was not easy to catch. Besides being slippery by nature, he had made his house on Friar's Creek a headquarters for the carpetbagger faction. All day and all night he was surrounded by assorted pistol-toters, and Sam knew the thing would not be easy to bring off.

When his chance came, it came unexpectedly. Sam was riding at night down a lonely, brush-bordered road when he ran head-on into a large party of Scalawags. It would not do to hesitate or turn back. He kept his horse at a walk and rode right through the band, saying nothing and keeping his eyes open. Early rode a white-faced horse, and Sam was watching for that white patch.

As he came to the last man in the group, he saw what he was looking for. His pistol came out and up in one swift motion. The explosion shattered the country quiet, and before the startled riders could turn in their saddles, he had disappeared in the brush. Early was rending the air with oaths and cries as he scrambled to get free of his dead horse.

Sam's first try had failed because the white-faced horse, thinking himself the object of Sam's dislike, had reared up just as the shot was fired and got the bullet in his own head.[6]

Nobody offered to go into the undergrowth after Sam, but there was much angry, threatening talk after the party got back to headquarters. Leading the chorus was the carpetbagger boss, Judge Hiram Christian, Chief Justice of the Military Commissioners for that district with headquarters in Belton. He was the best-hated man in that part of Texas, and the old Southerners damned him up and down as their most persistent persecutor. He and some of his friends, particularly one named Dr. Calvin Clark, had kept mum during the war, but as soon as it was safe to do so they revealed their Northern sympathies, got control of the local government, and improved every opportunity to get even with their old neighbors for past slights and injuries, real or imagined. High on the list of those they hated were the Hasleys and their friends.

Searching for some way to bring the authorities down on these people, Christian remembered the hanging of the three deserters near Reed's Lake. His henchmen were circulating a rumor that the saddles and saddle blankets of the dead men had been found in the attic of the Reed house. Then it came to his ears that somebody—probably a relative of one of the victims—was hounding the Military Government in Austin to make an example of the lynchers. Christian sent word to the capital that an investigation was in order.

Finally a detachment of soldiers arrived from Austin, shivering in the winter weather, and began arresting people. Among those picked up were John B. Reed, his son Ed, a Mr. Bell, and old Mr. Drew Hasley. Others who were wanted got word in time and made themselves scarce.[7] Sam Hasley's name was not on the list, of course, because he had been away at war when the lynching occurred. They would have to set another trap to catch him.

Christian had not been able to get everybody he hated, but the men in custody were all prominent and respected members of the Southern group. It was a great satisfaction to him to watch them being hustled off to Austin and jail. Most of them were certainly above suspicion. Only the Reeds could possibly have been implicated, and there was no proof against them. One and all they were herded off down the Austin road, however, and confined for several months in the clammy cells of an old stone prison.

It was no place for an elderly gentleman in poor health, and Sam's father suffered severely from exposure and privation. When they finally let him out, without ever bringing him to trial, he was a broken man and lasted only a few years more.[8]

This was what made a feud out of Sam's campaign against John Early. Out there in the post oaks a faction grew up united by a resolve to make Early, Christian and Clark pay dearly for their sins. Sam Hasley gave his name to this faction, but he kept in the background as usual and let other people do the loud talking. By now he had a brother-in-law named Jim McRae who was a brave man, but as noisy as Sam was quiet. McRae was the front man, but Sam did the thinking and planning.

There is no real evidence that Sam and his friends were mixed up in the undercover work which went on during the next few months—but who else could or would have stepped in to combat the lawlessness which the Union officials were powerless to stop? Sam was the only man in Bell County with the men and the motive to do it.

Like the rest of Texas, Bell County was almost at the mercy of horse thieves and other criminals.[9] There were rumors of secret organizations like the Alphebit of the forties,[10] and every sort of crime seemed to be profitable and safe. One farmer had his gentle stock cleaned out twice. Another had the same horse stolen three times, and the last time the thief was shot off the animal's back. And it was practically suicide to go after these bandits. They killed without compunction.[11]

When their patience ran out, the citizens took matters into their own hands. It was done so thoroughly and so quietly and so well that it began to look like an organized campaign. In April of 1866 half a dozen of the worst outlaws were done away with, including the leader of the Shackleford gang.[12] So expertly were these killings planned and so neatly were they executed that no one knew or cared to guess who the executioners were.

There was a lull during the month of May as the thieves ran for cover. Then in June the bullet-torn bodies of Jasper Lindley and Sam Miller were found floating in the Little River near Three Forks. Miller was a Bell County boy and Lindley was from down around San Antonio. They had been dead for several weeks, the papers said, and added that they had been liquidated "for horse stealing."[13]

The vigilantes, whoever they were, had shown what they could do and were now ready for bigger game. There were no denunciations or blacklists or warnings in the newspapers. It was all done as usual secretly and silently. But the word went around, and there was quaking and dismay in high places.

Judge Hiram Christian must have heard the quiet word of warning, and it must have come to him suddenly in the midst of his labors.

On July 2 he called his court to order as usual and went through the day's business. Then somehow he found that his number was up. He left the courthouse without signing the minutes, and before the dawn of July 3 broke over Bell County, he was long gone.[14]

Even so he left too late. The vigilantes were hard on his heels and he could not shake them off. They caught up with him in Missouri and killed him with their usual unobtrusive efficiency. No man's name was ever mentioned as the killer. The story of that chase has never been told.[15] Whoever managed the affair was a master at arranging these things and preventing the leakage of information afterward. George W. Tyler thinks that Sam Hasley was responsible.[16]

Now, however, some of the vigilantes' chickens were coming home to roost. About the time Christian folded his tent, the killing of Jasper Lindley began to cause trouble. Jasper's father Jonathan Lindley and his brother Newton left their home near San Antonio[17] with a warrant for the arrest of two men named Duncan and Daws. Duncan was a respectable ranchman who had lost a fine horse a little before Lindley's death. There was no other apparent reason for connecting him with that event. Daws was an inoffensive old Englishman, a sheepherder for Duncan. Their names were never mentioned as members of the vigilantes, but then nobody else's name was ever mentioned either. Those old Southern frontiersmen stuck together then, and for years afterward, protecting each other and laying all their troubles at the door of Christian, Clark, and the Yankees.[18]

Toward the middle of July, Lindley was ready to make his play. He rode up to Duncan's house, dressed in a United States Army uniform and accompanied by his son Newton and fifteen soldiers under the command of Major Carpenter of the Sixth Cavalry. Duncan and Daws gave up at once. Since there was nothing on the record to incriminate them, they had no serious qualms. Lindley apparently was also aware that if he got any satisfaction, he would have to get it by his own efforts.

They had a very short ride. In the middle of the prairie both of the captives were shot from their horses. "The officer alleges that Lindley did the shooting and fled," the Texas papers reported, and a Bell County correspondent demanded bitterly: "Can it be possible that

President Johnson will much longer inflict such a state of things upon us?"[19]

The outrage stirred up the men of Bell County as nothing ever had before. A public meeting was held in the Belton courthouse on July 19, 1866, to make vigorous protest. It was unanimously and indignantly resolved that the troops had gone beyond "their legitimate duty of preventing insurrections to intermeddle with private feuds," and the President of the United States was called upon to remove the soldiers.[20]

Colonel Morris, the Commissioner at Austin, came up to see what was going on and what could be done about it,[21] but the citizens found a way to solve the problem themselves. When Jonathan and Newton Lindley, father and son, were brought back to Bell County to stand trial, a mob surrounded the jail, "attacked and dispersed the guard," and shot the prisoners. Strangely enough no one recognized a soul in the party, and it was "some hours" before any of the local citizens reached the scene of the crime.[22]

The Lindley case became notorious all over the nation. The radical papers seized upon it as a horrible example of Southern barbarism and *Harper's Weekly* for March 23, 1867, included a pen sketch of something like the Lindley mobbing in a two-page spread on "Southern Justice."

And where was Sam Hasley all this time? He was not a man to let his neighbors risk their lives mobbing the Yankees while he loafed in the background. It was his side, and probably his friends and henchmen, who did the dirty work, but if Sam was there he succeeded in keeping his name out of it. Since he was already on the black books of the Northerners, he probably took extra precautions and worked under cover as much as possible.

Most of the time he and his friends walked warily and kept to themselves. For two years they made their headquarters at the old Moses Griffin home near Three Forks out in the post-oak country where there was plenty of cover. Here lived David Griffin, who was a brother-in-law of Jim McRae, who was a brother-in-law of Sam Hasley. The Griffins were people of some wealth and considerable respectability, and they had many friends. The other side conceded that they were "considered as good people, with one exception" (meaning McRae). Of McRae they remarked that his character was "too well known throughout the State to require a notice. Suffice to say his record in this county has been a record of crime."

It was McRae who began to be talked about now as the bold, bad man of the outlaws, Sam Hasley still keeping his head down. In the summer of 1869 McRae had progressed so far in the enmity of the other side that a movement was set afoot to bring his career to an end. On July 21, the papers reported, "a meeting was held by twenty odd citizens & a card published offering their services to bring McRae's band to justice."[23]

McRae was not the quiet type, and when he heard of this he put on a good dramatic performance describing what he planned to do to the signers of the card. He meant every word of it, too, as he demonstrated when on July 27 he and a few followers crept up to John Early's house and took a shot at a young man named Morrison who was enjoying a moment of peace on the front gallery. The ball struck above his head and did him no harm, but the way he sprang to life and removed himself from the line of fire seemed very funny to the attackers. McRae described the scene with howls of laughter when he got home, and he repeated his intention of making some people skip for their lives, mentioning particularly Dr. O. C. Powell, who had written the petition offering the services of the Citizens' Committee to the military.

The single shot fired at Morrison had a wonderful effect, for when Lieutenant Holt and a company of soldiers set out on the day of the shooting to run McRae down, only four members of the Committee came forward to assist—Dr. Powell, Robert McDaniel, Amos Morrison, and J. C. Ballard.[24] Before the day was over, this band made contact with McRae and had a brush with him and some of his men. They thought they winged McRae himself but could not be sure, and the action had to be classed as indecisive.

The feud was now nearing its climax and fear settled over the land. "All of the country between Belton and Reed's Lake up and down the north side of Leon and Little River was in a state of semi-war," says the Bell County historian.[25] There was scouting and forting up and watchful waiting on both sides as the fighting men girded themselves for battle.

On the thirtieth John Early took a hand. He assembled a posse of his own and, armed with authority from Lieutenant Holt, set out "to capture if possible and to kill if necessary the leading men of this band of outlaws."

It was six A.M. when they started out, and the day was well advanced when they crept up to the Griffin house and found themselves almost in the midst of a family party. There they were—Hasleys, McRaes and Griffins—the whole tribe, great and small—having a watermelon feast. The anticlimax stopped the invaders in their tracks and they crept away again, whispering to each other that with so many women and children around it wouldn't be right to start shooting.

When they reached the Griffin pasture they halted and made up their minds to wait a while. Somebody was bound to make a scout through the woods before night, and there would be a chance to mow that somebody down.

Let the man who described the action for the Belton *Journal* tell the rest:

"They had to wait several hours for the hoped-for moment when McRea and one other supposed to be David Griffin rode in the direction of the party of Early.

"McRea and his comrade had a pistol each in the right hand swearing vengeance against their enemies when a volley from the opposing force dropped McRea from his horse. His friend fired four shots from his pistol, but the contents of four double-barreled shotguns fired at him reminded him of important business at some other place.

"McRea had on his person three sixshooters and fired them all out after he fell from his horse, wounding young McDaniels, as noble a boy as ever lived. He is shot about two inches below the joint of the right knee. . . . The balance of McRea's band fired from a cane patch. The women hovered over the body of McRea, and as McDaniel's wound was bleeding it was thought best not to charge them. McRea lived until 9 o'clock that night—was shot about 4, living five hours. He was one of the most daring men that ever lived or died, and made friends from fear."[26]

With McRae gone, the heart went out of the band, but it took a few weeks for the authorities to find out that their troubles were really over. In August, after trying in vain to find a citizen of the county who could or would serve as sheriff, the commanding officer at Waco authorized Sergeant George F. Mayne of Co. E, Sixth U.S. Cavalry, to act as sheriff until relieved.[27] Sergeant Mayne brought a few troops with him when he took over, but found they would not be needed. He sent them back to Waco with a report that the McRae party had broken up and gone away.

When Major Longley of the Austin *Republican* came up in early October to see how matters stood, he could report that he had never seen "a more quiet and orderly community than this presents at the present time."[28]

Again we wonder what had become of Sam Hasley, who had slipped away from Bell County to be seen in his old haunts no more. Where he finally put down new roots and began a new life we do not know, but he appears once more to bring the gory history of the Bell County troubles to a close. The Galveston *News* ran a story on March 2, 1870, which shows that Sam had not forgotten and had not left the trail:

"A telegram from Memphis, Tenn., last week announced that Calvin Clark, of Bell County, Texas, was killed in Arkansas by a desperado named Halsey who followed him from Texas. The Belton (Bell County) *Journal,* of the 26th ult., says: C. C. Clark, who in some manner was known to every citizen of this county, moved from here to some point unknown to us, and if he is not the man referred to in the telegram, we cannot conjecture who Calvin Clark was. If there was ever a citizen in this county named Halsey, we do not know it."[29]

It would seem that the editor of the *Journal* was on Sam's side.

The last piece in the puzzle refuses to fall into place—the end of the story cannot be told. What happened to John Early? Did Sam Hasley follow his trail to the end too? Did a stranger camped in some lonely Western canyon wake up one bright morning to see Sam looking at him over the sights of a Winchester, and did the coroner's jury rule that the man died of gunshot wounds inflicted by a person or persons unknown? Or did Early fly so far and so fast that even

Sam Hasley could not catch up with him? Maybe some Kansas farmer who died full of years, honored by his neighbors, was really John Early, while Sam went to his own grave with his mission unfulfilled.

Nobody knows; but after all that had happened one can't help believing that Sam finally met Early face to face.

Sam, you know, was a very determined fellow.

4. The Franks Case

The Civil War brought changes to San Antonio, but San Antonio was prepared for them. This free-and-easy, half-Mexican town had already been through some rough times and knew what to do with the tough and sometimes desperate men who made it their headquarters. The country produced its share of horse thieves and general plunderers who blew their money in its innumerable gin mills. The citizens let them carouse till they went too far. Then the vigilantes hanged them.[1]

War conditions did not improve the situation. San Antonio entered on a mild boom period as a center of Confederate activity, both military and commercial. Soldiers came and went. Wagon trains loaded with cotton rattled off to Mexico where it was easy to bypass the Yankee blockade. Refugees from West Texas and New Mexico trailed wearily in after the South lost out in the West. The town was full of strangers, and many of the strangers were full of sin.

Their drinking and carousing could be borne. Robbery and murder were harder to take, and the Vigilance Committee had as much business as it could handle.

The "Mob" in San Antonio was well organized long before the War, and had promoted some notable lynchings and street fights. Like the Regulators in Shelby County twenty years before, these men fell back on the idea that people have a "natural right" to hang criminals when there is no other way of controlling them. In at least one case a feud situation arose as the result of extra-legal rope work.

In 1863, when this trouble began, the vigilantes were at full strength and ready to go into action at a moment's warning. No membership lists were kept and the rank and file maintained a sort of shadowy anonymity, but the leaders were well known and probably proud of their distinction. The acknowledged head of the organization was a pious man named Asa (or Ase) Mitchell.

Ase was a paradoxical character. A prosperous citizen in his fifties, he seemed the soul of portly respectability. He loved to preach and pray in the Methodist churches. And yet he went joyfully about the business of strangling the strangers within his gates. He unquestionably thought he was spreading the gospel and doing the Lord's work. So have many greater men in former times who slaughtered their fellow mortals in order to save the victims' souls.

One good story about him has come down to us. R. H. Williams, who went through the war with the local defense troops and spent much time around San Antonio, mentions him under the name of "Minshull" in his book *With the Border Ruffians:*

"There was always that rope that the old fellow was supposed to carry in the tall white hat he invariably wore. The old rascal was preaching one hot Sunday afternoon in the Wesleyan church to a crowded congregation, and by his side on the pulpit platform he placed his hat. As he vehemently denounced sinners, and urged to righteousness his listening flock, the perspiration trickled down his forehead so fast that he paused, and stooped down for his handkerchief lying in his hat. But, in his excitement, he quite forgot what else his hat contained, and hurriedly seizing his handkerchief, drew out with it a coil of rope."[2]

Most of Mitchell's activities seem to have passed without remark, possibly because he was too good a workman to leave any evidence; possibly because his fellow citizens approved of his labors and aided them by keeping silent. One time, however, his foot slipped, and he made news.

In the summer of 1863 a case came to the attention of the Mob which they felt they could not overlook. A Mexican arrived in town with a tale of robbery and murder. Ben Franks, a well-to-do cattleman from down in Atascosa County a few miles south of the city, had some cows to sell.³ Two Mexican ranchers visited the ranch to look the stock over. They had their money along—real hard silver dollars. The sight of so much money, according to the witness, was too much for Old Man Franks and he killed the visitors to get their wealth.

Since Franks was never brought to trial, nobody knows how much of the story is true.

The law was still functioning in San Antonio, though perhaps not as vigorously as the Mob, and the officers went down to Atascosa County to pick Franks up. In July of 1863 they brought him in to jail.

He never got inside the walls. The Mob was waiting for him, and in the time it takes to pull on a rope, he was hanging from a chinaberry tree near the jail entrance. To do Mitchell justice, he was not there to officiate, though one of his close relatives was.⁴

It so happened that Franks had two boys, both under twenty-one. They were serving in Williams' company of State Guards at the time and were not in the neighborhood, but they had been raised according to the Texas system and knew what was expected of them. They found out who the lynchers were and bided their time.

When the war was over and they were able to take up their private business, they went to work. Williams gives the names of seven men they settled with, though the names are probably fictitious. Three got away to Mexico. The others had to move fast to keep ahead of the Franks boys.

How strangely these things work out is shown by the story of Sam Childress, the same age as young Alse Franks. Sam's father was one of the men the Franks boys were after, but Sam and Alse were on fairly friendly terms. Old Man Childress hid out in Mississippi and so saved his hide, but as time went on he grew homesick for the sight of the mesquite and huisache of his native land. He wrote to Sam and told him to ask Alse Franks if he could come home now. "He says he wants to come home to die," Sam said. "Will you let him?"

"Sure," replied Alse, "and damn quick."

Presumably Old Man Childress did his dying in Mississippi.

According to the late R. R. (Railroad) Smith of Jourdanton, another fugitive was not so lucky. They located him in Louisiana and laid elaborate plans to trap him. In order to keep ahead of pursuit, if there should be any, they set up a series of relay stations, with horses saddled and ready, clear to the Louisiana border. Then they walked into his house and told him to get ready to die.

The man was tubercular and down in bed with his last illness. "I haven't got much time left," he pleaded with them. "Let me live a little longer."

"You've lived too long already," they told him, and finished him then and there.[5]

Such stories as this grow up, whether true or not, wherever a feud breaks out. From newspaper columns and court records, however, a few facts can be put together. John Turnbull, who was jailer at the time of the hanging, was indicted in 1865 as one of the murderers. He had already left the country when the indictment was lodged against him, but later on he was located in Rains County on the Sabine in East Texas. On November 23, 1871, he was brought back and placed in the San Antonio jail.[6]

"He has changed very much since the war," commented a reporter, "and although only 47 years old, is very gray." No doubt he had been doing some worrying.

His trial was finished on April 3. The jury was out ten minutes and agreed that he was not guilty. "The other two men charged in the same indictment were clearly proven guilty of the hanging," remarked the San Antonio *Herald*. "Those men have, however, not resided in the State, and perhaps not in the United States, since the conclusion of the late 'onpleasantness,' and we do not suppose anyone knows positively the whereabouts of either."[7]

Turnbull admitted watching the hanging, but was able to prove that he had tried to stop it and had given up only when "a pistol was put to my head, and I was told to be quiet or be killed."

Public opinion seems to have been with the Franks boys in the prosecution of their revenge. Mrs. Frances Farris (late of Coronado, California), who grew up in the prickly-pear pasture country south of San Antonio, used to tell how Alse Franks sometimes hid out on her father's ranch. She could remember tagging along when the grown-ups took supplies to him and playing with the handsome buttons on his shirt as she sat on his knee. It never occurred to her that he was a fugitive from justice. According to the code of her time and place he was a brave man who had risked his life to set things straight.

Mrs. Farris and her people were not low-class citizens with little respect for law and order. If anything, they were the aristocracy of their frontier country; and what they did, most of the good people of Texas would have done in their place. They simply recognized, as we all do at times, an ethical principle higher than the laws on the statute books.

BEEF and SALT

All existing civilized communities appear to have gone through a stage in which it was impossible to say where private vengeance for injuries ended and public retribution for offenses began, or rather the two notions are hardly distinguished.

Sir Frederick Pollock,
The King's Peace in the Middle Ages.

5. *The Hoodoo War*

The night of February 18, 1875, settled down quietly enough on the roofs of Mason, Texas, a German-American community a hundred miles northwest of San Antonio. The yellow light of kerosene lamps bloomed here and there behind the trees and shrubs. One by one the merchants closed up and hurried home to warm suppers and comfortable fires. Mason was no honky-tonk town, and people stayed home after dark.

Then suddenly a woman began to scream—terrible, gasping blood-curdling shrieks that could be heard blocks away through the still air. I have heard old men say that those screams still rang in their ears after seventy years.[1]

It was Mrs. John Wohrle who was rending the night with her cries. She was watching a band of masked men who had knocked at the door and crowded into the house when her husband answered. They were now busily engaged in tying him to a chair and fastening a gag in his mouth.[2] Mrs. Wohrle was pregnant and feeling nervous any-way. This completely unexpected violence took away her last shred of self-possession, and she let go with everything she had. Somebody in the mob (legend says it was Dan Hoerster, though no positive identification was possible) shouted, "Hit her in the mouth and she'll shut up." That set her off louder than ever.

It seems the masked men wanted the keys to the jail, and also wanted no interference from the jailer, who happened to be Mr. Wohrle. When they failed to find any keys in his pockets, they left him as he was and slid out into the night while Mrs. Wohrle collapsed.

Ranger Lieutenant Dan W. Roberts had come into town that day from his winter quarters at Menardville in order to buy grain for his horses.[3] He was just getting to sleep in his room at Hunter's Hotel when the commotion broke loose. Before he could get his clothes back on, there was a thundering knock at his door and Sheriff John Clark, breathless and wild eyed, ran into the room shouting, "Get up! A lot of men are mobbing the jail!"

Together they ran down the stairs and headed for the lock-up, accompanied by James Trainer. A dark knot of men was huddled together outside the jail-house door and they heard the steady thump of a battering ram.

The officers never quite reached the spot. With twenty steps to go, they heard a sharp "Halt!" And they halted.

"Keep your distance if you don't want to get shot," said the stern voice. Being sensible as well as courageous, they backed off and crossed the street diagonally to the courthouse. Roberts and Trainer stopped at the door. Clark went on to the second floor and put his gun through a courtroom window. "The first damned man that touches that jail door, I'll kill him!" he announced.

Immediately ten of the forty mobsters detached themselves and came across the street. They brushed past Roberts and marched upstairs for a conference with the embattled sheriff. "We don't mean any harm to you or to the county," they said, "but we're going to have those men in the jail and you're going to get hurt if you try to stop us."

Clark looked at the masked faces. Maybe he knew who was behind the masks and maybe he didn't. People still wonder about that. Finally he said, "I give up."

Without another word the delegation went back to the jail, which by this time was open, and the mob disappeared inside. In a matter of minutes they came back out with five men—the Backus gang. They had Lige and Pete Backus, Charley Johnson, Abe Wiggins, and Tom Turley. A sixth prisoner, not much more than a boy, they left behind while they concentrated on his elders and badders.

While this was going on Clark was doing what he could. "You stay here and watch which way they go," he said to Roberts, and left at the double in order to get his horse and round up some help. By the time he had collected five or six citizens who were willing to help him, the mob had made its way through the darkness about a mile to a draw beyond the south edge of town and were proceeding to string their prisoners up to a big old post oak, which is still standing.

When Clark, Roberts, and the little posse came up at a trot, the hanging was pretty well along, but in order to make sure of their victims some of the lynchers began to fire at the dangling bodies. The posse was not sure who was being shot at and started throwing lead themselves. Immediately the dark figures ahead of them began to scatter and everybody had disappeared when the officers arrived on the scene.

They cut down four men. Later they learned that Charley Johnson, the tenderfoot cook, still had his feet on the ground when the shooting started. He threw the rope off his neck, cleared a fence which under ordinary circumstances he would have had to climb over, and tore down the bushes for half a mile of frantic flight. Three days later he showed up at Roberts' camp, "footsore and wild." Tom Turley also survived, though he was practically dead when the rescuers got him down. Lige and Pete Backus had been successfully hanged, and Abe Wiggins had most of his head blown off.

This was the first, though unfortunately not the last, appearance of the "Hoodoos" who gave the Mason County war its odd name. They were the members of a vigilance committee which attempted, by ambushes and midnight hangings, to get rid of the thieves and outlaws who had been holding a carnival of lawlessness in Mason County, as in other parts of Texas. Negroes used to call the Ku Klux Klan by the same name.[4] Lee Hall's Texas Rangers down on the Rio Grande had earned the same title.[5]

As usual some good people, driven to desperation, were undercover supporters of the mob. It is still said behind closed doors in Mason that Deputy Wohrle was no unwilling victim, and that the tying and gagging was just an act. If this was true, his wife was not entrusted with the secret. She had a miscarriage as a result of her experience.[6] If she was acting, she carried her dramatics pretty far.

If Wohrle was not putting on an exhibition to save his face as a peace officer, he must at least have known that the masked mobsters were men he had grown up with and been intimate with for years. The majority and maybe all of them were Mason County Germans—Dutchmen, as the "Americans" called them—one or two generations from the Old Country. They were still pretty much German in customs and language, but they were beginning to get the hang of one American custom: the use of rope, steel and lead to maintain peace and property rights.

At the start the Dutch had most of the right on their side. They were good thrifty people whose fathers and grandfathers had landed in Texas in the fifties or before after a nine-week voyage from Hamburg to Indianola. Some of the immigrants stopped at Fredericksburg; some pushed on to Loyal Valley;[7] the hardiest ventured across the Llano to Fort Mason and farther still, settling in lonely spots where only God and a good rifle were any protection against Indians and outlaws.[8] The family cemeteries grew rapidly, and it can still be noted how many of the graves were dug for little children.[9]

The Civil War helped to toughen these bearded German pioneers further. Most of them leaned toward the Union or tried to be neutral (which to a Southerner was the same thing),[10] and between the Home Guard and the Comanche Indians they had about all they could handle.

After the war better times were terribly slow in coming. The Rangers did not bring the Indians under control until 1875[11]—the year the feud broke out—and the outlaws rode high and wide until they were wiped out or run out by the feud itself.

Organized bands of these human coyotes were at work even before the Indians were neutralized, ranging up and down the frontier and running off small bunches of livestock. Some of the local ranchers were not much better than the thieves. Trail herds were made up every spring, and many times the trail bosses were completely indifferent as to whose cows they drove. Even reputable ranchers helped things along by picking up strays and mavericks. Charley Lehmberg down at Loyal Valley had a standing offer of five dollars a head for unbranded calves, and a thing like that was bound to cause trouble.[12]

"Accommodation marketing" made matters worse. A man who

found a neighbor's steer in his herd was supposed to sell the animal with his own stock and return the profits to the owner.[13] More trouble!

Then there was the brand registration law which allowed a rancher to record any brand he wished, provided there was no similar brand registered in the county. Still more trouble!

Even geography was an encouragement to lawlessness. Cows were always drifting from the eastern portions of the county into the higher, wilder country farther west. Had there been no rustlers at all, many a cow would have disappeared of her own accord. As things stood, a man who coveted his neighbor's ox had only to wait awhile and one would be along. A man who could keep his hands entirely clean under such conditions would have been a little eccentric.

In the 1870's things had grown so bad that the population could endure no more. Little ranchers and small farmers, to whom a small loss was important, were the hardest hit and the most resentful. To a rustler a milk cow was just a cow. To a farmer whose children needed her milk she was a family institution. So it was the little men who took the first steps toward a clean-up about two years before the fighting began.

Since these little men were mostly Germans, the trouble took on the appearance of a war between races, or at least nationalities. A Mason correspondent for the Austin *Statesman* explained that about three-fourths of the population was of German origin, and that most of the outrages had been "perpetrated almost exclusively on Germans as a class, by a numerous and bloody band of outlaws gathered from all the surrounding frontier counties. . . . Though in perfect accord with the Germans in opposing the doings of the outlaws, the American population take no open action against them lest they, too, should fall before the bullet of the concealed or midnight assassin. Therefore the Germans are left alone to combat these malign scourges of civilization. . . ."[14]

At first the Germans tried to get out of the mess they were in by peaceful means. It might help, they thought, if they could get some honest men into the county government. In 1872 they elected Sheriff Clark and Cattle Inspector Hoerster to office—"honest men," the

Mason correspondent called them, "whom neither the cajolery, threats nor money of the clique could seduce. . . ."[15]

Clark was indeed an honest and courageous man, an ex-soldier, who seems to have had a genuine desire to put down stealing and crookedness, though his reputation is clouded by the support he gave to mob methods. Hoerster was a famous fighter during the feud, a big, bold fellow with corn-colored hair and a great yellow beard.

Then came the year 1875 and a tidal wave of rustling which made all previous outbreaks seem puny. In February Sheriff Clark called on the citizens to help him break it up. Already trail herds were being gathered at various places in the county, and two posses were organized within a few days of each other for the purpose of reclaiming stolen cattle from these herds and arresting the men who had rustled them.[16]

In their first sweep the Sheriff and one posse caught up with a group of men out west of Mason on Brady Creek. The Backus brothers and eight of their boys were readying a herd belonging to almost everybody in Mason County but themselves. It is said that only three of the cows they had gathered belonged to them. In rounding up the gang the officers let three get away. The remaining five they took to Mason and lodged in the jail.

The second posse pushed farther south and west to the James River where another herd of stolen stock was being held. They found the cattle, but the rustlers had become alarmed and allowed the herd to scatter, so nobody was arrested.

The plan to lynch the Backus boys may have been hatched among the members of this second expedition. Tom Gamel, a posse member who wrote down what he remembered of their transactions, actually blames Sheriff Clark for the first proposal. To the suggestion that they all combine to "get rid of" the men in jail, Gamel replied: "That's all right. Those fellows can't get out of jail, and we have our cattle, and they are bound for the penitentiary. And anyway if we should send every man to the penitentiary that ever stole a cow, there wouldn't be any citizens left in Mason."

He adds that Dan Hoerster also proposed "taking the law into their own hands" and again he refused to cooperate. From this time on

Gamel was a supporter of the American side, and his accusations may be taken for whatever they are worth.

The posse returned to Mason that afternoon, and the jail was broken into during the night. That touched off a fuse which threatened to explode the whole countryside into civil war. All sorts of rumors and counter rumors circulated. First one man and then another was talked of as the next victim of the mob. Tom Gamel heard that he was marked down for slaughter and, being a tough Texan, he started looking for the men who were looking for him.

The only reasonably full account of the early stages of the feud—written to the San Antonio *Herald* by Major Henry M. Holmes, an ex-Englishman and former Union soldier who had set up a law practice in Mason—picks up the story at this point:

"On the 24th or 25th of March, Mr. Thomas Gamel learned that the mob was about to hang him, what the source of his information was, is unknown to the writer; but evidently it was considered serious by him, as he summoned his friends and came into town to see about it. The sheriff was in town when they arrived, but at once left, though as he never called on any citizen of the place for assistance it is not thought that he considered himself in any danger.

"Mr. Gamel's party behaved very well, and left the next day after, which I think was Saturday, and on the following Monday, the sheriff returned to the town, followed by sixty-two men, mounted and armed, and it was at once remarked that every one of the gentlemen following him were Germans, not one American amongst them.

"The town was held by this party in a kind of semi-military manner for the remainder of the week. Saturday Mr. Gamel came in again with a party, and peace was proclaimed, under the agreement that there should be no more mobs or hanging: who made the agreement or who was authorized to do so, I cannot inform you. I would add here that the party with the sheriff behaved admirably while in town."[17]

Ernest Lemburg remembers when that truce was ratified. The Germans were grouped on one side of the square when the others rode in. There was a big pow-wow which came to a peaceful end. The men stacked their arms on the courthouse square and appeared to mingle as friends. Ernest's mother gave a sigh of relief and said, "Well, maybe they are going to make up and stop fighting."

The armistice turned out to be a very short breathing spell. Behind the scenes the men of violence were almost ready to take the fight away from the good but exasperated people who had started it. The clean-up, as usual, was about to become a reign of terror, and the Williamson business on the thirteenth of May was what set the prairie afire.

Tim Williamson was a prominent and popular "American" who worked as foreman for Charley Lehmberg at Loyal Valley. Lehmberg was the one who had offered five dollars a head for unbranded calves, and his foreman was said to be picking up a little extra money on the side. There was talk about that.

More important, Tim was at outs with Sheriff Clark. Tom Gamel says they had "a dispute over some taxes" and adds that Clark abused Mrs. Williamson over this matter one time during Tim's absence but backed down when Tim "tried to get a fight out of him."[18]

We do not know how much bad there was in Williamson, but we can be sure there was some good. Some years before, on a drive to Kansas, he had picked up an orphan boy named Scott Cooley who had been carried off by the Indians after his parents had been massacred up in Palo Pinto County.[19] He brought the frightened, miserable youngster back from Oklahoma, took care of him, and sent him to school during the three months of the year when they had any.[20] Mrs. Williamson nursed him through an attack of typhoid fever. Both of them gave him a rough-and-ready affection which he valued more than they knew.

Maybe the terrible experiences of his early childhood did something to Scott Cooley. Maybe there was a queer streak in him. His picture reveals a look of brooding intensity, as if there were hot fires banked up inside, and there was something morbid and terrible about both his loves and his hates.

He grew up into a heavy-set, powerful man so dark-skinned that people wondered if he might not be part Cherokee, but his feelings toward Indians were too bitter for words. After he left home, he served for a year or so in Company D of the Rangers under Captain

Perry, seeing action in several skirmishes. He behaved himself well at the Loss Valley Indian battle on July 12, 1874,[21] and won the respect of his comrades. They noted that when he came up with the red raiders he "fought them hard and close."[22]

The old men at Mason remember that he once brought Mr. Schuessler, the saddle maker, some long strips of heavily tallowed hide to be braided into a quirt. When Mr. Schuessler found out that the stuff was Indian hide, he ran Cooley out of the shop.[23]

It was also said that Cooley was subject to some sort of fits "at certain periods of the year throughout his life"—supposedly the aftermath of a rattlesnake bite.[24]

In 1875 he was cultivating a farm over near Menardville in perfect peace and harmony with his neighbors.

On a Thursday in May, 1875, Deputy John Wohrle rode down to Lehmberg's ranch to arrest Williamson. The offense—stealing a yearling—was an old one, and Tim had made bond some time before, but bondsman Dan Hoerster had withdrawn for some reason and a new bond had to be made. Charley Lehmberg was perfectly willing to put up security and save Williamson a trip to town, but Wohrle said no—Tim would have to go in with him. People remembered his insistence later on.

They remembered also what he did about the horses. Tim's mount was famous for its speed, while Wohrle's horse was old and slow. Wohrle made Tim change mounts with him.

Only a short distance from the ranch they were waylaid by about a dozen men. Tim is said to have begged Wohrle to give him a chance to run for it, but he must have known he had no show. One story says that Wohrle shot the horse out from under him to keep him from making a break. In a matter of seconds Tim was lying in the road badly wounded.

At that moment the leader of the bushwhackers came up and Tim recognized him in spite of the blacking on his face.

"Pete," he pleaded, "this is all foolishness. I've got a family and you've got a family. Let's stop it now."

The leader looked at him and said: "I've blowed my coffee and now

I'm going to drink it." With that he shot Williamson dead and rode off.[25]

"Pete" was Peter Bader, a farmer and rancher of German ancestry who lived thirty miles east of Mason across the line in Llano County. He played a major part in the feud from now on as hatchet man for the "Germans." Peter was pretty rough and ready, given to noisy demonstrations and full of bluster, but quite ready to make good his boasts. Many people didn't like him, but naturally enough they were people on the other side. He is described as a dark man, not large though very rugged, who wore sideburns and a mustache but shaved his chin and neck. He had a brother Charley who was perfectly innocent, but who had to pay for Pete's sins.

The Williamson murder brought the whole countryside back to quivering tension.[26] Scott Cooley burst into tears when he heard of it[27] and vowed he would get the men who did it. All of Tim's friends ground their teeth and started cleaning their guns. The Germans grimly kept their mouths shut and carried their weapons wherever they went. When they had to come to town, they came in groups.

Peace-loving people had hoped that the July term of court, which was to convene in Mason on May 12, would somehow bring better times, but they hoped in vain. The Grand Jury did absolutely nothing. Charley Johnson, the cook for the Backus outfit who had used his legs to save his neck, was brought in by Lieutenant Roberts and questioned at great length. What could he tell them about the men who had tried to hang him? He couldn't answer; he was unable to remember; he didn't know. Roberts always suspected that some members of the Grand Jury might have been among the men who stormed the jail. He was not anxious to tell what he knew, either, so nothing was done.[28]

Even some of the Germans felt that such inaction was a shame. Henry Doell and his boy were riding with two of the mobsters one day, and Mr. Doell told them how he felt about it.

"It was too bad what you did to the Backus boys and Williamson. They were no worse than the rest of us. You've mavericked and sleepered and I've mavericked and sleepered; and besides, those weren't Tim's cattle. He was just working for Lehmberg."[29]

The two men changed the subject and asked him how many calves he had branded that year.

Maybe that was how Henry Doell came to be the next man killed. He was on a cow hunt on the West Bluff Creek with John Doyle, Fritz Kothmann, August Keller, and John Lindsey. They had eaten supper with one of the Gamel boys, who lived near by, and had gone to sleep in their camp on high, open ground where they should have been safe from ambush. About two hours before day, however, they were fired on. August Keller was shot through the foot, and Henry Doell was wounded fatally in the stomach. He lived four days after the shooting.

The story was spread that Indians had done it, but nobody believed that. Henry Doell, named for his father, told me it happened over a red cow with white ears which Mr. Doell well knew to be his own. When they found her, the V of his V6 brand had been changed to a number.

"I'm going to keep this cow," Doell said quietly, "but there won't be any trouble."

The attack occurred that night. Afterward the man who did the shooting used to stop by young Henry's house once in a while and borrow a chew of tobacco, but Henry did not find out that he was the assassin until long, long afterward.

And now it was time for Scott Cooley to play his brief and bloody part on the Mason County stage. While all this was happening, he had been going about quietly, talking a little and listening a lot. He came to Mason, where he was not known, put up at a hotel, and kept his ear to the ground. As soon as he was sure of what he wanted to know, he took his gun to Miller the gunsmith for some repairs. When he picked it up, he remarked that he was about ready to use it now.[30]

Deputy Wohrle was his first target. John was busy just then over on the west side of town helping Charley Harcourt dig a well. During the afternoon of August 10 the two men and a boy who is remembered only as "Doc Harcourt's little Yankee" were digging away when Scott Cooley rode up and began a conversation. What happened next is never told twice the same way, but this is the story the newspapers got:

"[Cooley] began conversing with Wohrle in the most friendly manner, stating among other things that he was looking for two horses. He asked Wohrle for a piece of leather with which to fasten his gun to the saddle, which request was complied with. While the villain was apparently fixing the leather to his saddle, Wohrle and another man who was present began hauling Harcourt up from the bottom of the well. While they were thus engaged the stranger took advantage of the opportunity to shoot Wohrle through the back of the head, the ball coming out near his nose. Wohrle fell dead, his companion, being without arms, fled, and Harcourt fell to the bottom of the well, a distance of forty feet, where he remained senseless.

"The murderer then fired six shots into the dead body of Wohrle stabbed it in four places with his knife, and finally took his scalp. Whereupon the fiend mounted his horse and rode off."[31]

Cooley rode away to the west with Wohrle's bloody scalp in his pocket. The posse which was soon organized to pursue him seems to have ridden off with great energy in the opposite direction.

From that moment he was not the same man. His friend Tom Gamel says he avoided all his former cronies and refused to shake hands with anybody for fear of being caught at a disadvantage. "He developed a habit of wearing his hat pulled down over his eyes and did not ever notice anyone in particular."[32]

Soon he became known for the tricks he played with Wohrle's scalp. Once he was taking a drink at Keller's store with several of his friends and when the time came to pay up, he pulled out that awful piece of skin and hair and threw it on the bar. The bartender flung up his hands and said shakily: "The drinks are on me, fellows."[33]

The gang which Cooley assembled around him were a pretty desperate outfit. They included four prominent gunmen named George Gladden, John and Mose Beard, and John Ringgo. The Beards were from Burnet in the second tier of counties east of Mason. Ringgo was from nobody knew where. And Gladden, whose place was a headquarters for the gang, lived at Loyal Valley, sometimes called Cold Spring.

They were all handy with guns and wouldn't run from a fight. In fact Dan Hoerster, the cattle inspector, and George Gladden had had a fist fight some time before the Wohrle murder and it took strenuous efforts on the part of Anton Hoerster to keep them from killing each other.[34]

Sheriff Clark heard about the gathering of Cooley and his crowd at Loyal Valley. He and his party went into council and decided to attempt an ambush. They wished to do this at minimum risk to themselves, however, and started off with a bit of strategy. They hired a Mason gambler named Cheney to go down and tell Gladden and Mose Beard that they were wanted in Mason. Cheney delivered his message and burned the road up getting back home. Beard and Gladden followed more slowly, and when they passed Keller's store at the old settlement of Hedwig's Hill about ten miles south of Mason, they found themselves suddenly and unexpectedly engaged in a battle for their lives.[35]

They were two against an estimated sixty men who included Peter Bader, Dan Hoerster, and Sheriff Clark. Beard and Gladden backed up fast and the Germans pursued, firing heavily. Gladden was wounded in the face and fell into the water at the Beaver Creek crossing. They were about to finish him, but he pleaded and promised so feelingly that Charley Keller was moved to mercy and said he would blast any man who offered to shoot him again. Beard was killed a little farther down the creek.

The old folk story about the dead man's ring is told of Beard and Peter Bader. Bader liked the looks of a gold band on Beard's finger. When he was unable to remove it, he got out his knife and took away finger and all. The sequel to this tale says that years later John Beard (who left the country after the trouble) was seen in Montana wearing the ring.

"Yes, that's the ring Pete Bader cut off my brother's finger to get," he admitted. "I had to cut off Pete's finger to get it back."

Major Holmes reported to the *Herald* that for a couple of days after the battle the Keller house was turned into a garrison, all ready for the expected counter-attack. But no reprisals were made. Beard took his brother's body back to Burnet and the Germans left.

"Last night," Holmes added, "a petition was in circulation to the

Governor to 'come over into Macedonia and help us;' Whether he can do any more now than he could after Tim Williamson's murder, when he was petitioned before, remains to be seen."

Cooley's men did not delay in taking their revenge. Before the month was out George Gladden's wound was in good shape, John Beard was back from the burial, and the gang was ready to go. Early in the morning on September 25, eight of the most dangerous of them slipped into Mason. Ringgo and a man named Williams rode on through town and out to the home of Cheney—John Clark's catspaw —on Comanche Creek north of town. Cheney asked them to get down and eat. They accepted his invitation. And while their host was washing his face, they killed him.

Then they rode back and had their breakfast at the Bridges Hotel, apparently in high spirits, though they sat with their rifles across their laps.[36]

Cooley is said to have remarked, while his men were out after Cheney, that Mrs. Bridges might like to know that there was some fresh meat up the creek.[37]

The men hung around Mason for several days, obviously looking for somebody else to kill. Three days after their arrival (it was September 28) things began to warm up. When Tom Gamel came down to his saloon that morning, he found John Beard standing inside with the muzzle of his gun out of the window. Tom had seen Sheriff Clark loping down the street a few minutes before and he said, "I just saw your meat riding down the road."

"I'll get some of them before I leave town," replied Beard, grimly.[38]

Scott Cooley, John Gladden, and a friend named Bill Coke waited around for half an hour more at Gamel's place and then walked over to the barber shop that stood across from the old Southern Hotel just off the northwest corner of the square. Something was going on up the hill in front of David Doole's store a little farther out of town, and they were watching intently.

It was a little knot of men on horseback carrying on a conversation with Doole himself. Dan Hoerster was there. So were Peter Jordan and Henry Pluenneke—all prominent Germans. Like unsuspicious flies they waved goodbye to Doole and rode toward the hungry spiders waiting at the barber shop. When they were within range, Beard and Cooley fired from behind the building. Just as the shooting began, the barber was stropping his razor. He gave such a start that he cut his strop in two.

Hoerster dropped out of his saddle, dead, with four buckshot in his neck. Jordan and Pluenneke leaped from their horses, ran around behind the Southern Hotel, and entered from the rear. They slowed down only long enough to grab rifles—then charged out onto the porch and began throwing lead. There was a brisk exchange of shots, but nobody was hit except Jordan. He had his scalp creased by a bullet and was soon covered with blood.

With no more chance of surprising anybody, the Cooley gang withdrew, had a drink at Gamel's bar, got somebody to bring their horses around, and started to leave town. As they rode past the hotel, Jordan opened up on them again. A bullet struck George Gladden's six-shooter as he was returning it to its holster, giving him a nasty wound in the hand, but he rode on.[39]

The posse organized to pursue these men caught up with only one. They found Bill Coke at John Gamel's on Mill Creek the next day. Six deputies took him in charge and started back to Mason, but when they arrived Bill Coke was not with them. They said he had "escaped," and maybe he had; but Lieutenant Roberts was never able to find any trace of him, though he sent out a search party. Tom Gamel states that Clark was put on trial for this supposed murder, but got out of it when a woman who knew him very well refused to identify him.

And where was John Clark during the three days the Cooley party spent in Mason? Most of this time he seems to have spent at Keller's store, where he had a number of men stationed in expectation of an attack from Loyal Valley. Major Jones of the Frontier Battalion of Texas Rangers found him there the day after Cheney was murdered.

It was the Major's habit to spend as much time as he could with his troops stationed out on the frontier, sharing their life and observing first-hand what was going on. On this trip he was intercepted at Loyal Valley by a courier from the Adjutant General who had been informed of the terrible conditions in Mason County. He wanted Major

Jones to send a detachment into town to hold the lid on. Two days later, on September 28, the Major reported from Loyal Valley what he had run into when he scouted toward Mason.

In passing Keller's, on the Llano en route for Mason, I was surprised to see fifteen or twenty men, armed with Winchester carbines and six-shooters, rise up behind a stone fence, in a fighting attitude.

Halting to ascertain the meaning of this demonstration, I was informed that a report had reached them that the Gladden party of Cold Springs and the Beard party from Burnett, some thirty men in all, were at Cold Springs and intended coming up today or tonight to "burn out the Dutch" consequently they had assembled to defend themselves and their property. Seeing us coming up the road they mistook us for the Cold Springs party and got into position for the fight. They were headed by a Mr. Clark, the sheriff of the County, were well armed and had a strong position in the angle of the Llano commanding the ford of the Llano and the approach from two directions for four or five hundred yards.[40]

Clark's story induced the Major to go back to Loyal Valley to try to locate the Cooley forces. He found "the houses closed and a death-like stillness in the place and an evident suspense if not dread in the minds of the inhabitants." He could find scarcely any men at all in the village, and nobody told him that they were all at Mason hunting for Germans to kill. Next day he reached the town a few hours after Hoerster had been shot down and found the population in a state of "terrible excitement."

Immediately he sent out three parties in pursuit of the killers but said he had small hope of catching them because "the National prejudice is so very bitter here—American against German and vice versa."[41] Nobody seemed willing to help, and to make matters worse, the Major found that there was no law.

All the justices of the peace except Wilson Hey had resigned and Hey would not turn a hand. He said "he had not given any papers to Sheriff Clark for several months and would never give him any more." The next day, however, under pressure, he did issue warrants for the arrest of Clark and seven or eight others, all of whom came in and surrendered within a few days.

Clark was the only one held, and the charges against him fell through. Within a very few weeks he had resigned from his office, left the country, and was never heard of in Mason again. Scott Cooley had boasted that there were not enough men in Texas to keep him from killing Clark,[42] but John got out in time. Alf Baird took his place and proved himself capable until a new sheriff was elected.

Meanwhile Jones was giving his best efforts to getting his hands on Cooley, Beard and Gladden. Scout after scout clattered off after them, and each time the men came back empty-handed. The Major fumed and fretted about it, knowing what was wrong but unable to find a remedy.

The trouble was that Cooley had been a Ranger himself and the boys didn't want to catch him—in fact, were taking pains not to catch him. Finally, as James B. Gillett tells it, Jones decided to face the issue squarely. He called his troop together and went over the ground with them. At last he said:

"Men, I now have a proposition to make to you. If every man here who is in sympathy with Scott Cooley and his gang and who does not wish to pursue him to the bitter end will step out of ranks I will issue him an honorable discharge and let him quit the service clean."

Fifteen men stepped forward. The Major paused to look them over —then went on.

"Gentlemen, those who do not avail themselves of this opportunity I shall expect to use all diligence and strength in helping me to break up or capture these violators of the law."[43]

This action solved one of the Major's problems, but others came fast upon him. Some of the citizens (he thought Major Holmes was one of them) sent a complaint to the Governor against the Rangers. They said that Jones and his men had taken sides and were fighting for the Germans.[44] The Major defended himself with dignity and vigor in a letter to his chief, and then went off to answer a loud cry of distress from Loyal Valley.

Clark and his party had been in a few days before, searching houses and behaving in a high-handed manner. Now Cooley and his men had sent word that they were on their way in to clean up their enemies in that section. Jones came on down as requested. He reassured the brave, persuaded the frightened not to leave their homes, and left a small detachment to take care of emergencies.

By the end of the month he felt that it would be safe for him to leave, and on October 28 he set out for Coleman County, leaving the force in charge of Lieutenant Ira Long, a capable officer who won the respect of the citizens and kept after Cooley and his friends.

Mason was quiet enough when Jones left, and there was no further murdering in the town itself; but the killing was not over yet. Scott Cooley was still around, and as determined as ever to revenge the death of Tim Williamson. As long as Peter Bader was above ground, Cooley meant to pursue him.

Sometime in November Scott took his trusty knaves with him and rode over toward Llano where Peter lived. It seems strange that these men should go astray in a country they had ridden over many times, but go astray they did. They went to Charley Bader's place instead of Peter's. Charley "was in the field that morning hauling top fodder," says Tom Gamel, "and they rode up and shot him down—killing an innocent man."[45]

Before they could try again, Cooley and Ringgo found themselves, to their astonishment, locked up in jail. Little publicity was given to the details of this revolutionary event, but they must have run up against a man who wouldn't back down. They were charged with threatening the life of Sheriff A. J. Strickland of Burnet.

They seem to have had many friends thereabouts, for as soon as the cell door had clanged shut behind them, the bad boys got together and very soon "an armed body of men were dashing through the streets intent upon a rescue."[46] Sheriff Strickland decided that he had better get his prisoners out of town.

He took them, under a strong guard, to Austin. When they reached the capital, a curious but not uncommon thing happened. A mob of peering people surrounded them showing great curiosity about the appearance and habits of the desperadoes. A senator or an actor or an evangelist couldn't have brought out half the crowd. Newspaper reporters had a field day.

"Arriving in the city," one of them babbled, "the whole party stopped at Salge's snack house for lunch, and while there a large concourse of people gathered to see the two men who have in the past few months, with others, been on the rampage. . . . The prisoners were apparently cool and reserved, and chatted as freely as any of the guard, and each recognized a person or two in the crowd. Cooley, who is said to have been a very quiet man until about a year ago, is a short, solid man, about twenty-eight years old, and looks like he might have some Cherokee blood in him. . . . Ringgold, who is taller and perhaps older than Cooley, is said to have taken an active part in the Mason County war. . . ."[47]

As nearly as we can tell, it was on the first of January that Strickland made these trouble makers eat crow. On January 2 he had them locked up in Austin. They were to be held until District Court met in Burnet on the fourth Monday in the month. But something caused a change of plans and instead of standing their trial the two men were removed once more to a jail in foreign parts. This time they were sent to Lampasas County, just north of Burnet. There they found sympathizers again, and in May some forty of these Helping Hands broke them loose. One bank robber named Redding was being held in jail in August for his part in engineering this escape, but other details are scarce. It is obvious, however, that Cooley's ruthlessness and daring made him look like Robin Hood to a lot of people.

Then for a little while it seemed as if the days of '75 were back again. It was reported that Cooley and his gang had "gone into camp, and that they defy the law and the authorities, and that there is no protection for life and property."[48] Bands of thieves were said to be running off stock again, and many an honest rancher must have had moments of despair over the prospect of ever living in peace again.

Another murder deepened the gloom. Peter Bader was lying low over near the settlement of Castel on the road to Llano, but shortly after Cooley and Ringgo were put away, Gladden and Beard found out where he was. They watched his movements for a while—then hid behind some large rocks beside the road and ambushed him neatly and effectively.[49]

The Fredericksburg *Sentinel* thereupon printed an editorial under the heading "More Blood," pointing out that the men of Mason were up to their old tricks. This was too much for the disgusted Masonites to take. They held a mass meeting at their courthouse on January 27 to protest the "unmerited slur" on their county. They wanted the Fredericksburgers to know that this murder had happened in Llano County and did not belong to them.[50]

All through the summer of 1876, however, they suffered under the terror of lawlessness. In August, Cooley's gang was reported to be driving off cattle from Mason County ranches, and the citizens were calling for military aid.[51]

This was the last flare-up of the disease. In a little while the menace died out, partly because the price of stolen horses declined, and partly because Scott Cooley left Mason County and the world for good and all. He went out of the country as spectacularly as he had entered it. The old-timers at Mason think he was poisoned.

It was probably in the fall of 1876 that he rode into Fredericksburg, stopped at the Nimitz Hotel for dinner, bought a bottle of whiskey, and headed south. A few miles from town he was taken sick, stopped at a friend's house, and died in a short time.[52]

Ranger James B. Gillett tells a different tale: "Having lost his friends and sympathizers in the rangers, Cooley returned to Blanco County, where he had formerly lived. Here he was stricken with brain fever, and though tenderly nursed, shielded by his friends, he died without ever being brought to trial for his killings."[53]

Either way, he ceased being a trouble to himself and the State of Texas.

The rest of the gang fared little better. Beard escaped to New Mexico, became a peace officer, and was killed by the man he succeeded, according to stories that came back to Mason.[54] Gladden and Ringgo were arrested by the Rangers under Sergeant Robinson, assisted by Sheriff Bosarth of Llano County, at Moseley's ranch on November 7, 1876.[55]

Ringgo seems to have beaten the rap and left the state. He is the same Johnny Ringgo who died under peculiar circumstances at Tombstone, Arizona, some years later, probably by a bullet from the gun of the notorious Buckskin Frank Leslie.[56]

Gladden, charged with the murder of Peter Bader, got ninety-nine years and headed for the penitentiary in December.[57] Years later he was pardoned out and came back to his old haunts in Mason. Some of the boys threw a celebration for him at a saloon next to Schuessler's saddle shop and just around the corner from Hell's Half Acre. They gave him a horse and saddle, and a fine sentimental time was had by all. Afterward the honored guest drifted west, was picked up again for mishandling stock, and is supposed to have died in the penitentiary.[58]

There was a sort of epilogue to the feud when the old courthouse burned on January 21, 1877.[59] It was a Texas custom at this time for people with many indictments on the books to destroy the records by burning the building. We don't know who poured the kerosene and lighted the match, but whoever he was he eliminated for all time to come the last traces of the Hoodoo War.

Symbolic of better times was the new silver-domed courthouse which soon rose in the center of the ample square. The old town which surrounds it is today one of the most interesting—and one of the most peaceful—communities in Texas. Its streets are broad and airy. Its houses are always neat and shining with fresh paint. The old names—Kothmann, Schuessler, Lemburg, Zesch—still decorate the store windows, and the old German ways have not been lost.

Well-to-do and conservative, those old German families avoid any innovations which might disturb their civic and personal tranquillity. They don't even want a railroad. Two or three times the octopus has extended a tentacle, but always something happened to prevent action. The burghers of Mason are glad of it. There will never be any shacks, weeds, tin cans, and assorted paper down along the railroad tracks, because there will never be any railroad tracks.

It looks as if there won't be any more feuding, either.

6. *The El Paso Salt War*

MAN FROM MISSOURI

One morning in the early part of 1872 a grim and dusty stranger appeared on the streets of the frontier hamlet of El Paso, followed by an obsequious Negro who obviously considered his master a most important person. Strangers were rare in this remote outpost, and El Paso inspected the newcomer thoroughly. What El Paso saw was a Missouri lawyer named Charles W. Howard, a bulldog of a man with a barrel body, a menacing, heavy-featured face, and a carriage which testified that he had been a soldier.

It took only a glance to tell the old hands that this man was dangerous. "From the first moment I saw him," said one of them a long time afterward, "I feared him."

As time went on, more facts about him accumulated and were retailed in Ben Dowell's saloon, where the handful of Americans gathered for companionship and whiskey. Entering the Southern army as a trooper in Wood's Regiment of Missouri Cavalry, Howard had gained his lieutenancy just before the end[1] and had built up, as the Texas papers noted later, "a great reputation for the daring and coolness with which he carried out the most dangerous enterprises."[2]

When peace came, he had decided to try his fortune in Texas, had spent the previous winter in Austin, and had now arrived at the ends of the earth, hoping to make his fortune in the green valley where there would one day be a railroad. His politics? Well, he was a Democrat.

At first that seemed so strange as to be unbelievable, for El Paso was a hotbed of entrenched Republicanism. What El Paso did not realize for some time was the fact that Charles Howard had come as a missionary. In cold blood he had made up his mind to start a political career in the very stronghold of the opposition. As Edmund Stine phrased it after Howard's race was finally run, "He considered it his duty to convert El Paso to the true faith of the Democratic party."[3]

In some ways he could have been better prepared for his job. For one thing he kept his mouth shut most of the time—something which has been true of no Texas politician before or since. For another he drank no whiskey, and this too made him eccentric.[4]

On the other hand he was well educated and in most ways a gentleman. He was a "good and fluent speaker," when it was necessary for him to talk, and overflowed with determination and aggressiveness.[5] More important still, he was a famous marksman—"probably the best pistol shot in the state, his feats with all classes of firearms bordering on the miraculous."[6]

With such gifts as these a man could go far in a frontier community in 1872, but Howard had one final advantage—he had come at the right time. Texas Democrats were on the march; radical rule was crumbling; it was time for all patriots, whether Democrats or conservative Republicans, to give the tottering structure of carpetbag rule a final push. So the man from Missouri looked around at the little kingdom which he hoped to rule, and found it good.

Once on the throne, he would certainly be free from outside interference, at any rate, for El Paso in 1872 was about the lonesomest community in the United States. San Antonio lay far to the east across seven hundred miles of Apache-infested wilderness, and the California settlements were even harder to reach. The stage came in three times a week over the old *Camino Real,* but sometimes it had to fight its way through, and even without interruptions it took six days of bone-racking travel to make the trip.

Even the Government seemed to have abandoned the place when, earlier in that same year, it had withdrawn the two small detachments of troops from Fort Bliss and Fort Quitman, leaving the country to the Indians and the border thieves (who were plentiful).[7] The international situation was unhealthy, too. The Mexican press took pleasure in damning all the gringos and their government,[8] and the Americans who congregated in Ben Dowell's combination saloon and post office felt themselves to be far out on a limb.

There was just a handful of them. Of the five thousand inhabitants of the Valley on the American side, only seventy-five or eighty were not of Mexican blood. During the Civil War their numbers had been reduced even further, but now they were beginning to drift back—some to get away from trouble; some to get into politics; some to buy and sell; some to invest their money and wait for the railroad which would surely come.

They should have been contented in their little oasis which seemed, in comparison with the country round about, like a somewhat sandy corner of Paradise. The great river flowed through a fertile area twenty-five or thirty miles long and five miles wide at the widest, and the corn and beans, fruit and melons, grapes and gourds, were irrigated (when the river did not overflow or go dry) by rippling *acequias* of clear water. Everybody lived in adobe houses shaded by ancient cottonwoods, loafed in the perpetual sunshine, drank the famous El Paso wine, and worried very little about the tumults and tragedies of the world outside.

At the head of the cultivated portion, where the Rio Grande emerged from the Pass of the North, the Mexican town of Paso del Norte (they call it Juarez now) squatted comfortably on the river bank. With three hundred years of history behind it and a population of something like seven thousand, it was the Big Town of the valley. On the opposite bank was the American hamlet of El Paso, and down river on the San Antonio road a handful of sleepy old towns dozed around their dusty *plazas*.

First came Ysleta, founded by fugitive Indians from New Mexico after the Pueblo revolt of 1680; then Socorro; and finally San Elizario, the most important settlement on the American side in those far-off days.[9] It was also the prettiest town in the Valley and the most typically Mexican. The old ways were still dear to the people. San Elceario, a little statue in eighteenth-century knee breeches and short beard was carried in all the religious processions and treated with great respect. In return he interceded diligently for the prosperity of his people.

What complicated matters most was the difficulty of convincing the Mexicans that an International Boundary meant anything. The people on the left bank of the river were supposed to be American citizents and their cousins a hundred feet away on the other side of a sometimes non-existent stream were supposed to be Mexicans. Most of them paid no attention. They and their ancestors had passed and repassed the river at their pleasure for ten generations, and the idea of a "Boundary" set up by a handful of gringos who had moved in only twenty-five years before was a little comic.

Even today the border is more of a temptation than a barrier, and it takes many Border Patrolmen with lookout towers, radios, and fast automobiles to keep part of the population from changing sides every night.

Since for all practical purposes the gringo colony was living in Mexico, its members had to conform to the customs of the country or get out, and most of them conformed without visible effort. They ate *chile colorado,* took siestas, married Mexican wives, and learned to talk the language. Since they were all politicians in office, out of office, or running for office, they also paid particular attention to the Mexican voters. It was part of their routine to stand as godfathers for Mexican babies, get brothers and fathers out of trouble, make alliances with patriarchs and clan leaders, and play the game the Mexican way.

It was Charley Howard's misfortune that he never did adjust completely to this method of doing things. And there were other Mexican peculiarities that neither he nor his fellow Americans could accept without question—for instance the Latin attitude toward private property. In Spanish times the *pueblo* or community owned the land adjacent to it, and the *alcalde* portioned out to each man as many *varas* of ground and as much river water as he needed.[10] This system worked very well for them, but when the Americans came in and tried to apply their notions about the sacredness of private ownership, the result was a monumental confusion which still makes money for lawyers who specialize in tracing titles back to the Spanish grants.

Uncle Ben Dowell complained bitterly that he couldn't keep the Mexicans from herding cows on his pasture land, never stopping to think that they had been doing it for at least a hundred years before his arrival.[11]

There was one other quirk of the Mexican mind which no Missouri lawyer could ever accept, and that was a fine, frank disrespect for written codes of law. Among those humble *peones* and proud *ricos* flourished a set of democratic ideas which went beyond anything an American had been able to subscribe to since 1776. They knew that power originates in the people and they reasoned that what the people agree on must be right regardless of the law books. "They were the people, and the people were the law." That was the argument used more than once to justify what the Americans called mob action.[12] It was the argument they used to justify what they did to Charles W. Howard.

All these things contributed to what was about to happen, but there was one more ingredient necessary to complete the devil's brew and bring it to the boiling point. This was the greed and jealousy of the Americans themselves. They quarreled, hated each other, and finally got to the point of committing murder.

Behind it all was the humble, harmless, necessary thing we call salt.

SALT
TROUBLE

A hundred miles east of the Valley towns Guadalupe Peak lifted its sheer granite wall nine thousand feet above the level plain and the low foothills. In its shadow was a thing of great value—a vast deposit of salt lying under a thin skim of water in a chain of lakes which glistened against the dusty tans and greens of the desert.

The Valley Mexicans must have known about the existence of these deposits from the earliest times, but until the outbreak of the American Civil War they let them alone. Custom and a good road had led them from time immemorial to the Tularosa or San Andrés *salinas* a long two-days' journey to the north in New Mexico.

In 1862 they made up their minds to open up the beds under Guadalupe Peak.[13] The quality of the salt was better, and there was a rumor that private owners might close off the Tularosa supply. They all got together and cleared a road from Fort Quitman, an army post on the river below San Elizario, across the sand hills and *arroyos* to the lakes. The distance from Quitman was seventy waterless miles. Two days and nights were required to make the trip each way. Apaches added the fear of death and mutilation to the other perils and difficulties; but still the traffic flourished.

It was an international business. Men from the interior of Mexico made long journeys after salt for their families and neighbors. Men from the Valley followed their creaking carts far into Chihuahua and Sonora. When farming or politics failed to yield a living, a Mexican could always fall back on the salt business. All he needed was a wagon, four mules, a scoop shovel, a couple of water barrels, and the love of God to protect him from the Indians.

It never occurred to these people that their salt might be taken from them, but the Americans were shrewder. As soon as the road was broken from Quitman, they scented plunder. They knew that the lakes were on public land which could be taken up by anyone with enough state bounties or land scrip to cover it.

The El Paso politicians thought about these possibilities a good deal, but while they were trying to find a way to do the thing and make it look good, an outsider moved in and nearly took the booty away from them. Samuel A. Maverick of San Antonio got together enough scrip to cover two sections of land, and in 1865 he came out to preempt the best locations in the salt-lake area.

At first the Mexicans were very sad over this, and the Americans were completely chagrined. Then it was discovered that plenty of salt lay outside the boundaries of the Maverick grant. Immediately the wagons re-commenced their creaking journeys and the politicians, scared into hasty action, organized a company to take up the deposits which Maverick had missed.

The names of these organizers loom large in early El Paso history: W. W. Mills, A. J. Fountain, Gaylord Judd Clarke, A. H. French, B. F. Williams, and J. M. Lujan. They were known as the "Salt Ring," and when Fountain fell out with Mills in 1868, he became the leader of the "Anti-Salt-Ring" faction. At the time of Charley Howard's arrival, these two parties had long been at each other's throats.

The strong man of the Salt Ring was W. W. Mills, a powerful Republican leader who had been in El Paso before the war, and had fought for the Union cause. Lincoln had made him Collector of Customs, and he had made himself the political boss of the region. He was a small, intense man with a black goatee and a sharp tongue who made high drama out of his many quarrels, wrote letters to newspapers about them, and accused his enemies of terrible crimes, some of which they had committed.

Closely allied with Mills, and hardly second to him in influence, was a middle-aged Italian named Louis Cardis, the local stage contractor, whose chief political asset was the affectionate regard in which he was held by the native population. Old Mexicans half a century after he was gone still spoke of him with regret as the best friend their people ever had. Born in Piedmont in 1825, he had been a captain in Garibaldi's army before coming to the States in 1854. He had lived in El Paso since 1864 perfecting his Spanish, which was very good, and getting a firm grip on the confidence of the voting population.

In person he was inclined to plumpness, but was extremely elegant for a frontier character, usually appearing in a Prince Albert coat, spotless linen, and a black bow tie. His delicately featured face was set off by a black mustache and chin whiskers. Unlike most border politicians, he was no fighter, preferring to pull the strings from behind the scenes. The Mexicans, and consequently everybody else, pronounced his name Car*deese,* with the accent on the last syllable, but mostly they addressed him with respectful familiarity as "Don Luis."[14]

In 1866 Mills and Cardis were joined, for a while, by another striking character named A. J. Fountain, a New Yorker who had traveled to the Orient, studied law in San Francisco, and come to New Mexico during the war with the California Column of Union troops. Like a good many of his comrades, he had married a Mexican girl and settled down to making a career in the new country. Eventually he became Mills's assistant in the Collector's office. Fountain was a big man and a bold one, as shrewd and ambitious as Mills himself, and their relationship from the first was loaded with dynamite.[15]

Mills, Cardis and Fountain shared the leadership of the Salt Ring with a character more extraordinary than themselves—Father Antonio Borrajo, the parish priest of San Elizario and a greater power among the Mexicans than even Don Luis. People are still alive who bent before the rod of his will and the lash of his tongue seventy and eighty years ago.

In person he was a tall, slender old man with bent shoulders, long gray hair, and black, blazing eyes set in a thin, white face. Temperamentally he resembled a volcano—was always sure he was right, and was always determined to have his own way. He didn't like women because they wouldn't do what he said without arguing, and he didn't like anybody else who crossed him. The story is still told about the time he fell out with a workman who had been brought in to cast a new bell for the church. He chased the poor fellow out of town and cast the bell himself—very badly, so that it had to be done over again.

To balance his irritability where human beings were concerned, the old man was passionately fond of good horses. He had a pair of well matched and high-spirited geldings, and he loved to go whirling about the countryside in his buggy.

In religious matters he was desperately in earnest. No couple need apply to him for wedding rites unless both of them could go through the catechism, the Hail Mary, and a good deal more; but if they knew all the answers, he might contribute a cow out of his own corral to start them off as householders.

Religion was behind his dislike of the American invaders of his stronghold. They set up secular schools under his nose; they even prevented him (for sanitary reasons, they said) from burying his dead in consecrated ground beside his church. He became a very bitter man over all this, and often shook his gray mane in exasperation as he uttered his favorite ejaculation: *"Ba, ba, ba, que burrada!"*—what asininity![16]

For a while these four strong personalities worked in some kind of harmony, but by 1868 the quadrumvirate was falling to pieces. Mills and Fountain became bitter enemies. A "Conservative" Republican, Mills supported the candidacy of his father-in-law A. J. Hamilton for governor. Fountain came out for the other side and backed the "Radical" candidate, E. J. Davis. Davis won; Fountain went to the State Senate; and Mills ate crow. In the spring of 1869 Mills received his *coup de grace* when he was ousted from the Collectorship of Customs to make way for a carpetbag politician from Michigan. Mills raised a tremendous outcry, but he was out and he stayed out.

He blamed Fountain for his misfortune, and attacked him with every means at his disposal. Letters went off to the Austin papers in which he "exposed" Fountain's shortcomings, which ranged all the way from impersonating an Assistant Collector of Customs to misappropriation of public funds. When the newspapers had finished printing what he had to say, Mills collected his diatribes and published them as a pamphlet. Then he had his former friend and assistant indicted in the United States District Court on eighteen separate counts.

Fountain delayed the trial as long as he could, but eventually, in the spring of 1872, he was brought to Austin and underwent a sensational examination which brought him an acquittal.[17]

The salt question was the major issue which brought on all this conflict among the Republicans. Fountain himself said that he had only one plank in his platform when he won his seat in the State Senate—he was going to secure title to the salt lakes for the people of El Paso County.

Shortly after the election Fountain received a call from Father Borrajo. According to him, the interview went something like this:

"Senator, what do you intend to do about the salt lakes when you get to Austin?"

"I intend to secure title to them for the people of the El Paso district."

"Well, such is not my desire. And don't forget what I did for you in the election."

"I haven't forgotten it."

"I suggest, then, that you yourself acquire title to the lakes. Then you can put a reasonable price on the salt, and if I advise my people to pay it, they will. You will grow rich, and so will I, for we will divide equally."

"No," said Fountain, with emphasis. "I won't do it!"

At that the priest flew into a furious rage—told Fountain he would never hold another public office—assured him he would be lucky if nothing worse happened to him—and took his temper away with him.[18]

Cardis was just as anxious as Borrajo to keep Fountain from defeating the purposes of the Salt Ring and he joined the priest in a sort of defensive alliance aimed at preventing the new senator from carrying out his campaign promises.

Fountain's first move was to suggest to the Valley people that if they would raise money to pay for the surveying, he would provide enough scrip to cover the unlocated portion of the lakes. Cardis and Borrajo immediately went to work and persuaded them that Fountain's offer was just another trick of the wicked politicians.

Next Fountain readied for the Legislature a bill calling for "the relinquishment to the County of El Paso, for the use of her citizens forever, all right, title, and interest of the State of Texas in and to the unlocated portion of the Guadalupe Salt Lakes in El Paso County." On his way to Austin with his document, he stopped at San Elizario to read it to an assembly of citizens. He thought they were pleased. But after he had laid his proposal before the Senate, he received a petition from four hundred of his constituents—an impressive number then—asking him not to push the matter.

Cardis had gone out into the highways and byways and persuaded his friends that Fountain was trying to get the deposits for himself. There was nothing for Fountain to do but withdraw his bill and start the long journey home.

Things had been happening while he was gone. The Ring and Anti-Ring forces were making a final desperate attempt to get together. A. H. French, a former Mills man who had made friends with Fountain and had been rewarded with a commission as captain in the State Police, brought Cardis around for a conference. Borrajo did not come, but he sent a letter authorizing Cardis to act for both of them.

Fountain listened while Cardis talked, suggesting a reorganization with jobs and patronage distributed among members of both sides. And what about Borrajo? Well, he didn't ask for much—just complete control of the schools, a free hand in appointing teachers, and a definite understanding about the salt lakes.

Cardis felt that this called for some explanation. "Borrajo has salt lakes on the brain," he said. "He seems to think he can make a fortune out of them."

"Why don't you and Borrajo locate the lakes yourselves?"

"Because we can't afford to make money that way. It would destroy our influence with the people."

"Supposing I do what Borrajo wants, how do you know I won't keep all the profits?"

"Because," answered Cardis with the simplicity of truth, "it would cost you your life if you did, and you know it."

Again Fountain refused to entangle himself in these schemes, according to his own story, and the meeting broke up with less than nothing accomplished.

All this happened in the late summer or early fall of 1870 and led directly to one of the worst of early-day El Paso tragedies. On December 7, 1870, B. F. Williams, a lawyer who belonged to the Salt Ring and hated Fountain with an alcoholic passion, had too many drinks at Ben Dowell's place and commenced abusing Fountain and District Judge Gaylord Judd Clarke. Clarke, though he was an old schoolmate and an intimate friend of Mills, had been appointed through the influence of Fountain.

At the height of the storm Fountain unluckily stepped into the saloon and Williams switched from Billingsgate to bullets. Fountain was wounded twice and badly hurt but he defended himself vigorously with his cane. His derringer empty, Williams went up to his room nearby and barricaded the door. Fountain started home after his rifle and on the way met Judge Clarke, who took over from there.

He ordered Captain French of the State Police to arrest Williams, and the two of them tried to break the man's door down. Exasperated by this assault, Williams stepped out and killed Clarke with a double charge of buckshot fired into his heart at pointblank range. A long rifle shot from Fountain and a pistol ball fired by Captain French put Williams out of business permanently.

There was much bitter feeling over this shooting, and worse might easily have followed. Fountain in particular felt that his life was in great danger, and after he had fought off the charges against him in the U.S. District Court at Austin in the winter of 1871-72, he decided that he had better go somewhere else. In 1874, when his term in the Legislature was up, he moved his family to Mesilla, New Mexico, and thenceforward made his talents as legislator, editor, and Indian fighter available in his new home.

It was into this explosive situation that Charles W. Howard stepped in 1872. For a few years there was a lull. The panic of 1873 destroyed the dreams of many who had hoped to see El Paso boom. Many of them moved away and business fell off. The embers of the salt quarrel died down. If it had not been for Charles W. Howard himself, the feud might have died out entirely. As time went on, however, he became the center of a whirlwind of violence which dwarfed what had gone before.

RISING TEMPERATURES

Charley Howard was no man to avoid trouble, and his assertive and pugnacious character seldom left him long in doubt as to which side he wanted to be on. Before he had even got acquainted, he was piping that theme song of all politicians—Throw the Rascals Out! The Radical Republicans had to go.

Now the boss of the Radicals in this last citadel of carpetbag rule was A. J. Fountain, no easy man to push around. But just as Howard found a made-to-order opponent, so he at once acquired a set of hand-me-down friends. Cardis and Borrajo and their supporters took him in immediately, well knowing that the thing they needed most was just such a ferocious battler as he.

For a while Cardis and Howard could not have got along better. Their ends were the same, and their talents dovetailed nicely. Cardis was not much of a speaker; Howard was. Cardis liked to work in the shadow; Howard was a good front man. Cardis could handle the Mexicans; Howard could bully the Americans. So they went to work.

His first taste of combat brought Howard up against J. P. Hague, a brilliant twenty-two-year-old youngster who had been brought out from East Texas the year before by the Fountain forces to be District Attorney. Howard ran against him in the November elections, and though Hague was a fiery and courageous fighter, he was no match for the Cardis-Howard combination. Howard won by a vote of 477 to 120.[19]

And then such harmony and happiness as there was between these two ambitious and unscrupulous men! Howard could not say enough for Cardis. He even wrote a letter to the San Antonio *Herald* telling the world how much it owed to Don Luis for engineering this "great political revolution":

"For months and months preceding the election, unassisted and alone, with an energy and perseverance absolutely astonishing, Mr. Cardis worked day and night to rouse up the people. . . . I think no county in the State deserves more credit than El Paso, and no man more than L. Cardis."[20]

Cardis did not make public his opinion of Howard at this time, but who could resist flattery like that? He must have loved Charley with a passion; otherwise their political honeymoon would never have lasted for almost two years.

In 1874 they combined again to put Cardis in the State Legislature. Father Borrajo was on the bandwagon with them. It is said that he "went from house to house threatening that those who did not vote for Cardis should not be buried in consecrated ground, but on dung hills, like dogs . . . he gathered his flock like a herd of sheep, and marched them to the polls, sprinkling holy water over the Cardis tickets and distributing them."[21]

Howard boasted to a friend in Austin that "but eleven radical votes were cast in the entire county."[22] And no wonder, after a campaign like that.

In April, only two years after his arrival in the little kingdom he had chosen for his own, Charley Howard began to rule. The District

Judge, S. B. Newcomb, was a non-Texan political appointee whom the Legislature saw fit to remove.[23] Next day they gave Howard the job.[24] Cardis had paid his debt, and Howard was now the supreme judicial authority in a district some four hundred miles from one end to the other.

To celebrate the victory he got married. His bride was Louisa Zimpelman of Manor, Texas, daughter of a well-known soldier and banker with business headquarters in Austin. The day after the ceremony—it was New Year's Day, 1876—Judge and Mrs. Howard set out in a team and buggy, escorted by two Negroes, to cross the eight hundred miles of cactus, Apaches, and wind-swept desert between them and an adobe home in El Paso.[25]

Lou Zimpelman was a quiet girl and apparently not made of pioneer stuff, for in the early summer of 1877, after a lingering illness, she died in her new home as quietly as she had lived.[26]

No one ever saw very deeply into Charley Howard's murky interior, and it is impossible to say how much affection he felt for Louisa, or how much her death grieved him. The only sign he gave of internal disturbance was an increased arrogance in dealing with his political allies, and that could have come from his assumption that he was now "the head of the party."

This arrogance—this fierce and steady scorn for any obstacle, human or not—was the engine by which he rose, and the trap through which he fell. Within six months after his return as a husband he had made a deadly enemy of Louis Cardis, and his good days were over.

It was the salt again that set men at odds. There is evidence that Cardis and Borrajo tried to get Howard to agree to some sort of arrangement about claiming it, and that Howard was outraged.[27] Cardis told Fountain that "Howard had violated his pledges"; Howard told Fountain that he had broken with Cardis and Borrajo "on account of their trying to force him into some monstrous schemes."

It would seem to add up to a revival of the salt mania. Whatever it was that estranged them, Howard and Cardis could hardly have detested each other more. Howard accused his enemy in print of being "a liar, a coward, a mischief maker, a meddler; such a thing as could only spring from the decaying carcass of an effete people."[28]

The Constitutional Convention of 1876 made a public scandal of this private feud. Delegates were elected in June, 1875, and both men were candidates. Howard beat Cardis at both the precinct and the district convention, while Cardis trumpeted to the newspapers that it was done by fraud and trickery. He had his inning at the election in August when he ran as an independent candidate and got 365 votes to Howard's 115.[29]

After that it was war to the knife, and it seemed that something happened nearly every day to widen the breach between them. There was the matter of the ditch project in San Elizario, for instance. The State was slow in giving the citizens the help they thought they ought to have; Cardis told his Mexican friends it was Howard's fault; and they came near mobbing the Judge when he passed through on his way to Presidio to attend District Court.[30]

Then came the next regular election. Howard went out as District Judge but Cardis was returned to the Legislature by a large majority.[31]

Howard, being Howard, wanted to fight. He never could corner his enemy at home, but once in Austin and once in San Antonio he gave Cardis a public beating.[32]

"Why don't you shoot him?" they asked Cardis. He shook his head and made no answer. It would take a braver man than he to face Charles Howard with a gun.

Cardis may have been urging his friends to do what he did not dare to do himself. Ben Dowell warned the Judge every few weeks that they were laying plans to get him, but no open moves were made.[33]

Then Howard took his first fatal step. In the name of his father-in-law, Major Zimpelman, he filed on the unlocated portion of the salt lakes and took over the claim staked out ten years before by Samuel Maverick.

Many men were shocked by this act, but they need not have been surprised. Major Zimpelman had spent several months in El Paso while his daughter was dying, and his plans had been made openly. Nevertheless the Mexican population was deeply disturbed. The old men remembered long after how Don Luis came down to Ysleta and had the *tombé* sounded to call everybody together. He told them not to go to sleep, and warned them that their rights were in danger.

While the words were still in his mouth, Howard was already far along with his plans. At first he could get no one to haul salt for him, but finally he induced Ismael Ochoa, John Atkinson, and Juan Armendariz to sign contracts. They were to get a dollar and a quarter a *fanega* (two and a half bushels) for bringing the salt in. Howard expected to sell it for two dollars a *fanega*.

He might as well have told the Mexicans that he intended to sell air at so much a breath. The salt was all that stood between some of them and starvation. The river had been dry for a month; the corn was dying; the people were desperate; and now the little they could pick up by hauling salt was about to be taken away from them.

They were all sure that they had a right to the salt. It was still possible a few years ago to talk to men in the Valley towns who had been through this trouble—men like Clemente Candelaria and the two Rodela brothers of Ysleta. They remembered vividly how Don Luis did all he could to keep the salt for his people, even traveling to Washington (or was it Austin?) with four Ysleta Indians and bringing back a paper justifying the Mexican claims. Did any of them see the paper? No, but Andres Paz did. It was a big writing with four seals.[34] Probably none of them could have read the legendary document even if they had seen it, but the legend was enough. The salt was theirs.

Some of the educated class thought so too. Among these was Father Ortiz, the priest of Paso del Norte. After the blood had stopped flowing, he wrote a letter to General Hatch stating that the Spanish Government had actually granted the salt lakes "to all the towns of the river in common."

In honesty Father Ortiz had to note one flaw in his argument: the fact that there was a time limit for filing claim to such grants after the Americans took over. The people, "because of the robbery of the archives of their town by the expedition of Colonel Doniphan, did not have the records; and although they might have been able to produce other proofs, they are ignorant in the extreme. . . ."

He added one more damning detail: "Moreover, from what I have learned, the inhabitants of San Elizario and of the other two towns made a pact with Lawyer Howard that he should act as defender of their rights, and try to establish them, but they were deceived."[35]

Major Jones of the Rangers used the word "vague" in describing the Mexicans' claim to public ownership of the salt. True, they had no claim which would have stood up in an American court—but they had a claim. From their point of view, they had about as much on their side as our forefathers did in resenting the Stamp Act.

ACTION AT SAN ELIZARIO

Down the river at San Elizario, Padre Borrajo heard of Howard's rape of the salt lakes and turned an apoplectic purple. Now the last straw was added to an already intolerable burden. It was the Americans—always the Americans! How he hated them!

Charley Ellis was the one he hated worst of all, though Charley was not easy to hate. Ellis was a prosperous, affable little man with a brown mustache who had come in with the Union forces in 1862, set up a store and mill just where the El Paso road entered the town from the northwest, and married a Mexican girl. From 1871 to 1873 he had been sheriff and tax collector.[36]

When the day's business was over, he went home to Doña Teodora and the fine house they had built beyond the church at the other end of town. The señora was not a pretty woman, but she was large and stately and gracious, like her house. It was a many-roomed adobe with two patios, a ball room with painted walls and ceiling, and a little private chapel for the mistress. With such a wife and such a house and such a business, Charley Ellis should have been Father Borrajo's favorite parishioner. But he was a gringo, and more than that he was a friend and supporter of Charles Howard. So Borrajo hated him.

He took a dim view of the other Americans in the community also. These included Nick Kohlhaus, a roly-poly German who kept a store and loved to play Santa Claus for the children at Christmas time, and Mr. Campbell, Ellis's miller, who was supposed to be a Mormon with many wives bestrewing his back trail. Finally there was Atkinson, the village Mephistopheles—long and lean, thin-faced and ironical, quarrelsome and dictatorial.[37]

Atkinson's "mean streak" may have been aggravated by a slight difference in the length of his legs, though this handicap did not impede his running. At least he is said to have run rather well when Mr. Campbell caught him being agreeable to his wife (or one of them) and took out after him with a pistol. He had some mercantile interests but liked to take time off for politics. He had been Ellis's deputy when Charley was sheriff, and though his chief was too easy going to cause much trouble, Atkinson had succeeded in making enemies for the two of them.[38]

It was during their term in office that Borrajo had begun to spit venom. They were the ones who tried to restrain him from burying his dead in consecrated ground lest he contaminate the water supply. What was the water supply in comparison with the welfare of a human soul? When he was told officially in 1871 to do his burying elsewhere, he defied them by burying a child in the old place the very next day.[39]

It was these two also who had raised all the trouble about the schools. The education of boys and girls was naturally the business of the Church. How else could they learn about religion and grow up to be decent citizens and good Catholics? And yet these Americans tried to tell him that the laws of the State required all children between the ages of eight and eighteen to go to American schools where religious instruction was strictly forbidden.

And that was not all. They crowded grown boys and girls, twelve or fifteen years old, into the same room with each other. Any Mexican, and presumably any civilized person, knew that only the smallest children were ever taught in the same room with boys and girls together.

"*Ba, ba, ba, que burrada!*" growled Father Borrajo, and he went out among his people telling them to pay no attention to the crazy American laws.

Telesforo Montes, an ex-Ranger captain and a great man in San Elizario, had a daughter sixteen years old when Ellis was sheriff. She was a young lady, not merely too old to be in school with boys, but too old to be in school at all. Consequently she did not go to school. Others followed her example. Ellis was reminded repeatedly that he had a duty to perform, and finally he did it. He put Telesforo Montes and two of his friends in jail, where they enjoyed martyrdom for three weeks. At the end of that time Ellis turned them loose to save worse trouble.[40]

Father Borrajo shrugged his stooped shoulders and chuckled. He had been too smart for the Gringos that time.

But nobody can win forever. Early in 1877, when he least expected it, an order was issued from Rome removing the left bank of the river from the jurisdiction of the Bishop of Durango and attaching it to the Diocese of Tucson. Borrajo was a secular priest under the supervision of the Bishop of Durango, and he should immediately have given up his charge and gone to Mexico. But he was loath to leave the game when he was ahead. The Americans appealed to Bishop Salpointe at Tucson when they saw that Borrajo was going to delay as long as he could. The old priest heard about it and said he was not leaving at all.

Finally the good and gentle Bishop Salpointe had to come over to see about it. He set out from El Paso one morning, but was stopped at Socorro by Borrajo and a band of his followers. There was a terrible scene. The Bishop heard himself called by hard names and threatened with dire consequences if he proceeded. The driver of the Episcopal carriage raised an expressive shoulder and advised against going on.

Nevertheless the Bishop went ahead and succeeded in reaching San Elizario without loss of dignity. Nobody in town dared take him in, however, and he had to camp out for the night. In the morning he returned to El Paso.

Borrajo was triumphant again. He jibed at his enemies, it is said, even in the pulpit, calling them *pelados,* Protestants, and worse. Ultimately the case was acted on by the Bishop of Durango, and Borrajo moved to a smaller parish at Guadalupe on the Mexican side of the river, but he did not go in peace. The Reverend Pierre Bourgade, later Archbishop of Santa Fe, eventually took charge of the parish. He testified that Borrajo "used his influence to estrange the people of my parish from me," and even "tried to make the people believe that he would come back here again."[41]

All of this was part of the web of destiny which was drawing tighter every day around Charles Howard, though he refused to believe it. Through April and May his friends kept reminding him that he must not push his luck too far, and he shrugged them off. Then came the end of June and he found out for himself that he walked with death.

Early one morning he climbed into his buggy and set off for Quitman and the salt lakes in order to complete his survey. Surveyor Blanchard, McBride (Howard's agent), three Mexicans, and three Negroes brought up the rear. At San Elizario the Mexicans dropped out. Don Luis, they said, had told them not to go any farther. Howard was short-handed and short-tempered when he halted at one end of abandoned Fort Quitman to camp for the night.

Just for something to do, he took Blanchard and went out to see if he could find any surveyor's monuments. When they reached the other end of the post, where Cardis's stage company had a station, whom should they run into but Cardis himself making an inspection of his equipment! The minute Cardis recognized them, he dashed inside the station like a scared rat. It was too good a chance to miss, and Howard went in right behind him.

Five minutes later he was back, looking baffled. "He ran under a table and acted so cowardly I didn't have the heart to shoot him," he explained.

As for Cardis, he was more frightened and angry than he had ever been before. Back in El Paso, he filed charges against Howard and had him indicted at the September term of the District Court.[42]

To a man of Howard's courage and fighting instinct all this fuss was funny. He laughed at it and went about his business—namely, salt. After finishing his survey at the lakes he posted notices that the deposits belonged to him and that he would prosecute anybody who raided his property. Probably he hoped that somebody would try it.

For a few days no Mexican moved to brave his wrath, but they talked about it. It came to Howard's ears that José María Juarez and

128TEN TEXAS FEUDS

Macedonio Gandara of San Elizario had declared publicly their intention of going after salt whenever they felt like it. He had them arrested. It was time for him to hold court at Fort Davis and he had to pass through the Valley towns *en route*. At San Elizario he called on County Judge Gregorio N. Garcia and asked to have the two offenders brought in for examination.

At first the hearing seemed to be getting nowhere. Gandara was questioned first and he very wisely said as little as possible. Since there was no real evidence against him and he refused to accuse himself, Howard asked that the charge against him be dismissed. After spending a little more time on Juarez, he said, "I reckon we will have to dismiss the case against him too." He laughed as he said it.

Juarez spoke no English, but a scornful laugh is understandable in any language and he reacted at once. "You are a fool," he shouted at Judge Garcia, "and you have no right to try me. I will go for salt. I do not care about the law! If others go to the salt lakes, I will go too, and maybe I will go anyhow!"

Garcia sighed wearily and did his duty. He put Juarez under a peace bond and turned him over to Sheriff Charles Kerber.[43]

That was all it took to bring out the mob. There was a *junta* with speeches. Don Luis was in town, and they sent to see if he had anything to suggest. He told them to stand up for their rights but not to do anything violent. Then he left hurriedly for El Paso, not wishing to be in the same town with Charles Howard if anything broke loose.

Luckily for him, and for Howard too, the Judge had already climbed back into his buggy (Cardis had refused to sell him stage transportation) and jogged off toward Fort Davis. Fifteen miles down the highway a party of twenty-five men was lying in wait for him, expecting, as he told Colonel Fountain later, "to ambuscade and kill me as I passed and say it was Apaches." But he didn't find out about that until later.

In the streets of San Elizario strange things were happening. The leaders of the mob sent a committee to wait on Justice of the Peace Porfirio Garcia. "Give us a warrant for Howard's arrest," they demanded. Don Porfirio explained that he could not legally do what they wanted, so they took him out and locked him up.

Next they called on Porfirio's younger brother, County Judge Gregorio N. Garcia.[44] Don Gregorio came of a fighting clan, but prolonged sessions with the bottle had weakened his spirit and his nerves were not very reliable. He suffered a severe shock when, about ten o'clock that night, the Committee assaulted his door. After much cautious unbarring, he let three of them in and they explained what they wanted.

"Well, make out your complaint," he said. "There must be a complaint first; then a warrant."

"But we haven't any complaint. Howard has not harmed us personally, but it is the will of the people that he should go to jail."

"But in the United States. . . ."

They cut him short. "If you can't issue a warrant, we will lock Howard up anyhow." Then they left.

When he stepped out into the street on nervous tiptoes some time later to see why everything was so quiet, he ran into a very tough Mexican named Desiderio Apodaca who put a rifle against his back and conducted him to the house of Leon Granillo, where he spent the night. In the morning they moved him to Mauro Lujan's house near the church and locked him up in the same room with his brother the Justice of the Peace.[45]

Meanwhile Howard was having troubles of his own. After finishing with Juarez and Gandara, he drove six miles down the road to a place called the Quadrilla, where he and his Negro man Wesley Owens set up camp. About midnight McBride came in at a fast trot. He had heard of the ambush farther down the road and had ridden hard to head his employer off before it was too late.[46]

In the morning the three of them crossed the river and rode back toward El Paso on the Mexican side in order to stay out of trouble. Howard seemed to be brooding deeply on the wrongs he was having to endure from that "coward, thief, sneak, and liar"—Cardis. He said to his servant, "Wesley, when I get back from Fort Davis, if Cardis don't let me alone I'm going to kill him. I'm going to kill him anyway, for he has been bothering me long enough."[47]

When they came opposite Ysleta, Howard made up his mind to cross over and see what Charley Kerber thought about these goings-on. At Kerber's house he learned of the excitement that had sprung up behind him and took the sheriff's advice to stay right where he was. The Mexican signal corps had gone into action, however, the moment he showed his face in town, and the next morning he awoke to find the house surrounded.

Whatever else is to be said about Charles Howard, he was a man and not a mouse. Taking McBride with him, he went out to face the music. Chico Barela of Ysleta and Leon Granillo of San Elizario, the leaders, told him they had come to take him prisoner, and when he threatened to resist, they seized him forcibly. A week later he described what followed to Colonel Fountain at Mesilla:

". . . I was seized by two of the men and dragged through the streets of Ysleta, surrounded by forty armed men, hooting and jeering at me. Near the plaza they were joined by twenty-five or thirty more and I was then forced on horseback and taken to San Elizario. The whole mob followed, and yelled, hooted and jeered the whole way. I omitted to state that Mr. McBride was taken with me.

"On reaching San Elizario, I was taken to the house of Dona Apolonia Lujan. There I found from 200 to 250 more Mexicans under arms—and a more sullen, ferocious looking body of men, I never saw —I was taken to a room in the house, and immediately placed under a heavy guard. Thus I was kept for three days and nights; at all times surrounded by three or four hundred armed *pelados,* raving and raging like hungry *coyotes.* I was not allowed to see my friends or write to anyone. I was told that unless I would agree to certain conditions that the mob would impose, I would be killed. For two days I refused to subscribe to the conditions required or in any way treat with the mob. On the third day, finding there was no assistance, that could be had in time to save my life, and that the mob was growing more ferocious every moment, and that not only my safety was involved, but also that of every American in the county, I agreed to sign any papers required of me, and late in the evening of the third day of my confinement did sign a document. . . ."[48]

Father Bourgade handled the negotiations. The leaders called him in when they could not agree on the question of putting their prisoners to death. He asked Howard what he would do if he were allowed to go free.

"I won't prosecute them," Howard said, "for they are ignorant men; but they may be prosecuted for what they have done to the Judge."

Still trying to decide what to do, the mob sent a messenger off to Don Luis at El Paso with a request for advice. Sheriff Kerber had already had an interview with Cardis the night before and had dropped some strong hints about what might happen to certain people if Howard suffered any harm.[49] Cardis apparently advised his friends not to shed blood, and they drew up the paper which Howard signed.

The two judges were required to resign their offices, a step which seems to have caused them no grief.[50] Howard had to promise "voluntarily" that he would "forget all that has passed," let the courts decide who owned the salt lakes, leave the country within twenty-four hours and never return, give bond for his future conduct, and confess that his prosecution of Juarez and Gandara had been "unjust, improper and without cause."[51]

Four leading citizens of San Elizario put their names to his bond— John G. Atkinson, Charles E. Ellis, Jesus Cobos, and Tomas Garcia.[52]

Even then he was not out of danger. The mob looked grim as he appeared in the doorway of Mrs. Lujan's house. But Father Bourgade put a hand on his shoulder, walked by his side to the waiting carriage, and did not leave him till he had passed Ysleta.[53]

Convinced at last that there could be no trifling, Howard drove on up to Mesilla, where A. J. Fountain gave him sanctuary. The telegraph line from the north came that far, and he made use of it at once by wiring the Governor of Texas that there was danger of an invasion from Mexico.[54] The wires buzzed with other messages. Sheriff Kerber tried to get troops sent down from Fort Craig in New Mexico. District Judge Allen Blacker fired off a message from Fort Stockton, where the line from eastern Texas ended, to the Governor: "Civil authorities powerless. . . . Life and property still in danger."[55]

When the Governor, much concerned, looked into the possibility of sending a detachment of Rangers, he found that the nearest company was five hundred miles from the trouble, that it could not be moved in less than a month, and that the men were "over-taxed in their present occupation."[56]

His Excellency was much relieved when Louis Cardis took his turn at telegraphing on October 9: "The late disturbance in this Co. is over and everything seems to be quiet. It is mainly through my efforts that peace has been established, though reports may come to you to the contrary. Full particulars by mail."[57]

The full particulars never arrived. Cardis had actually taken steps to organize the leading men of the Valley towns for the purpose of restoring order. If he had lived, he might have had something to report, but his time was almost up.

At Fountain's house in Mesilla, Howard was burning with anger. He knew he had signed the mob's papers under duress and could not be held to his promises, but he could not swallow the humiliation he had suffered. "It was entirely his [Cardis's] creation," he wrote, "designed and arranged long before." "What," he asked, "ought to be the punishment of that infamous monster who has brought these poor, ignorant, deluded and credulous people, into this trouble for his own cowardly and selfish ends. I can think of nothing in Earth or Hell, bad enough for him."[58]

DEATH OF
A CHIEFTAIN

On the seventh of October, with only three days left him, Louis Cardis was quite cheerful and confident. His friend G. W. Wahl of Ysleta, the County Clerk, came to see him in the morning and remarked that it would be dangerous for him and Howard to meet. Cardis raised the tails of his long black coat and placed his hands on the butts of two pistols. "There is no danger," he said. "I am always prepared."[59]

Before going to bed he made the last entry in his diary:

7th, evening.—The express has returned, and brought answer showing good disposition on the part of the people to meet us and harmonize. Rucker with

twenty men and Howard came in this morning. Captain Courtney advised me
to be on my lookout, for Howard is making "desperate threats at my life."[60]

Howard had indeed driven down that very day from Mesilla under
the cottonwoods now fast turning a ripe yellow. With him rode a
company of soldiers from Fort Bayard, ordered by Colonel Hatch to
San Elizario. From Sunday to Wednesday he remained quietly in
El Paso. About two o'clock on Wednesday, October 10, after eating
his noon meal at the hotel, he said to his colored man, "Wesley, I feel
very restless and must have my revenge."[61] With that he picked up a
double-barrelled shotgun and left the room.

Two minutes later Frank Faudoa saw him turn the corner into San
Francisco Street. When I talked to Frank he was ninety-four years
old and almost blind, but he could still see *El Indio* (the Mexicans
called Howard "The Indian" because he was so dark and silent)
rounding the corner of Don Inocente Ochoa's store and heading west
down *Calle San Francisco*. Frank and a couple of cousins who worked
with him in the store ran out, knowing that there was a feud and that
blood might flow at any moment. They saw their man disappear
into Solomon Schutz's store, a place he had not entered for months.

Inside Schutz's place of business[62] Howard paused momentarily as
he searched the cluttered room with his eye. Across from him he saw
a black-coated gentleman sitting in a rocking-chair with his back
to the entrance. It was Cardis. He did not like to write letters, especially in Spanish, and he had just finished dictating one to Adolph
Krakauer, the bookkeeper.

Joe Schutz did what he could. He called loudly, "How do you do,
Judge Howard." Cardis knew he was being warned, jumped up
quickly, and stepped behind a tall bookkeeper's desk. It was poor
protection, covering only the upper part of his body, but it was all
that was available.

"Krakauer, come away from there!" Schutz barked at his bookkeeper, who sat behind another desk. Krakauer dived for the door
as Howard brought up the muzzle of his shotgun.

Schutz tried to stop him. "Don't shoot here, Judge! Respect my
house and family."

"I will," replied Howard, "if he'll come out in the street."

Then he fired a charge of buckshot under the desk into Cardis's stomach and gave him the second barrel in the left breast as the man staggered out into the open.

All accounts that have appeared in print since that time assume that Cardis made no attempt to defend himself, but when Howard got back to Mesilla he told his friends (for publication) that as Cardis went behind the desk "his right hand held a pistol which was also exposed below the desk," and that he "observed the latter raise his pistol, from below the desk," just before he himself fired.

The point is important because it makes Howard's act seem a little less cold-blooded, and because it would probably have saved the Judge's neck if the case had ever come to trial. The discovery of a previously unknown file of the *Independent* has made it possible to give Charles Howard this sorry bit of credit.[63]

Cardis seems to have died without a word; and without a word Howard walked out of the door, threw away two empty shells, and handed his gun to Wesley Owens, who came running to meet him.

Krakauer, bursting with excitement, was two steps behind. He saw Frank Faudoa just coming up to the door and sent him off to Juarez for a doctor—there was none in El Paso. Frank finally located Dr. Ramirez, about two hours too late.

Meanwhile Howard had gone directly to the Customs Office to see what Joe Magoffin, the Inspector, thought he ought to do next. Magoffin told him to get out of town. So Wesley hitched up the Judge's horse and the two of them drove back up the Mesilla road under the yellow globes of the *alamos* with no apparent hurry, and in no apparent alarm.

Back at Schutz's store Gabriel Valdés and Edmund Stine placed Cardis's body on a piece of plank, first removing a cartridge belt with a big revolver, half-cocked, still in the scabbard. Only one man noted that there was another holster attached to the belt, and that it "was entirely empty."[64] If Cardis did bring two guns with him into the store, some of his friends had found a reason for concealing one of them.

On the floor beside him was the letter he had just finished dictating, stained with his blood. It was for Cipriano Alderete of San Elizario, and told of yesterday's meeting at Ysleta, which he considered "very satisfactory" as a move toward peace.[65]

By nightfall the whole Valley had heard the story. A few were glad that the deed was done. Sheriff Kerber at Ysleta said that Howard had done a good thing, that "if it was any other country but this a monument would be erected to his memory for delivering us from a tyrannical and unscrupulous scoundrel."[66]

Most people, however, realized that this bloody act had endangered the life of every American in the Valley. Immediately after the murder, as fast as the wires could carry it, a telegram[67] went off to Colonel Hatch:

> Don Luis Cardis was killed this moment by Chas. Howard, and we are expecting a terrible catastrophe in the county, as threats have been made that every American would be killed if harm came to Cardis. Can you send immediate help for God's sake?
>
> S. Schutz & Bro., and all
> Citizens of Franklin, Tex.

A JOB FOR THE RANGERS

Down river, at San Elizario, every nerve was taut as an Apache bowstring. By twos and threes men from Mexico plowed across the waterless bed of the Rio Grande, squatted under the cottonwoods with their American *compadres,* and talked in low bitter tones. Some of them quoted Father Borrajo, who was holding forth these days with redoubled vigor on the wickedness of the Gringos.

For two weeks this continued. On both sides of the river there were midnight messengers, secret conclaves, and even some drilling in military formation.[68] Men were set to watch for a chance to murder Howard. Day after day this dance of shadows went on, and every American in the region lay down on his bed at night wondering if he would rise up in the morning. Sheriff Kerber was heard to say that he didn't dare make an arrest. There was no more law in the Valley.

At Ysleta a meeting was called to discuss ways and means of getting rid of County Judge Gregorio Garcia. Some were for killing him at once to save trouble, whereupon Martin Alderete rose to remind them that they were American citizens. At once the assembly was on its feet shouting, "No, we are Mexicans till we die—*hasta la muerte, hasta la muerte!*"[69]

The word came to Major Jones of the Rangers to go and see what was wrong. He might almost as well have been ordered to China. The quickest way of getting to West Texas was to go to Topeka, Kansas, pick up the Santa Fe down into New Mexico, and continue by stage-coach from the end of the track. Ten days after he received his orders Jones reached Mesilla, where he spent Saturday and Sunday with Fountain and Howard.[70]

On Monday he came to El Paso, which he found in a state of great fear and excitement. A message from San Elizario had come in say-ing that the mob had served notice on Howard's bondsmen to pay up or suffer the consequences. The day after the Major arrived an-other message was smuggled out—a letter signed by Atkinson, Ellis, Cobos, Ball, Garcia, and others. "Some eight or ten of us have got together," they said, "and will fight till we die; we are in Atkinson's house—send us help for the honor of the *Gringos*." There was a post-script to Sheriff Kerber: "Help us Charlie for Christ's sake, and we will do our damndest in the meantime."[71]

Kerber himself showed this appeal to Major Jones and Lieutenant Rucker in the Major's hotel room. In the council of war which fol-lowed they discovered that none of them could do anything. Kerber and Jones had no men to work with. Rucker's orders forbade him to interfere unless he was sure that the mob was enlisting aliens.

Since he must do something, and since there was power in the very name of the Texas Rangers, Jones decided to face the mob himself. He went down to San Elizario and sent word to the leaders that he wanted to see them.[72]

They seemed frank and courteous enough as he faced them in the *sala* of Mauro Lujan's big house. José M. Juarez, lately in court for threatening to take salt, was there. So was Cipriano Alderete, Cardis's friend. So were Luciano Fresquez, Agaton Porras, and Ramon Sam-brano, leading agitators. The real organizers, Chico Barela and Sisto

Salcido, were absent, though they were probably not far away. Father Bourgade did the translating.

"What are you going to do with the men who signed Howard's bond?" the Major asked them.

Apparently they were expecting a different question, for their reply was to produce a book containing the Texas Constitution as proof that they had a right to assemble. Jones met them on their own ground. He explained carefully the difference between a legal assembly and a mob assembly. "If your rights to the salt lakes have been invaded, the courts will settle it. You have no right to appeal to arms to settle it yourselves."

"But there is the bond," they argued. "We have a right to collect the bond. We cannot get it through the courts, but Howard came back and the money is rightfully ours."

Jones answered as best he could, promising that Howard would have to account for his deeds if he ever set foot in Texas again. The leaders looked at each other, hesitated, weakened, and gave in. "All right," they said, "we will do what you say."

That afternoon the Major made a fatal mistake which undid all he had accomplished. He let it be known that he intended to organize a company of Rangers to hold the lid on after he left. The Mexicans became suspicious once more. At night there was another *junta,* and presently Jones was asked to come around again. When he and Father Bourgade arrived, they were plied with questions. Was he intending to organize a company of State troops? He was. Was the force going to be recruited locally? There was no other place to recruit it. Would there be any Mexicans in it? Yes, if they were loyal.

"Let us raise our own company and elect our own officers," the spokesmen said. "Or if this is impossible, let the United States troops be called in."

"No," said the Major regretfully, "I can't do either of those things."

They went away angry and sullen, and Jones knew he had accomplished nothing. In the morning he returned to El Paso and began recruiting. Three days later, on November 12, he wired the Adjutant General requesting a second lieutenant's commission for John B.

Tays, who was to head a new detachment of Company C of the Frontier Battalion.[73]

The twenty men of this troop have endured, for their conduct during the next thirty days, the bitterest criticism. All that can be said for them is that where the sheriff had despaired of raising a posse, these men were assembled out of holes and corners. Not a one of them would have been a Ranger under normal circumstances.

Their leader was just an ordinary man, like the rest. He was a brother of the Reverend Joseph W. Tays, the first Episcopal minister in the Valley. A Nova Scotian by birth and a British subject, he had passed most of his life in the United States. The previous year he had spent in Austin, where his brother had been chaplain of the State Senate. Until his new distinction had been thrust upon him, he was "no hand for trouble"—just a sort of handy man around the Reverend Joseph's combination house and chapel where he made furniture, dug wells, and puttered around. He took a long time to finish a job, but he was honest and loyal. Major Jones considered him "cool and determined," and his fellow citizens testified that he was "a man of unblemished integrity, cool, courageous, and discreet."[74]

Whatever his qualities were, there was nobody better to be found. He took command, and as soon as arms, ammunition, horses, and instructions could be provided, his detachment went into quarters at San Elizario.

Judge Howard did a little recruiting for Major Jones and wrote to him from Mesilla on November 13, "I have found two good quiet men, who will start down tomorrow to El Paso to enlist."[75] The Mexicans, and some of the Americans, made a good deal of Howard's help and complained that the new company was just a gang of thugs assembled and paid by him. Jones did not bother to explain to them that he always tried to be on good terms with both sides when he was called in to keep the peace. Instead he spent the evening of November 16, 1877, in paying a call at the home of Mr. Joseph Magoffin.

The Magoffins were entertaining at dinner when the Major's knock was heard. Mr. Magoffin went to the door and found himself in the presence of Jones, Tays, half a dozen Rangers, and a proposition.

"Mr. Magoffin," said the Major, "I am expecting Charley Howard tonight. I sent for him to come down and I want you to go with me to see a justice of the peace. We must work fast and quietly. I haven't spoken of this to anyone, not even my lieutenant here, and I think we can carry it through."

Magoffin pulled thoughtfully at his beard. "All right. As soon as I get through dinner, I'll come to town and see you."

Two hours later they presented themselves at the door of Guadalupe Carbajal, the local justice, a Mexican of some culture but with little English and less law. He was of the opinion that in this case he could waive examination and admit the accused to bail (it was a decision that was much debated later), so Jones and Magoffin went home in an easier frame of mind while Charley Howard's horse jogged down the road from Mesilla in the small hours before dawn.

Charley himself appeared with Jones and Magoffin before Justice Carbajal betimes in the morning and was arraigned for the murder of Cardis on a warrant sworn to by Magoffin and issued to and executed by Jones. The prisoner waived examination and was admitted to bail in the sum of $4,000. Magoffin and Tays signed the bond, and Howard put down the name of his father-in-law, from whom he had power of attorney.[76]

"Now, Charley," admonished Magoffin, "for the Lord's sake stay away from here until court meets."

"I will," Howard promised. "I am thinking of making a trip to Chihuahua." And he walked out, a free man.

Howard's massive self-confidence always misled him into thinking that when he had won a battle the war was over. He knew that Ben Dowell and others would testify, when his case came to trial, that he had been in danger of assassination from Cardis's friends, and that Cardis was aiming a pistol when he was shot. There was nothing more to worry about, and he was in no hurry to get out of town. Instead he appeared on the streets and even went out of his way to make up with several men who had threatened to shoot him on sight. One of these was Benigno Alderete of Ysleta, who said he had regarded Cardis as a second father.

Major Jones shared some of Howard's confidence and felt that it

was safe to leave for Austin. On his arrival he received a letter[77] from
Lieutenant Tays, dated November 29, 1877:

> Things are about the same as when you left the Mexicans gave Howerd a
> scare the other nite on his way down to franklin at the ranch 15 miles above
> Franklin his man shot a dog belongen to the ranch as they past and fifteen
> armed men rushed out on Howerd with the entention of killen him but for
> some nice talks and $100 he got off but badly scared he is now in Franklin.
>
> > Yours respectfully
> >
> > Lt. J. B. Tays
>
> P.S. How is it about doctoreing dose the State pay for it or not how is it.

SHOWDOWN　　　　John McBride, Howard's efficient and
unpopular agent at San Elizario, slid
off his horse in front of the El Paso
Customs House and hurried inside. It was the second of December
and the day was crisp and cool, but horse and man were sweating.

Collector Slade and Inspector Magoffin listened to McBride's tale
with startled faces. A wagon train of sixteen *carros* and sixty yoke of
oxen had left the Valley towns for the salt lakes. A good many men
from Mexico were among the drivers. All three realized that this was
the showdown.[78]

Magoffin stirred his stumps. He squeezed his portly figure and
Old Testament beard into a buggy, picked up half a dozen mounted
soldiers, and went to have a look. As he passed through Ysleta and
Socorro, he questioned and listened, and what he heard made him
very uneasy. This was no two-by-four revolt. The entire Mexican
population on both sides of the river was mixed up in it. Antonio
Barela, *presidente* of Father Borrajo's little town of Guadalupe, had
resigned his office to run salt in from the United States, and he was
one among many.

At San Elizario Magoffin spent the night with Cipriano Alderete,
who was openly defiant. "We have marked everything down," he
said "from the time when the rooster trod the hen until she laid her
last egg. Everything is going to be paid for now, and we do not care
what happens here after we have evened the score. You can take all

these old houses. What are they worth? We will go across the river or somewhere else."

Much disturbed, Magoffin went on to the turn-off at Quitman, where he noted that several ox teams had come from Mexico and taken the salt road. He followed their trail all day, and at night found himself near the camp ground half way out. Three loaded wagons were already there and a camp fire was going. Magoffin halted his party a little way off, set up his own camp, and then went forward to investigate.

They were ready for him. Six or eight men, all from the other side of the river, presented guns and demanded his business. He explained, and told them they would have to go back with him next day. In the morning, when he went over to take up the matter where he had left off, he found only cart tracks and three loads of salt dumped on the ground.

It was probably just as well. He learned later that they had debated a long time whether to stay and kill him, or make their escape.

Meanwhile Howard had sent McBride to start legal proceedings. On December 12, the day the wagon train was expected back, he got a writ at Ysleta to sequestrate eight hundred bushels of salt taken "forcibly and with violence." Sheriff Kerber was to attend to it and report when court reconvened. Sheriff Kerber never made that report.

There was going to be trouble. Judge Hague knew it. He had stepped into Cardis's shoes as the Friend of the Poor, somewhat to his own embarrassment, and got credit for being a conspirator against Howard. In October he had written his wife from Fort Davis: "I will try and be home the last of the month if not before—but I don't want to get into any of the troubles there—I have had no connection with the affair and I don't want or intend to have."[79] He was dragged into it anyway. On December 12, when the storm broke, he had gone to San Elizario to try to persuade the Mexicans to think before they acted. While he was on the road his horse ran away, smashed the buggy, and broke one of Hague's legs. He was lying helpless in Mauro Lujan's house when the shooting started.

Father Bourgade knew. He wrote to Major Jones that "three fourths of these fellows are already starving in consequence of their bad crops and are determined to get something from the salt or fight to the death."[80]

Captain Blair knew. He had come down from Fort Bayard under orders not to interfere unless aliens were implicated. He told Lieutenant Tays, "In four hours after I get the word, I will be in San Elizario without fail."[81]

The Governor of Texas also knew. On December 10 he sent a telegram to Sisto Salcido, Leon Granillo, and Chico Barela in care of Sheriff Kerber. "I call on you to obey the laws," he said. "You can control your people if you will, I am informed. Do so."[82]

Kerber stopped at Barela's home in Ysleta and read him the message. Barela seemed unimpressed. At San Elizario the Sheriff learned that Granillo had gone out after salt and Salcido was in Chihuahua,[83] so he got together as many men as he could in Mauro Lujan's house and told them, in the presence of Judge Hague and his shattered leg, what the Governor had said. They did not seem impressed either.

Howard might still have turned the tide, bad as things were, if he had been a little less stubborn; but he was as hard as ever. "If they take salt, I will prosecute them," he declared, and on the afternoon of December 12 he went down to San Elizario to make his word good. At his request, part of the Ranger force had come up that morning to act as escort.

The San Elizario Mexicans had known that he was coming when they saw the escort trot off toward El Paso. All morning they moved restlessly about. In the afternoon the men assigned to outpost duty went off to take their places. Father Bourgade watched them go and reported to Lieutenant Tays at the Ranger quarters. "There is big excitement up the road," he said, "and many armed men."[84]

Tays began to worry. Should he have told Howard to stay at home? Should he have gone himself? Finally he took half a dozen of his remaining men and started for Ysleta to meet the escort.

At the edge of town he came upon a body of armed and excited Mexicans, several of whom he knew to be aliens. At once he sent off one of Captain Blair's messengers to ask for troops.

At the head of the little army was Francisco, or "Chico," Barela. A man of no education who is said not to have known the first letter of his name, he was a leader of much force. They say he was a quiet fellow, fair complexioned for a Mexican, with light skin, brown hair, and blue eyes. For years he had lived peaceably as a farmer at Ysleta, and according to some of his descendants he would never have been in trouble had it not been for his daughter Pancha, who had been engaged to Cardis. Chico's son-in-law Francisco Gonzalez, was alive until a few years ago, and he used to tell how *tonto* (bullheaded) Chico was—how much he resented the death of Pancha's betrothed, adding that the girl herself never married and died very young.[85]

We might add here that gossip at San Elizario has Don Luis engaged to Cipriano Alderete's daughter Angela, who died not long ago, old and widowed and blind. Whatever Cardis's amatory situation was, Chico Barela thought he had a personal reason for going to war.

Tays met the escort at Ysleta and turned back with them, prophesying battle and murder. "I have sent a man off for Captain Blair," he said.

"Do you think Blair will be as good as his word and come down?" Howard asked.

"I have every confidence in him."

"I'm afraid he won't," the Judge grumbled.

About six o'clock, just as the last crumbs of the desert sunset were being cleared away, the party arrived at the Ranger headquarters. The men had taken over a house along the highway at the north side of the village. From the door one could look west down the main street on which were situated the stores, the mill, the post office, and other places of business. Howard remained inside long enough to eat supper and receive visits from a few of his friends. Then he came out and walked a few steps westward to Ellis's mill, where he had a talk with his friend Charley.[86]

Meanwhile Captain Blair had received Tay's message. About dark his troop passed through Ysleta, fourteen men, including an unarmed musician. By nine o'clock he was near San Elizario and began to encounter armed Mexicans who said they were guarding animals from the Indians. As they reached the edge of town, under a bright moon, their way was blocked by many men who told Blair that their *Capitán* forbade him to go any farther. Blair demanded to see their captain "at once" and deployed his men along the road. Half an hour later Chico Barela appeared.

"No," he told the Captain, "you cannot come into town. We are going to take Howard, and nothing can stop us. We will fight you if you try to free him."

They argued for some time. Once Blair tried to enter the town alone and they would not let him pass. Finally Barela dropped a remark which determined the outcome: "There is not a man among us who is not a resident of this county. This matter is none of your business."

Blair believed him, and went away. In the morning he wired his commanding officer that the affair was local and that the trouble had been greatly exaggerated. On the following Saturday he again rode down and interviewed the leaders of the mob, and again he accomplished nothing. If Blair had had the determination to force his way in, he might have headed off the tragedy that followed.[87] But he threw in his cards and the last hand was played without him.

While this was going on, bigger forces were being set in motion. Governor Hubbard telegraphed President Hayes on December 15 asking for aid in repelling "this invasion of our territory." His request was heeded, but it was too late for troops to reach San Elizario in time.

NOW
IS THE TIME

Inside Ellis's store on that moonlit December evening Howard found a dozen men gathered, on their guard but not especially alarmed. Ellis in particular was confident. Why shouldn't he be? He had lived among these people for years and done them many a good turn.

The moon rode westward. Ellis and Howard were beginning to think about going to bed (Howard planned to sleep in the store) when they became aware that something was going on outside. Ellis stopped in the middle of a sentence, got up, and peered out of the door. He came back looking very grave, thrust the revolver from his cash box into his boot, and said to Judge Howard, "You had better go to the Rangers and ask for protection." Then he stepped out into the moonlight.

The disturbance seemed to be centered some distance down the street in front of Leon Granillo's house, where a man was making a speech. Ellis came closer and saw that it was Chico Barela. He was telling how he had run Captain Blair off. When he got through with that he described how the *Presidente* at Paso del Norte had refused to give them arms and had forbidden his own people to cross the river. Chico thought they would get along all right anyway, and promised that they would deal with Howard in the morning.

Ellis listened for some time without attracting attention. When his presence was noticed, the men thought he had come to spy on them.[88] Corporal Matthews heard someone shout "Stop him! Stop him!" half an hour after Ellis left the store. It seems that when he found he could not get away, he tried to reason with the men, calling them *muchachos*—boys—and advising them to do nothing rash. In the midst of his desperate plea Ramon Sambrano (the "crazy" one of two San Elizario brothers) raised his voice in a cry which went through the crowd like an electric shock: "*Ahora es tiempo. Ahora es tiempo!*"

"Now is the time!" A dozen voices took it up. Eutemio Chavez got on his horse, loosened his rope, cast the loop around Ellis's body, and started to drag the poor storekeeper to death.

Of the two or three hundred men who saw Ellis hauled away, only County Commissioner Juan Nepa Garcia told what he saw, and he did not dare acknowledge the authorship of his article in the Mesilla *Independent* until the trouble was over. Even he could not tell how Ellis met his end, but the old men at San Elizario say there was a witness. Manuel Carrasco was hiding behind a *garanbullo* bush when Eutemio Chavez, Pedro Holguin, and old Manuel Lopez dragged Ellis past and stopped. Ellis was begging for his life, but Lopez advised them to stick a knife in him at once, and they did.[89]

In the Ranger quarters there were twenty men and a few guests, including Howard, Wesley Owens, and Deputy Sheriff Andrew Loomis of Pecos County. Out in the corral were the detachment's horses; in the house was ample food; the cistern held enough water to last a long time. Tays assured everybody that they could hold out indefinitely.

Even so, it was a long night for men who had never stood a siege before. In the morning they felt no better, for when Tays looked out he saw a line of pickets all around his block of buildings. Beyond that was a second line and what looked like a third. Before long a bullet crashed through a window. The battle had begun.

Howard at last looked the facts in the face. He said to Wesley Owens, "I think I'd better give myself up. I might as well let them kill me and be done with it."

Wesley thought the Rangers would protect them.

"It wouldn't do to rely on those fellows," he remarked thoughtfully. And when he heard a Ranger grumbling about being kept a prisoner on his account, he set his jaw and said, "I'm not going to stay here and have all of them killed for me."

At that moment someone pounded on the door and demanded to be let in. It was limping John Atkinson. On his back he carried a small but heavy trunk which he set down with a sigh of relief. Howard looked on with interest, for Atkinson was one of the men who had signed his bond and suffered as a result. Recently he had sold his business, expecting to leave town, but he had not got out in time. Now he was claiming sanctuary for himself and about eleven thousand dollars in money, drafts, and other valuables.[90] How he got by the pickets is a mystery, but he did. Tays welcomed him as one fighter more and sent him with three Rangers to take possession of the roof of Postmaster Clark's house, next door.

Almost as soon as these men were in position, they heard a hail from the street. Two men stood below them, one being Barela's lieutenant Sisto Salcido, a fat Mexican with one eye and an odorous reputation.[91] "We want Howard," he said. "You have three hours to give him up. If you refuse, we will take him by force and shoot him. The same thing may happen to you and Tays if you oppose us."

"We are only trying to enforce the law," Atkinson told him, whereupon Salcido grew angry and shook his fist.

"This is none of your business," he shouted. "Why are you defending this man? We will burn your house down if you keep on talking."

Atkinson and his companions were relieved when he went away and they were recalled to the quarters.[92]

Mid-morning came. As Sergeant C. E. Mortimer was walking between Atkinson's house and Ellis's store, a single shot fired from a window in Nick Kohlhaus's place across the street passed through his body and gave him a mortal wound. It was told among the Mexicans that he provoked the shot by making an insulting gesture at them, then "deliberately turned his back and insulted them again. The officer had scarcely removed his hand when a bullet took its place."[93]

Mortimer staggered a few steps; then crumpled up quietly in the middle of the road. Lieutenant Tays saw it. He heard the firing start up from all directions. Without an instant's hesitation he stepped into the street, picked up his man, and carried him inside. People forgot about this when they later charged Tays with cowardice. Mortimer died just before sundown, but it was through no negligence on the part of his superior officer.[94]

The firing continued all day. That night after the moon rose, one of the besiegers brought up a flag of truce and said they were tired of fighting, but when Ranger Santiago Cooper, taking them at their word, climbed up on the roof to get a blanket he had left there, all hell broke loose on top of a building a few doors away. He tumbled back inside with bullet holes in his hat and strong opinions about Mexican flags of truce.[95]

The second night was as long and sleepless as the first. When it was good daylight, the men saw that the lines had closed in under cover of darkness and that an assault was in preparation. Before long the Mexicans charged the horse corral but were driven back by rifle fire. Twice more they tried and twice more they failed. Then they resorted to Indian tactics and crept around to the rear of Ellis's store. Here too they found the garrison ready.

They did accomplish one thing: they got action from Mrs. Campbell whose husband, the miller, was one of the two American men in the store. She marched off under fire to deposit her two children in the Rangers' house and to ask permission for her husband and his companion, Frank Kent, to come over. She said that the mob was breaking through the adobe wall between Atkinson's and Ellis's stores, and that Captain Garcia had no hope of holding out.

When night came a wave of mobsmen stormed Ellis's place and killed Captain Garcia's son Miguel. The rest of the defenders scurried for cover in the town or across the river in Mexico. The victors immediately started piling sacks of flour in the store windows, and bullets were soon coming at the Rangers from another direction.

The siege, which had begun on Wednesday night, dragged on through Friday and Saturday. The mob made assault after assault, and the sleepless Rangers fought them off. Five or six of the mob are said to have been killed, but it is impossible to be sure.[96] On Sunday two determined mothers came down from El Paso. One was Mrs. Campbell, the miller's mother; the other was Mrs. Marsh, whose son Billy was the youngest of the Rangers. They browbeat the Mexican leaders into letting them take Campbell's wife and two children out, and got Billy Marsh as far as the edge of town, but there the Mexicans decided that Billy was big enough to be dangerous and they led him off, a prisoner.[97]

It was Mrs. Marsh who brought the Rangers their first news of Captain Blair's retreat. Howard said, when he heard of it, "I should have known better than to depend on him."

Then it occurred to Mr. Loomis, Deputy Sheriff of Pecos County, that he too might be more useful elsewhere. Tays obligingly hung out a flag of truce for him, and the Mexican leaders said he might leave. They suggested further that fighting should be called off for the night in preparation for a *junta* in the morning. Tays agreed, and the Mexicans did not fire any more.

Tays did not know that Loomis was still in San Elizario, locked up in an adobe prison. He did not hear the sounds of digging during the night. But when Monday morning arrived, he saw that he had been tricked again. Staring him in the face were rifle pits and breastworks. The flag of truce appeared once more, and this time the emissaries were not even polite. "Give up Howard," they demanded, "or we will blow up your house. We have undermined the building."[98]

Tays knew better than to trust the tale, and yet he was afraid not to. His slow-moving mind gave him no help. The Mexicans observed his bewilderment. "If Howard gives himself up willingly," they promised, "and if he gives up all claim to the salt lakes, no harm will come to him." Tays went back to quarters to confer with Howard.

The Judge had already made up his mind. "I will go. It is the only chance to save your lives. But they will kill me."

"Then don't go. We are here to protect you, and we will do so to the very last."

"No, I'll go. McBride, take care of my money and papers. Good-bye, boys."

He shook hands, smiling cheerfully. "It's your only chance to come out alive." And then this brave but stubborn man stepped out of the building, as Corporal Matthews remembered it, "apparently unconcerned."[99]

Tays went with him to the Mexican headquarters at Guillermo Gandara's house. Barela was so glad to see Howard that he is said to have thrown his arms around him and "hugged and kissed him."

Howard had little Spanish, so a messenger was sent back for Atkinson, who left his eleven thousand dollars and came at once. He was not brought into the room where Howard and Tays were waiting, however. They took him into another part of the house, and there he entered into an agreement which gave the Mexicans what they wanted. No one will ever know how it came about, but Chico Barela persuaded him to turn over his eleven thousand dollars, which was close enough to the sum of Howard's bond to cancel that debt. Chico in his turn seems to have promised that all could go free if the Rangers surrendered and Howard left the country forever.

"Well," Atkinson remarked, "you have received a better price for us than we would bring if sold at public auction."

At once Chico sent off a messenger to Father Borrajo advising him that a settlement had been reached. Borrajo, according to a story which may or may not be a malicious fabrication, sent back this reply:

"Shoot all the gringos and I will absolve you."[100]

Atkinson played the game out. Within half an hour of his leaving, he was escorted back to the Ranger quarters. "Everything is peacefully arranged," he assured the men. "You will not lose your horses or guns." The Mexican escort joined in and promised to place a guard over their property so nothing would be stolen. "Tays is waiting for you," Atkinson added. "Come on down."

They swallowed the bait. As they reached the mob headquarters, two or three at a time, they were disarmed, shoved into a "dirty room," and placed under heavy guard. One by one they stretched out on the dirt floor and dropped into exhausted sleep.[101]

Tays, unaware of all this, argued for a long time with the leaders, who kept telling him that he must take his men and go away, now that they had Howard. "I will not leave till Howard goes free," he said again and again. Finally a dozen of them picked him up bodily and shoved him into a room they were using as a guard house.

There he found himself face to face with Andrew Loomis, and the idea began to penetrate into his benumbed mind that they had made a fool of him.

SUDDEN
DEATH

There was a mighty crowd in San Elizario that day. The other villages in the Valley, on both sides of the river, were practically depopulated. When the people heard that their enemy was taken at last, they gathered in the plaza, many hundreds of them, and set up a death chant which echoed in Charles Howard's ears as he sat in his prison room in Leon Granillo's house:

"Máte le! Máte le!" they roared. "Kill him!"

Presently a committee of twelve or fifteen men entered the house and reappeared soon after, shoving him ahead of them. He walked erect and steady with his hands behind his back. They marched him to a vacant space between the houses, where he halted and turned around to face half a thousand men who a moment before had been yelling like savages. They were silent now, waiting to see him die.

A firing squad of five men filed up under command of Desiderio Apodaca. Every one of them was from the Mexican side of the river.

Howard spoke to them in his halting Spanish: "Three hundred men—" he said. "You are going to kill three hundred men."

He meant that a good many of them would have to pay for his murder with their lives. It was his last public speech and it was a complete failure. Seeing this, he braced himself and gave the command, "Fire."

The volley rang out, and he fell to the ground, writhing in his last pangs. Jesús Telles, a well known horse thief of Ysleta and Mexico, ran up with a machete swung over his head and aimed a furious blow at Howard's face. The dying man twisted away, and Telles cut off two toes from his own foot. While he went off to bleed, others with better aim hacked and chopped at the body.[102]

Atkinson and McBride were brought out next, in spite of frantic objections from Chico Barela. McBride had slept through all the noise and excitement of Howard's execution. It was a terrible awakening for him when he was snatched up from his corner and hustled out of the house. The spectators noticed how sad and dejected he looked. Atkinson, however, was bold to the end. He made a speech in excellent Spanish, reminding the mob that Chico had sworn to let them go.

"Will you violate your oath?" he demanded.

"Finish them!" yelled half a dozen of the Mexicans. "*Acábanlos!*"

"Then there is no remedy?"

"No! No!"

"Then let me die with honor. I will give the word."

He took off his coat and unbuttoned his shirt, leaving his breast exposed. "When I give the word, fire at my heart."

At the word of command, he received five bullets in his body, but he did not fall. "Higher!" he screamed. "*Mas arriba, cabrones!*"

Two more shots. He fell, but was still alive. A man from Sonora named Jesus Garcia came up. Atkinson motioned feebly to his head, and Garcia killed him.

McBride was next. He never said a word, but just stood there until they shot him.

There were loud cries of "More blood!" and "Shoot all the Gringos," but Chico Barela would have no more. He stood up and said his men would fight if there was any more killing. The bodies were dragged away with ropes tied to the saddle horns of Mexican horsemen. Stripped and mutilated, they were found later in an old well half a mile away.

Then the mob fell to looting. Many a man across the river had brought his wagon, just in case. Now cart after cart drove away loaded with bolts of cloth, boxes of dishes, bundles of clothing from the stores. Doña Teodora Ellis's furniture was taken. So were her dead husband's clothes—even her food. When she asked the robbers to leave her something to eat, they laughed in her face. Thirty thousand dollars in money and goods disappeared in forty-eight hours. The fiesta of Guadalupe was in progress on the other side, but it broke up because nobody came.[103]

The Rangers, who had been sent back to their quarters, were disposed of next morning. A mass meeting was held just outside which Corporal Matthews described for the *Independent* later on. There was a "dress parade," followed by passionate speeches demanding death for all the Americans, and then Chico Barela made a few remarks which settled the business. He said the Mexicans had what they wanted now, and if men from the other side killed another American, he "would turn his men loose on them."[104]

Chico gave the civilian prisoners their liberty first, and they scattered like frightened quail. Then he brought out the Rangers' horses and told them to ride. "In the name of the State of Texas, I demand our arms," said Tays, still unbowed. But all he got was an escort of Chico's men as far as Ysleta.

Back in El Paso, Tays wrote a report to Major Jones, concluding: "When I arrived here the greatest excitement prevailed, and found Captain Blair making preparations to start to my assistance with his command of 18 men some time next spring."[105]

And now that it was too late, help began to pour in from every side. The Secretary of War had ordered troops to march from Fort Bayard, Fort Stanton, and Fort Davis. Colonel Hatch arrived in El Paso on Friday evening and took charge of his assembled troops, many of whom were Negroes.[106]

Meanwhile Sheriff Kerber had received instructions from Governor Hubbard to assemble a posse, and since he was unable to raise a force in Texas, he appealed to the citizens of Silver City, New

Mexico. Thirty individuals answered the call and appeared in El Paso as the military forces were assembling on Friday. The new recruits were hard faced and battle scarred. Some had no arms; some had no horses; but they nearly all had reputations. They reported to the Sheriff and acted under his orders.[107]

When all these clans had gathered, the invasion of San Elizario got under way—first Hatch and his soldiers; then later in the day Tays's Rangers and the exhibits from Silver City. They were accompanied by Isaac Campbell, who drove a wagon containing four coffins for the bodies of the murdered Americans. All were in a pretty revengeful mood. Corporal Matthews expressed their feelings when he wrote: "Howard and Atkinson . . . met their fate like brave gentlemen fully believing we would avenge them, *and we will.*"[108]

Their first opportunity came on the outskirts of Ysleta at the house of Crescencio Irigoyen. They found him in possession of a pistol and a carbine which had belonged to the Rangers. He also had a small arsenal of ten old muzzle loaders, which they smashed before proceeding into town with Crescencio in custody. Several other guns were confiscated here and there, and an Indian named Santiago Duran was also made prisoner. By then it was growing late, and they decided to spend the night at the house of Ranger Price Cooper.

Next morning, paying no attention to the Sunday bells of the ancient mission church, they clattered away down the San Elizario road followed by the wagonload of coffins. Seated on the wooden boxes were the two prisoners, bound hand and foot with leather straps. They had been told that they were to dig the graves. Halfway to San Elizario, however, they were shot.

Lieutenant Tays, who was riding in advance, reported officially that the captives had been killed in trying to escape. When Colonel Hatch saw the bodies half an hour later, however, he was convinced that Tays was mistaken.[109] Nothing was ever done about it.

The next stop was at Socorro. Kerber's men reported that they were fired on from the house of one Nuñez and that Sergeant Frazer was hit in the boot. Immediately an assault was made. Nuñez was killed and his wife was left screaming on the floor with a bullet through her lungs. The Rangers said the first shot was fired at them from inside the house through a closed door. Subsequent investigators could never find any bullet hole in that door.

Jesús Telles, the one with two toes missing, lived in Socorro. Tays sent five men to bring him in. He saw them first, tried to run to the church as he fired his rifle wildly, and was cut down by bullets. Another Mexican, Cruz Chaves, was shot but not killed in Socorro, and by that time Colonel Hatch had come back with the news that it would be best not to go any farther. From there on "the brush was full of armed Mexicans" acting as a rear guard while their families fled across the river into Mexico. The Rangers stayed at Socorro that night, and in the morning reinforcements arrived which made it safe to go on.

By now all organized resistance was a thing of the past, but the Rangers and the recruits from Silver City camped at Ysleta till Christmas. The New Mexico detachment clouded still further the damaged reputation of Tays's group. Some of the visitors cultivated an already over-developed faculty for stealing—especially wines and tobacco. Some committed worse wickedness. J. Williams and F. Johnson, for instance, called at the house of Juan de Dios Alderete and raped his sister-in-law. Similar attempts were made elsewhere until Captain Blair had to write a letter of protest to Sheriff Kerber, advising him that men, women and children had fled in terror and "are now perishing for want of food and from exposure to the cold in and around Saragossa, Mexico."

The recruits began quarreling among themselves. On New Year's Day, 1878, First Sergeant Ford killed Sergeant Frazer, and other desirable homicides might have followed if the Silver City "Rangers" had not been mustered out on January 10.[110]

Lieutenant Tays's resignation was sent in to Austin on March 25. He is still known to fame (of a sort) as the only officer of the Rangers who ever surrendered to an enemy.

All that was left to do was to conduct an official investigation, a task which was undertaken by the Congress of the United States. On January 22, 1878, three of the four members of the Board assembled in El Paso. Major Jones, the Governor's appointee, did not arrive until February 19, but the others—Col. John H. King, Colonel William H. Lewis, and Lieutenant Leonard Hay—went ahead with the taking of testimony.[111]

They had considerable trouble finding out what they wanted to know. Some witnesses refused to answer; some forgot; some had moved away. On March 16 they adopted a final report and a set of recommendations. Major Jones, who had been dissatisfied all along with the method of conducting the investigation, continued taking testimony after the adjournment and filed a minority report on March 22.

He differed from his colleagues mostly on two points. He held that only the international aspect of the affair concerned them, and that the Mexican citizens in the mob were more numerous and better organized than the majority were prepared to admit. He felt, in the second place, that the United States should demand that the Mexican Government punish its own criminals and make reparations for the looting. He estimated the amount of damage at $31,000 against the Board's $12,000.

He agreed with the recommendation of the majority that a military post should be reestablished at El Paso in case another Judge Howard should come to live under the Valley *alamos*.

These reports were printed, read, discussed, and forgotten, as was to be expected. Court convened in March. It should have done a rushing business in mobsmen, but there were no mobsmen present. No one was punished; no one was tried; no one was even arrested.[112]

Occasionally an American whose business called him across the river would see a happy family making use of Doña Teodora's blankets or Atkinson's horse and buggy, but such a one kept his mouth religiously shut. On the Mexican side it was the same way.

The Grand Jury of El Paso County indicted six of the leaders of the mob, and later the Governor offered rewards for Chico Barela, Sisto Salcido, Luciano Fresquez, Agaton Porras, Desiderio Apodaca, and Jesus Garcia. Not a Mexican turned a finger to collect the money.[113]

For long years there was bitterness, but no more dead men in the streets of San Elizario. Doña Teodora lived in her big house alone, as stately as ever, and oh, so courteous when she had had an extra toddy, but her glory had departed, and the glory of her little town had departed also. The walls of her great house cracked and sank. Her neighbors died or left. The railroad came—and passed the village three miles away.

The salt question troubled no more. A new agent, Sergeant J. C. Ford of the Rangers, was given authority to represent the Zimpelmans, and the Mexicans applied to him with great politeness for permission to haul salt.

The War was all wasteful and unnecessary, unless to prove to a pessimist that men can die bravely in a bad cause.

POLITICS
is MURDER

In perhaps a majority of those instances of note, the situation was so acute, on account of local politics, friendships or family connections, that a single indiscretional act of the arresting peace-officer would have touched a match to the powder-keg, the "explosion" of which would have instigated a relentless warfare between given opposing factions and reacted to the detriment of the community as a whole.

Jesse A. Ziegler,
Wave of the Gulf.

7. Boots and Sandals

THE LAREDO ELECTION RIOT

In front of the post office at Laredo back in the eighties were two old Confederate cannon.[1] Since the Yankees and the Indians had been run out or quieted down, there wasn't much for the ancient field pieces to do, and Postmaster J. Z. Leyendecker had converted them to civilian use. He sank their muzzles into the ground in front of his post office and made hitching posts out of them.

It was a comedown for what was left of a Rebel battery, but the old relics were at least useful, and nobody bothered them for a long time. Then came 1886; and in March, after an especially bitter election, one of them was put back in service and taken a-feuding—the only bona fide example of feuding with artillery in the history of Texas.

Since the Lower Rio Grande Valley yields to no other spot on the earth's surface in the promotion of political vendettas, the use of such a weapon should cause no great surprise. For at least a hundred years the Border politicians have used any and all lethal instruments that they could get their hands on. If they had possessed the atomic bomb, they would have used it.

In fairness it should be said that the Laredo field piece was rescued from rust and idleness only for ceremonial purposes. The campaigns of the year 1886 went beyond anything previously experienced in the little metropolis by the Rio Grande,[2] and there was need for all the old tricks and a few new ones. *La Política* is always an important and

dramatic part of life in these half-Mexican Border towns. The opposing parties talk about being Republicans or Democrats, but their
own local organizations are more important and command a fiercer
loyalty. They form clubs with badges and banners. They meet at club
rooms and encourage each other by passionate oratory. Their *juntas*
and rallies and parades are carried on with crusading zeal. And in the
early days, when gentlemen wore pistols much oftener than they
wore neckties, the excitement was intensified by the constant threat
of death and destruction for all.

In Laredo the division was between two parties who had somehow
become known as the *Botas* (Boots) and the *Guaraches* (Sandals). The
names reflected in a limited way the social standing of the members.
Boots were the ordinary footgear of the rich and influential, and
rawhide sandals (they make them out of cast-off automobile tires
now) protected the feet of the *pobres*.

The use of such catchy epithets—*Rojos* and *Crinolinas*, Reds and
Blues, *Botas* and *Guaraches*—is a trademark of political campaigns
in this part of Texas, and the custom goes back a long way. It has
been surmised that the Reds and the Blues were named when the
Valley people were so ignorant that it was about all they could do to
distinguish one color from another—at the voting places and elsewhere.[3]

In this case it was not entirely a matter of rich against poor, for
some important men sided with the *Guaraches*, and the *Botas* had a
considerable following of ordinary citizens who aimed to please their
patrons. It was possible, also, for both sides to muster a good many
voters who drifted across the river from Mexico at election time,
looking thirsty and willing. Nevertheless the *Guaraches* called themselves the Citizens Party and implied that their opponents were
wealthy and corrupt.

The *Botas* pretended to be the Laredo branch of the Democratic
organization and accused the *Guaraches* of Republicanism, but the
Guaraches squawked indignantly that this was pure political lying.
"There is," they declared, "as large a proportion of Democrats who
act with the Guaraches or Citizens party" as with the *Botas*.[4]

The leading Boots were Raymond Martin, a Frenchman who had

married into the powerful clan of Don Bartolomé Garcia, and an old-country Irishman named G. M. McDonnell who had come over in time to become a member of Terry's Texas Rangers in the Civil War.[5]

The foremost Sandal was Don Darío Gonzalez, long-time sheriff—now an ex-sheriff, having been removed from office shortly before the story begins. He had been replaced by a rather high Boot named Darío Sanchez, who gave up the office of mayor to specialize in law enforcement.

In Laredo, as elsewhere, money talked, and since the *Botas* had it they were in control of most of the city and county offices. The only *Guaraches* in office were two aldermen and City Marshal Stephen Boyard, and in 1886 the Boots were doing their best to enjoin the latter from holding his position. The Sandals were fighting mad about it, declaring that Boyard was under fire "solely in order that the Bota party might control every peace, as well as judicial officer, in the city and county."[6]

All attempts to remove the marshal eventually failed,[7] but both sides were in a terrible temper about it, and the *Guaraches* determined to make the effort of their lives to turn the bloated rascals out in the April elections. The *Botas* were just as unshakably resolved to stay where they were. Both sides campaigned, electioneered, persuaded and urged through the month of March. There were parades, torchlight processions, and speeches by the yard. The *Botas* were first to turn up with a new idea: they took to "shooting anvils" with gunpowder. That was when the *Guaraches*, in desperation, dug up Mr. Leyendecker's cannon.

They painted it yellow to look like brass. They put it on wheels. They even dressed one of their men (his name was Moran) in a red shirt and made him the official cannoneer.[8] It was very good theatre and probably caused much jealously and dismay among the *Botas*. One wonders why they did not dig up the other cannon and use it themselves. Later they undoubtedly wished they had.

The campaign itself was comparatively peaceful. There was only one murder, though several fights were narrowly averted. The fatality involved a ranchman named Alexander Meuly who, on March 28, killed a *Bota* alderman named Douglas after a game of pool at the Commercial saloon.

This could have upset the balance and turned a couple of ferocious mobs loose on the town. Consequently Sheriff Sanchez appointed a large number of deputies—all *Botas*—to keep the peace. The *Guaraches* were furious. They counted forty new deputy marshals and a hundred and fifty deputy sheriffs, they said, "each a walking arsenal —parading our streets for about three weeks before election time."[9]

When it came time to vote, their fury rose even higher. They found all those deputies on hand to see that the election was properly conducted. "It is also proper to state," said one of them, "that on election day the sheriff's armed deputies swarmed at all the polls and made a number of arrests." The *Guaraches* who were arrested found themselves in the lock-up. The *Botas* were turned loose.[10]

That was not all. In each Precinct the presiding officers numbered four *Botas* to one *Guarache*. In view of all these precautions, it came as no great surprise to anyone to hear that the *Botas* had elected all their candidates but two aldermen. However, the narrow margins of victory (thirteen to forty votes) seemed significant to the losers and they announced that they were going to contest the election.[11]

When the results became known, it was too late in the day for the defeated party to do anything but grumble, but the next morning the leaders assembled and the town buzzed with angry discussions. To work off their disgust the *Guaraches* got out their cannon, hauled it down near the school, and fired it off until the children and teachers became so jumpy that the principal had to dismiss classes for the day. Then the cannoneers hauled their smoking terror away and began to gather at the west end of the main street.[12]

Meanwhile the *Botas* had not been idle. Triumphant and secure, they were planning a celebration which would sweeten their victory and further humiliate their foes. The way to do it, they thought, was to have a mock funeral procession and bury the dead Guarache Party in effigy. This was not an unusual thing to do in those days and in that place, but it was a risky time to do it. Early in the morning of the day after election, however, a "funeral notice"[13] appeared on the streets reading as follows:

YESTERDAY

at six in the evening died

in this city, and in the FLOWER of their age,

THE CLUB GONZALES-GUARACHE

MAY THEY REST IN PEACE

Their · devoted supporters, in announcing to the Grand Democratic Society, LA BOTA and to the Society "Union Mexicana," such a sad, premature and unforeseen occurrence, beg their members and associates to have the goodness to raise to the Supreme Being the prayers that their piety teaches them, for the eternal rest of the deceased, and to attend the funeral services and burial which will take place at three in the afternoon.

The funeral procession will assemble in the hall of LAS DOS REPUBLICAS.

LAREDO, TEXAS, APRIL 7, 1886

It seemed to the *Guaraches*, especially the hot-headed younger ones, that this was going entirely too far. They sent word that they were not going to let any such thing happen. To make sure that it did not take place, they organized several squads of mounted riflemen who took positions at the street intersections which commanded the *Bota* club rooms above *Las Dos Republicas* saloon on Main Street.

Alarmed by all this, the *Botas* consented to hold a conference, which took place immediately in Judge E. F. Hall's office. They said they were willing to abandon their plans for the funeral but were determined to go on with the procession. The *Guarache* leaders were sure that this concession was just a subterfuge—that the Boots would go ahead with the funeral the minute the Sandals dispersed.[14] They wanted the whole thing called off. So the meeting broke up in a deadlock and the *Guaraches* went out to call in everybody on their side who owned a gun. They gathered until it looked to one observer as if the streets were "blockaded" with them, and the few merchants who had kept their doors open closed up in a hurry.[15]

From 3:30 till about 5:30 in the afternoon the two parties tried to wait each other out, the *Botas* in their club rooms and in the streets nearby; the *Guaraches* all around, watching them. Several citizens tried to get Sheriff Sanchez to try to break up the parties. He complied by trying to disperse the *Guaraches*. They, however, refused to budge, and their leader, Don Darío Gonzalez, told the sheriff he had lost control.

Then the *Botas* called on him. They were going to parade, they said, as was their right, and they demanded protection. Immediately Sanchez sent off to his home and to various stores for more firearms. "I was called upon to give them protection and I was going to give it," he explained when he was called to account later.[16]

About 5:40 P.M. the *Bota* band struck up and the procession swung off down Main Street, led by W. H. Adams and the Club banner. Behind him, in the front rank, came Sheriff Sanchez and County Judge Rodriguez; then the band; then about three hundred men, including thirty horsemen at the end of the column. They went east on Main Street to Flores, turned south until they reached San Augustín Plaza, and then east past Raymond Martin's house, where the ladies on the balcony showered them with flowers.[17]

Right behind them came the *Guaraches*—with the cannon. The main body of a hundred and fifty men turned south in the wake of the *Botas* while the cannon, red-shirted cannoneer, and ammunition box, rolled on another block east and took command of the street which the enemy would probably use in returning to the center of town. Sure enough the *Bota* column swung into that very street, and at once the battle opened.

Each side accused the other of firing the first shot, and nobody can say now which one was right. Both sides were certainly ready for business and lost no time in going into action. Everybody ran for cover. Snipers appeared on several buildings, especially Martin's storehouse, which had a parapet. Women and children cowered in their houses and were met by bullets when they showed so much as a nose. And then, at the height of the confusion, the cannon went off with a mighty roar.

It was loaded with everything metallic that could be collected—nails, bolts, and assorted scrap iron. It might easily have laid out the whole *Bota* clan, but fortunately it was two blocks from the head of the procession and was aimed a trifle high. Most of the charge went whistling over the heads of the warriors and lodged in the top of the nearby schoolhouse.

Half a dozen prominent *Botas* urged their men on. The snipers did severe execution from the roof tops. All that kept them from exterminating each other was lack of ammunition. When their supply of cartridges ran low, the *Botas* re-formed and marched back to their hall. Then the firing started up again, and it looked as if the battle were going to be fought all over.[18]

At this moment the United States Army arrived on the double. Colonel R. F. Bernard, in command at Fort McIntosh, had been expecting trouble, had observed that disreputable characters on the Mexican side were assembled and ready to cross at the first sign of belligerence, and had kept a private Intelligence Department busy bringing information. "I was determined," he explained in an interview, "upon the first outbreak of hostilities, to march my forces out and disarm every armed man I saw, and guard the river bank and stop any incursion."[19]

When he arrived, the men from the Mexican side of the river were swarming across. With the help of Sheriff Sanchez, the Colonel moved vigorously on the immigrants and soon had that invasion nipped in the bud.

No accurate count could be made of the dead and wounded, for each side tried its best to conceal the full extent of its losses, and some of the wounded got away to Mexican territory where at least two of them are supposed to have died. Seb S. Wilcox, the Laredo historian, calculates that at least eleven men were killed, including one bystander, a Mr. Poggenpohl, who was potted by a sniper when the fight was all but over.[20]

The rumors which always circulate wildly after such an affair now began to be heard. Men said and believed that several bands of outlaws were camped near town, waiting for the firing to start up again and hoping to loot the city. If such men were about, they were disappointed, for the firing did not start up again. The Belknap Rifles moved in, under orders from the Governor and bearing the bouquets presented to them by their female admirers on their departure. General Roberts moved in with a detachment of Rangers.[21] Newspapermen from San Antonio moved in. There was very little room left for the combatants, supposing any of them still wanted to fight.

The *Guaraches* petitioned to have Sheriff Sanchez removed from office because of his part in the riot, but the jury which sat on his case could not agree. He held his job and was voted back into authority at the next election.[22]

The outbreak was over, but in the Rio Grande Valley peace and quiet are apt to be temporary. *La Política* is always there to heat the emotions. In October of 1896 the Mayor and the Sheriff were in hot water again and were writing worried letters to Austin. Amador Sanchez, the Sheriff, made his plea to the Adjutant General:

"Owing to political feuds in this county there is danger of riots and lawless acts on the day of election. . . . I respectfully request that you send an officer and a detachment of rangers. . . ."[23]

So it was in the beginning, and it will probably be that way for a long time to come. In Texas, Politics is Murder.

8.

A Feud
for Miss Sue Pinckney

A heavy rain had fallen that afternoon. The trees were still dripping as the mellow April dusk gathered over Hempstead. Supper was just over in the little white house where Miss Sue Pinckney lived with her bachelor brother John. In 1905 John was serving his second term in the National Congress and they could have had a bigger dinner in a finer place, but Miss Sue loved her small home (she called it a "cottage") and was not about to live anywhere else.

"If you've finished, I'll clear away," she said to John and their brother Tom, who had come by for a meal and a visit. "I suppose you want to talk politics."

"What else is there to talk about," John replied, a smile on his rugged, mustached face, and he and Tom fell to discussing the events of the last few days.

The great campaign to run the saloon keepers out of their small East Texas town had ended in triumph, and they were feeling very good about it. They agreed that all that was needed now was a little help in enforcing the law, and Hempstead's desperate days would be a thing of the past.

"I don't think I'll go to the meeting tonight," Tom said. "I've listened to enough speeches."

"Well," his brother observed, "it's the last rally—just a wind-up; though there might be some argument about those resolutions for the

Governor. A lot of people think they're too strong and may cause more hard feelings."

"I doubt it, but anyway they won't need us."

John considered for a minute. "Oh, come on, let's go," he said finally. "This will be the quietest meeting we have had. The Lipscombs are all out of town."

Their sister came in to see them off and the three of them paused at the door a minute to listen to the concert going on outside. All the frogs in Hempstead (prohibitionists, naturally) had come out after the rain and were shouting joyfully in every direction. "Did you hear Tompkins' story about the frogs?" John asked with a laugh. (Tompkins was his secretary.) "It seems this man owned a big swamp that was full of frogs, and he contracted to deliver two carloads of them for frog's legs. But when he went frog hunting, he couldn't find a single one. All noise, no frogs!"[1]

For a moment Miss Sue watched them walk away, skirting the puddles and smiling over the deceptive nature of frogs. Then she closed the door.

It was the last happy moment of her life. Within the hour the wild melee still known in Hempstead as "The Courthouse Tragedy" had broken out and her brothers were carried home, dead or dying. Like many another Texas woman Miss Sue had lost everything she lived for in a swift blaze of gunfire, and the hopes and dreams of her sixty-two years lay about her in ruins.

Crushed as she was, she had to endure the further unbearable thought that her own strong will had helped to bring them all to this fatal hour. It was she who had roused her brothers to pull themselves up by their bootstraps—to live up to their birthright and attempt to rise in the world. But for her they might all be alive and happy in the log cabin they had started from. The irony of it could not have been more bitter.

It did seem that from the beginning her family had been reserved for some special fate. She herself had always lived a life a little apart. Outwardly she was a quiet citizen of Hempstead—the once hard-bitten little community which is still known, to the chagrin of its peaceful inhabitants, as Six-Shooter Junction. Inwardly she lived in a world created from her family traditions, the sentimental novels which she loved to read, and the dreams and ambitions which drove her to make something of herself and of her orphaned brothers.[2]

Her fellow townsmen accepted the fact that she was different, though there was nothing in her manner or appearance to suggest it. She was delicate and slightly stooped. Her eyes were weak, and when she was working with her flowers she shaded them with a white sunbonnet. Her dress was always plain black. In every way she could think of she tried to be modest and retiring. But the difference was there.

For one thing she did not go out. Hempstead was a sociable town, and in 1905 everybody had taken up a domino game called "42." The partying and visiting went on at a great pace, but Miss Sue never played. She enjoyed having her friends come to see her, but she never returned their visits. She did not even go to church, though she was an earnest Christian.[3] Nobody thought of criticizing her for such small foibles. She was Miss Sue Pinckney, and that was the way she was.

There was something else, however, which made her really extraordinary: Miss Sue Pinckney was an author; she had actually written a novel. Not only that—the book had been printed. Those who had seen it looked a bit baffled when asked for an opinion, but just the same it existed and could be read. It was called *Douglas: Tender and True*. It bore the imprint of the Nixon-Jones Company of Saint Louis, and was bound in Miss Sue's favorite shade of purple. Naturally Hempstead looked at her with a little awe.

She may have written as many as five or six novels, but characteristically she delayed until she was fifty before attempting to get into print, and then waited fourteen years more before trying again. In 1906 her two final volumes were published,[4] but they would probably have remained modestly buried beneath her voluminous scrapbooks had she not found herself in a desperate situation from which she wished to get as far away as she could—even to the other side of the world.

The professors at the state universities who lecture on The Facts and Backgrounds of American Literature have never heard of Miss

Sue Pinckney and her novels, and it is probably just as well that they haven't. They would have no patience with her mannerisms and affectations and might even treat her with contempt.

Her characters have names like Muriel Dacre, Guy Walsingham, and Lady Maud Villiers. Her favorite subjects are the affairs of English lords, Italian countesses, and Southern aristocrats. She deals with love stronger than death and death more beautiful than life. Her men and women never eat a meal; they enjoy a "light repast," a "tray of dainties," or a "sumptuous collation."[5] They never take a walk at dusk; they go for "an evening ramble."[6] A group of ladies is not a group of ladies at all, but "a bright parterre of breathing flowers."[7] In such a world one would never say "How queer!" He would exclaim in well-bred accents: "Strange, passing strange!"[8]

We are too sophisticated to enjoy such flights as these, but it is well to remember that Miss Sue constructed her imaginary world without benefit of travel or association with people who knew what the real world was like. Could she have been born fifty years later, she would have made a career for herself and might have earned the respect of even the professors at the State University. But she began her life in 1843, and women did not do these things, particularly in the South, until after her time was past.

She was not too easy in her own mind about her writing. It meant appearing before the public, and that was cheapening. Her mother had convinced her that any girl who went to more than one dance in a month was "common," and perhaps writing for money was common too. She told herself that authorship was really the only outlet possible to a woman of any breeding. "Not that ladies should compete with gentlemen," one of her characters says. "Ah, no, woman must fill a humbler, holier sphere—that of home. Yet it is her right to embark on the sea of literature."[9]

From such passages in her books the pattern of Miss Sue's life and thought can be pretty clearly made out. She was a Southern Lady of the Old School with all the characteristic reticences, timidities, and taboos, as well as the characteristic courage and pride. She was so sure that her formula was right and so ready to sacrifice everything to it! It was supremely ironic that such a woman should find herself in the midst of a savage feud—supremely tragic that just when the world she dreamed of had become a reality, the cloud-capped towers and airy pinnacles should be swept away forever.

People like Miss Sue do not just happen. They are produced by long chains of circumstance. We can begin to understand her by looking at her father, Thomas Shubrick Pinckney of Charleston, South Carolina. Thomas made his first trip to Texas in 1836 to escape the consequences of a notorious duel in which he had been an unwilling participant.[10] Later, when his family opposed his romantic marriage to a delicate, convent-bred girl from the North, he came to Texas to live, settling in a log cabin near Field's Store in what later became Waller County. His wife had to adjust herself to the most primitive kind of existence among the crudest kind of people, and his five children had little to look forward to but the same rugged life for themselves. The proud Pinckney traditions were for them part of a bright, unattainable dream.

Only for Sue did the dream become a reality when in 1848 at the age of five she went back to the Pinckney mansion in Charleston for her education. She knew comfort and even luxury, fed on the high history of her clan, and had a colored boy to carry her books.

She was thirteen when she returned to a family whose faces she did not recognize and whose ways were strange and uncouth. Of course she was homesick for Charleston, and her unhappiness made her family unhappy. Even her father was put out with her. "I wish that she was back there," he was heard to say. "I think she likes those people better than she likes us." Only John, two years her junior, petted her while she was readjusting herself, and she never got over being grateful to him for it.[11]

She found refuge in reading and writing. The reading was what an adolescent girl in the 1850's would naturally pick up—tender tales of sacrifice, devotion and death, mostly by female authors. Ouida was her first choice (she had a complete set of Ouida), but passages in her novels show that she was almost as fond of *St. Elmo* and *Beulah* as she was of *Under Two Flags*.[12] Among the poets she read Campbell, Byron, and "my favorite" Tennyson. When she wrote (and she was always scribbling) she let her starved imagination wander among rich, noble, and high-minded characters; she explored the agonies of unrequited love; and she lingered over the death bed of many a child who was "too precious a bud long to adorn her earthly home."[13]

Only once did a small private door to paradise seem to be on the point of opening for her. That was when she fell in love with Groce Lawrence, a vigorous and earthy young man of her neighborhood, the complete antithesis of her story-book heroes. It was an honest attachment for both of them, however, and Sue was deeply hurt when her father told Groce that he would rather see his daughter in her coffin than married to him. He said Groce drank too much and was a poor risk as a husband for a delicate, idealistic girl like her.

Groce urged her to go away with him and be married, but she would never have dreamed of defying her father. It was the supreme sin in the books she read, and it was against her nature besides. Later she admitted that it might have been better if she had run away, for her lover went off to fight in the War between the States and did not come back.[14]

Her parents never heard her mention his name again, but in three of her stories she described an episode in the Battle of the Wilderness when Lee ordered Hood's Brigade to assault a position and prepared to lead the charge himself. A young Texas soldier, "an eager look in his dark eyes, a flush on his handsome face," took Lee's bridle rein and said: "General, you must not risk your life. We will take the position." The boy was killed in the assault, but *"always* will the name of that young Texas soldier, Groce Lawrence, live with the memories of the wilderness and shine, side by side, with that of Robert E. Lee."[15]

She risked more than a lover in those battles. Her brother Robert was fourteen years old and John was sixteen when they marched away. No wonder Miss Sue pictured the Confederate soldier as a mere boy with an eager face and a manly desire to go home after the war and take care of his widowed mother. She was remembering that Lee himself arranged to have Robert transferred out of Hood's Brigade, remarking, "I did not know that I had babies in this army."[16]

She never got over the loss of her sweetheart, and she never had another. It was perhaps fortunate that she had precious little time to think of herself. Misfortune followed misfortune in the years after the war. Her father became a hopeless invalid as a result of wounds received in that youthful duel in Charleston. Her mother died. She had to take over the responsibility for the whole family. Many women would have become hopeless drudges under these burdens, but not Sue Pinckney. She never gave up—never stopped looking for a way to break the mold which was hardening around her.

There was not much to work with. The community at Field's Store was isolated and brutal. There was no money, and no way to get any. Household tasks took up almost all her time. But she had her brothers—four of them, John and Tom and Tucker and Dick (whose right name was Robert). They were growing up to be rough, good-hearted, undistinguished country boys, no different from their neighbors, but they were her raw material and she went to work on them.

She talked to them about the Pinckney name and the Pinckney blood. They were as good as their kinfolks in Charleston, even if they were poor. Blood would tell. A Pinckney would always be somebody. Why not read law? A lawyer could rise high—make a fortune —enjoy high social position—go to Washington, perhaps.

Somehow she struck a spark in those boys, especially in John. He was working full time as a cotton weigher, but he began reading Coke and Blackstone sitting on a cotton bale between jobs. Tom read law too, though he was never as successful a lawyer as John. When their father died, John took his place as Justice of the Peace and a few years later, as his ambition rose, he moved to Hempstead, taking the whole family with him.[17] In 1875 he was admitted to the bar,[18] and Sister Sue felt a deep but quiet satisfaction. Without her urging he never would have done it.

Hempstead was a good lawyer's town, being full of trouble in those days. Its feuds and difficulties were discussed familiarly in barrooms, livery stables, and barber shops all over Texas. The good people of the place were always in a commotion because of the drinking, fighting and hell-raising of a minority of the population. A restaurant owner once blew a man's brains all over the ceiling for stating mildly that a piece of pie was rotten. It was said that a thirteen-year-old who couldn't drink a quart of whiskey and fire off a pistol was run out of town. A typical anecdote illustrating the course of events in Hempstead describes a citizen perched on the curb in front of the Three Brothers Saloon. A friend approaches him and asks for a chew of tobacco. "It's in my hip pocket," says the man on the curb. "You get it."[19]

In Hempstead it was not safe to reach for the hip pocket under any circumstances.

The Pinckneys stepped into the middle of all this blood and thunder. Dick Pinckney became a peace officer and for the next twenty years his career was full of hair-raising episodes.[20] John hung out his shingle as a lawyer and in the course of time found himself on the outskirts of the worst of Hempstead's community feuds.[21]

When Sheriff Tom McDade was reelected in 1884, supposedly by cornering the Negro vote,[22] a majority of the white residents were fed up with him. One disgusted voter wrote a piece for the Hempstead *Courier* on the text, "How long, O Lord, how long?" In Hempstead, this article declared, a man could steal a pig and go to the penitentiary, but let him commit murder and he would not even be brought to trial. A sheriff who let such things go on must be either crooked or incompetent.[23]

It was not known who composed this blast, but McDade's son-in-law Dick Chambers was deeply offended. On the street one day he boasted that if he could catch the author, he would make him eat the article. Standing nearby when Chambers made this remark was Steve Allchin, a farmer and cattle raiser who also ran a dray line and had brains enough to have done the writing.

"I'll father the article," Steve said.

Chambers took him seriously and shot him down, whereupon All-chin got up off the ground and killed Chambers.

A couple of months later the tables were turned when Jack Mc-Dade, the Sheriff's nephew, and a friend named Dick Springfield caught Allchin off guard for a minute. They slipped up on him through an alley and started shooting before he was aware that there was any danger. He did his best to get to the Winchester on his saddle, but it was too late.[24]

In the fall of 1888 this particular feud situation came to a close when Tom McDade, an ex-sheriff now, was assassinated in his own yard as he stepped outside one night to get his sick son a drink of water from the well.[25]

After the Allchin killing McDade asked John Pinckney to defend the two boys, but John refused. Instead, he helped the prosecution so effectively that both of them got prison sentences. Miss Sue was very sorry about the whole thing, for the McDades and the Pinckneys had been good friends She even corresponded with Springfield while he was in the penitentiary and worked hard to promote a pardon for him.[26]

The gleam of comfort which came to her out of all this trouble was the spread of John's fame as a prosecutor after the trial. When Governor Coke appointed him District Attorney in 1890, she was again a proud and happy woman.

Still she was not satisfied. Ten years later she saw another opportunity and urged John to run for County Judge. He was not interested —had no political ambitions, he said; anyway he did not know enough civil law. But he ran. And he was elected.

Then in 1903 Tom Ball resigned from the National Congress, thereby creating a vacancy which had to be filled by special election. The last thing in the world that would have occurred to John Pinckney was to run for that office. It occurred to Sister Sue, however. She had, in fact, been dreaming of just such an opportunity for years.[27] John said he had never asked a man for his vote, and never would. But Miss Sue had no such inhibitions. She urged and pleaded and wrote endless streams of letters. Luckily, John's opposition came apart and the election simply fell into his lap, but he gave full credit to his sister. Without her urging, he said, he would never even have made the race.[28]

And so it happened, when she was over sixty, that Miss Sue at last had her chance to see what the world was really like. John insisted that she go to Washington with him. The idea made her nervous, but not nervous enough to keep her at home. She saw the Smithsonian Institution and the White House and the Capitol Building. She attended the inaugural ball. She bought souvenirs for everybody back home in Hempstead.[29]

For the first time she could exchange her world of beautiful dreams for a beautiful world of reality. Was she disappointed? She never did say. But it seems entirely possible that Washington seemed a little drab and commonplace in comparison with the European capitals in which she loved to set her stories.

Whatever joy she felt was not hers for long, for now the clouds of tragedy began to gather. The first blow came while she was away from home. In April, 1904, her brother Tucker Pinckney was killed by a gang of Negroes in the Sunnyside community where he had gone to buy a couple of cows.[30] Tucker had not been much of a credit to his people and had associated himself with another young man of good family who had gone against his raising and taken up with the Negroes. The shooting broke out at a Negro funeral, and apparently the assassins, who fired from inside the church, were aiming at the other man and killed Tucker by mistake. A telegram called John and his sister home.

The news nearly prostrated Miss Sue. If it had not been for some of her Northern friends (toward whom she had been more than a little stand-offish up to that time) she could hardly have done what she needed to do. After that she never could hate the Yankees so wholeheartedly.

As if there were not bitterness enough in the county already, the murder of Tucker Pinckney widened the breach which divided the citizens. It was the "Courthouse Gang"—long in power and tolerant of corruption—against the old-line Democrats. The division went back twenty years and more to the days of the McDade-Allchin troubles. The "ins" were wily, resourceful, and unscrupulous. They cultivated the Negro voters[31] and perhaps resorted in a pinch to methods even less tolerable. The Pinckney killing showed exactly where they stood.

Three Negroes, Abe Smith, Aaron Washington, and Jim Williams, were arrested for the crime, but their white friends in Hempstead were anxious that they should be put to as little inconvenience as possible. They were taken off to Houston and kept in jail for a while; then let out on bail. The names of seventeen men, both white and colored, appeared on their bonds.[32] The white men were members of the Courthouse Gang. The prisoners were defended by Captain H.

M. Brown, former District Attorney, and R. M. Hannay, former County Judge. The Pinckneys and their friends burned with a deep and steady resentment against these men.

Such troubles have been lived down or worn out in every county in Texas, but in Hempstead things had to get worse before they could get better. Just at the wrong moment a new crisis arrived to generate more heat. The Demon Rum was under attack again, and the embattled Drys were determined to drive out the saloon keepers once and for all. The Courthouse Gang, which was as wet as the Gulf of Mexico, stood on the defense. John Pinckney, a prominent Dry, was up for re-election and joined in charge after charge right up to the enemy breastworks.

Miss Sue was with him every step of the way. John Pinckney was a plain man of few pretensions—no knight in shining armor himself —but he felt, as she did, that the first duty of a Southern gentleman was the protection of women and children. When the Prohibition League was organized and the W.C.T.U. began appealing to the manhood of Waller County to save the helpless victims of drunken husbands and besotted fathers, Miss Sue Pinckney's favorite brother could not stand idly by.

He did put his foot down, however, when his sister told him she was about to take the extreme step of joining the W.C.T.U. "With the money I'm spending and the time I'm putting in," he said, "I don't see why my womenfolks should have to go before the public."[33] So Miss Sue stayed home and wrote a fiercely declamatory essay, which still exists in one of her scrapbooks, on the evils of liquor. In her stories she had already included more than one scene in which young love and happy childhood were blighted by drunkenness.[34]

God knows there was reason enough for Miss Sue's feelings. Since the beginning of settlement violence and whiskey had gone hand in hand. Even in the early days of statehood a strong wing of earnest citizens had stood for the regulation of the liquor traffic, though they would not stand for much else. The first provision for local option goes back to 1854, and from 1876 until recent times Texas has gone into frequent convulsions on this issue. The northern counties always felt some obligation to make an honest man out of the unwilling drunkard, but by 1904 the central district, including Waller County, had caught fire.[35] The women labored and pleaded and prayed. The Loyal Temperance Legion added the appeal of children's voices. And traveling exhorters worked their audiences into a fine frenzy.

Waller County was badly torn up by this contention. In 1903 the Drys had won a nominal victory, but the Courthouse Gang controlled the enforcement agencies and as a result conditions remained as before. There was as much rotten whiskey and synthetic gin as if the town had been wide open. The blind tigers down in the river bottoms sold potions which caused sickness and even death. And the town drunks rioted as scandalously as ever.[36]

It was John Pinckney's stand on the liquor issue which sent him back to Congress for a second term. His opponent was Judge Holt of Houston, a very strong contender. Nobody supposed that the country lawyer would have a chance against the brilliant city politician, but Holt was Wet and Pinckney was Dry, and Pinckney won.

In his home county, however, the Courthouse Gang managed to stay in office. These men, including the ones who were helping the Negroes accused of slaying Tucker Pinckney, were uncompromisingly Wet and opposed to John Pinckney and all his works. There were loud cries of fraud from the Pinckney party after the election.[37] John and Miss Sue went off to Washington for the second time, leaving behind them a community more deeply divided than ever.

They came back in the spring of 1905 to join their friends and supporters in preparing for a finish fight. April 20 was the day set for another prohibition election and the women were campaigning as never before. A powerful exhorter named Mrs. Zehner was holding tent meetings.[38] She had only one lung, but it was a good one, and she held forth almost continuously—meetings at ten A.M., four P.M., and eight P.M., with a ladies' prayer meeting in the tent at three in the afternoon while the men gathered in the Methodist church.

Everybody went to the meetings—there was no place else to go—and some amusing stories are still told about the old drunks who rose in befuddled obedience when Mrs. Zehner started trumpeting: "Show me the man who squanders his money on booze. . . ." The emotional tension which she created in the town was terrific. "I would wade

up to my knees in blood for Prohibition!" one old lady declared.[39]
And she came near doing it, too.

On the day of the election the women gathered as close to the polls
as the law allowed and prayed, sang and buttonholed. "Come over
and help us, is the cry," was their theme song. Even the drinking men
could not resist such assaults as these, and Waller County outlawed
the saloons again.

The Drys were jubilant but wary. They knew from past experience
that they could not trust their present officers to enforce the law, and
the result was a petition, signed by two hundred voters and addressed
to the Governor, asking that a detachment of Rangers be sent to take
over. The petition was very plain-spoken about the county officials.[40]
Some of the Drys would not sign it for fear of inflaming the feelings
of the community still further. It was decided that the Prohibition
League ought to hold one last meeting to discuss the petition, and
the members were asked to assemble.

Hardly anybody thought there would be trouble. The election was
over and the people had declared their will. It was time now to bury
the hatchet and not bloody it any more. That was why John and Tom
Pinckney almost decided not to go when meeting time came around
on that moist and peaceful evening in April, 1905. But they went off
through the scented dusk, listening to the frogs' evening hymn, and
stepped through the courthouse door into eternity.

About two hundred people were assembled in the court room on
the second floor. John Pinckney took his place on the rostrum with
a number of leading Prohibitionists, including Mr. and Mrs. Tompkins. Old Captain Brown, who seemed a little the worse for liquor,
was there on the front row talking to his neighbors against the petition and anxious to make a speech. Before the meeting was called
to order by J. C. Petty, he did manage to say a few words. Afterward
he got up and sat down several times, heckling and interrupting,
while John Pinckney delivered a brief address. He was still at it when
Mr. Tompkins rose to have his say. Tompkins would not pay any
attention to him, so Brown seized him by the coat and used some
language which Tompkins did not consider suitable. "My wife is
here and you must cut that out," he protested. "Turn me loose!"

As Tompkins resumed his discourse, Brown pulled out a pistol and struck him on the head with it. Brown's son Roland was sitting on a table at the rear of the room when this happened, and he moved forward in an attempt to get his father away.

Then it was as if a match had been set to a powder barrel. The whole place blew up. Somebody fired a shot, and in an instant the floor around the rostrum was full of struggling, shooting men.

John E. Mills, a strong Dry who had recently moved in from an outlying community, was killed. Tom Pinckney was shot twice through the small of the back and died next morning. Captain Brown was also shot in the back, the bullet penetrating his heart and killing him instantly. John Pinckney was hit four times and died almost at once. Roland Brown got a flesh wound in the breast.

Two of the dead men, Mills and John Pinckney, were unarmed.[41]

Could a massacre like that have been the result of spontaneous combustion? Some people today will tell you it was, but there are more who believe it was deliberately rigged up by the saloon keepers and the Wet politicians. A story was current at the time of the trouble that some undercover work was going on.

"It will probably never be known just how many people took part in the shooting," said the Houston *Post*. "The younger Brown went out of the court house after emptying his gun and a tall man who cannot now be placed was seen to hand him another gun and also to do some shooting. It is thought that some took a hand in the firing who escaped injury or detection."

The tall man has never been officially identified, but dozens of experts went over the ground after the fight, analyzed every shot, and calculated the angle of the bullets which had imbedded themselves in the walls and window casings. The conclusion arrived at by some of them was that men had been posted in the jury boxes in the towers at the corners of the court room which were reached by a flight of winding stairs and commanded every corner of the place. It may be that there was something to the story.[42]

The roar of the guns echoed from end to end of the little town and the streets were almost instantly full of frantic women. Many a sad scene[43] was enacted that night. Captain Brown's daughter Mary was rehearsing for her wedding, announced for the next day, when they told her that her father was dead.

It was worse at John Pinckney's house when they brought the brothers home to their sister Sue. John did not speak a word after he was hit. Tom was able to make a brief statement. "If I wanted to shoot a man," he said just before he died, "I wouldn't shoot him in the back."

For Miss Sue Pinckney the ruin was complete. Three brothers gone in eight months, including John, her special pride. Her mind must have wandered back to the log house at Field's Store—to Groce Lawrence and her early love—to the books and stories she had written and laid aside—to the beginnings of John's success with which she had had so much to do. Line by line and contour by contour she had forced the unwilling clay of their lives into a mold which should have brought them dignity and honor. And each step she had taken had brought them all closer to this. What bitterness must have been hers as she sat that night between a dead and a dying brother and wished herself back with her loved ones in the log cabin she had been so glad to leave.

Well, it was all over now—all but the last rites and eulogies which seemed so useless and empty. In Washington a session of the House was set aside to commemorate the old Confederate soldier who had taken a modest seat among the mighty. Half a dozen men, including a young Representative named John N. Garner, rose to give the dead man his due. A Congressional delegation appeared at the funeral and was lost in a concourse of mourners whose numbers showed the universal respect in which John Pinckney was held.[44]

None of it was much help to Miss Sue. The dream of her life was dead, and her estate in Utopia had shrunk to a lot in the Hempstead cemetery.

One final blow was reserved for her. While she was in Austin attending the trial of Roland Brown (who was acquitted), who should appear but Mr. Neale the publisher! He wore a frock coat and a top hat and had a bundle of contracts under his arm. In her distress Miss Sue was an easy mark. Without consulting anybody she signed Mr. Neale's papers, hoping to make ten thousand dollars and take her shattered heart abroad. She paid him $2000 to print two more books, two thousand copies all told, and all she got out of the bargain was fifty copies of each of them when they were published in 1906. What happened to the other 1900 volumes (if they were printed at all) nobody knows. Only a few specimens of *In the Southland* and *Darcy Pinckney* got into circulation, and they are hard to find now.[45]

On November 23, 1909, she died in Houston at the home of her niece, Mrs. George Scott, and she rests now in the Hempstead cemetery beside her brothers—as much a victim of the feuding spirit as if she had fallen in the "Courthouse Tragedy" with a bullet in her heart.

FAMILY TROUBLE IS the WORST TROUBLE

It is from the common prejudices which men receive from their parents, that hatreds are kept alive from one generation to another; and when men act by instinct, hatreds will descend when good offices are forgotten. For the degeneracy of human life is such, that our anger is more easily transferred to our children than our love.

Sir Richard Steele,
The Spectator.

9.

The Feud at Mitchell's Bend

Their cow-hunting activities that day had taken Cooney Mitchell and his son Bill over toward Comanche Peak, which rises almost in the center of Hood County, Texas, on the Middle Brazos. It was hard work, beating the brush for strays. The back of old Cooney's neck was wet under the long white hair which hung to his shoulders, and Bill's grim, mahogany-colored face was shiny with sweat.

They were just about ready to call it a day when they almost rode over a pitiful little group of human beings camped under an oak tree. The Mitchells were used to the sight of migrating families in all stages of destitution—Texas was full of them in the sixties and seventies[1]— but this lot was about the poorest they had ever seen. Cooney's tough old Texas heart was touched the moment he saw them, and even Bill's rock-like features softened for a moment.

The immigrants had absolutely nothing but a team of ponies, a light wagon, and a small mob of offspring, the oldest a big boy in his teens. One of the ponies was lying stretched out on the ground, dead, and it was obvious that this was the end of the road for that family. The Mitchells took one glance at the dejected faces, swapped a significant look with each other, and got off their horses.

Before night the Truitts had been moved to the Mitchell place down on the Brazos. The five boys—Jim, Sam, Ike, Lee, and Alfred— had been fed to bursting, and their elders had come to an agreement which made everybody happy. The Mitchells could use some help on the ranch, and the older Truitt boys looked big and strong. Cooney said he would help them build a log house and keep them going till they could take care of themselves. They could work out what they owed him.

Salvation had come just in the nick of time for the Truitts, and they went to work with grateful enthusiasm. There was a house to build—a garden to plant—a well to dig—a smokehouse to put together. Day and night they labored while the Mitchells looked on with approval and helped as much as they could. Bill Mitchell, impassive and silent as he was, seemed to feel friendly toward them, and Cooney took down meat from his own smokehouse and hung it in theirs as soon as they had it ready.[2]

All this happened in Hood County, something like fifty miles southwest of Fort Worth, about the year 1872—exact dates not available. The Mitchells themselves were comparative newcomers, having moved in shortly after the end of the war and found a stopping place in a great loop of the Brazos River which soon became known as Mitchell's Bend. The family included Nelson Mitchell, for some reason nicknamed Cooney, his wife, three sons named Bill, Dan and Jeff, and two daughters who in due time became Mrs. Mit Graves and Mrs. W. J. Owens. The family came to own a good deal of land, in fact almost the whole of the Mitchell Bend, and didn't need to ask favors of anybody.

The Mitchells were plain frontier Texans—rough and tough when their dander was up, but capable of great generosity. The clan spirit was strong in them, and it extended to their kinfolks and their friends. The Truitts belonged to a different breed. Poor as they were on the day of their arrival, they had in them a few seeds of aspiration for finer things. They worked like beavers to become independent, and they valued the fragments of religion and culture that were available to them.

The differences were summed up in Bill Mitchell and Jim Truitt, the two elder sons.[3] Dark-faced, rough-hewn Bill was the personification of the Texas frontier. Powerfully built, dour and enduring, he was a competent cowman and horseman, handy with an axe, expert with rope and gun. He was no hand for trouble, but he took nothing from anybody, and there was that in the look of his eye and the pride of his walk which said that he was somebody to let alone.

Jim Truitt, by contrast, seemed out of place in that rough country. He was a good-looking boy, very blond, with a thin, refined face. He liked to read books and think about them, and spent much of his time doing religious work for the Methodist churches of the county. He dreamed secretly of being a preacher. The Mitchells as well as his own folks were proud of Jim's gifts and encouraged him to make something of himself.[4]

Eventually the fathers of the Church were so much impressed by Jim's earnestness and devotion that they admitted him to preach "on trial" in what was then the Northwest Texas Conference. His first assignment was to the Chartersville Circuit, Weatherford District. He had been the Reverend Mr. James Truitt only a few months when the trouble with the Mitchells came to a head.[5]

In spite of the differences in their ideals and backgrounds the two families kept on good terms for years. The young people "passed each other friendly," as the country saying went, though Jim and Bill naturally did not have much to say to each other. But as the Truitts rose in the world, little things—trivialities—gradually chipped away the foundation of this good understanding. It may be that Cooney Mitchell was too conscious of the favors he had done for the Truitts and was tactless in his reminders. The Truitts probably resented his patronage and felt that they had repaid him in full for what he had done. The Mitchells may have suspected the Truitts of trying to be above their neighbors, and the Truitts could conceivably have felt that the Mitchells were a little crude.

It was so long ago—and there is so little we can really know about such things! But this we can be sure of: the first outbreak was brought on by a land dispute.

The Truitts were hard workers and did well. Eventually they bought land adjoining the Mitchell holdings near the settlement of Mambrino. There was a strip along the property line that both sides claimed. In March, 1874, they took their dispute to court. The court-house burned to the ground in 1875,[6] taking all records of the case with it, but the trial must have been a bitter one. There was so much backing and filling in the sworn testimony, so much "cross swearing," as a Hood County historian politely puts it, that each side accused the other of perjuring itself shamefully. Before the thing was decided, apparently in favor of the Truitts, hatreds had been aroused so violent that there had to be some blood letting.[7]

On Saturday evening, after the trial was over, the Truitts had covered some six miles on their way home when they were overtaken by Cooney Mitchell, Bill Mitchell, Mit Graves, W. J. Owens, and a neighbor of theirs, an old man named James Shaw. The stories which went off to the Texas papers said that Bill Mitchell and Mit Graves "immediately opened fire on the Truitts with double barreled shot guns, killing the second brother instantly and lodging nine buckshot in the back of the elder, who ran, followed by the younger, as yet uninjured. The little fellow Isaac—fifteen years old, being mounted upon a mule, soon fell behind, and was overtaken by the fiends and a fatal shot delivered at so short a range as to leave the plainest mark of powder burn upon his person; they continued the pursuit of the wounded brother, a mile and a half to the house where he took refuge. The murderers then retreated. The wounded minister laid down, and being perfectly sane . . . told the inmates all the shocking particulars. . . .

"Several members of the grand jury, being on their way home, came upon the bodies of the murdered boys laying stark and cold in the road and carried them to the same house where the elder brother had taken refuge. The poor dead boys were laid side by side on the porch. The elder lingered in mortal agony until 11 a. m. the next day, when he breathed his last."[8]

How much of this story is true, we can only guess. One detail at least was wrong: Jim Truitt did not die. The same tale was repeated in other accounts, however, with the addition of further horrible circumstances—for instance, "Little Isaac" was said to have been a cripple.[9]

The Mitchells didn't remember it that way at all. Their version is the one the old timers tell at Granbury today, though it seems never to have found its way into print. It says that the Mitchell group were on their way home after the trial and were jogging peacefully down the road some six or seven miles from town when they were overtaken by the Truitt boys. Old Man Cooney was unarmed, but Shaw and Bill Mitchell, riding well to the rear, carried shotguns, the stocks resting on their thighs and the barrels in the air.

The Truitts overtook and rode around them, making insulting remarks about the trial and singing some kind of song which implied that the Mitchells were hog thieves. When they had gone ahead a little way, they turned off the road, waited until the Mitchells had passed, and rode by them again. This time Little Isaac rushed at Bill Mitchell from behind, snapping a derringer at him. Immediately Shaw turned and shot him down. Bill, thinking there was going to be a general attack, turned his gun on Sam Truitt and killed him.[10]

There were no witnesses to this bloody business but the Truitts and the Mitchells themselves, and we have no way of reconciling the two stories.

Cooney Mitchell and his neighbor Shaw were arrested early in April. Bill and his brother-in-law Mit Graves eluded the officers. That was the beginning of the saga of Bill Mitchell, for his game of hide-and-seek with the law lasted for thirty years.

In December Cooney Mitchell, Owens and Shaw were placed on trial for their lives. The Reverend James Truitt, carrying the scars of Bill Mitchell's buckshot in his back, was the chief witness against them. He testified that Little Isaac was kneeling in the road begging for mercy when Bill Mitchell shot him in the mouth. Cooney, he said, had made himself an accomplice, though he was unarmed, by urging his side on and shouting "Give 'em hell, boys," during the shooting.

The jury was convinced that Jim Truitt had told the truth. They sent Owens and Shaw to the penitentiary,[11] where Shaw eventually died and where Owens languished till he was pardoned out. Cooney Mitchell was sentenced to die by hanging.

The grief and anger of the Mitchell family was deep and bitter. The old man was not afraid to die, but he did not want to be hanged like a dog. His family felt the disgrace of the sentence as keenly as he did and laid desperate plans to help him circumvent the hangman.

The execution was scheduled for Friday, October 9, 1875. "On Tuesday night previous," the Texas papers reported, "the guard about the jail discovered an armed man crawling towards them, and not knowing how many more there might be, fired. The next morning the lifeless body of Jeff Mitchell, youngest son of the doomed man, was found on the ground, the whole top of his head blown off. He was armed with a double-barrelled shot gun and a brace of Colt's revolvers. In his pocket was found a large vial of laudanum, which he was evidently conveying to his father.[12]

Jeff had climbed up the thirty-foot bluff from the river bottom—the only way he could approach the jail undetected—just before daylight in a last frantic attempt to save his father from the noose. The old man knew he was coming and had let down a string from his cell window to pull up the bottle in case Jeff made it.[13]

Jeff did not make it, however, and his death filled Cooney Mitchell's cup of sorrow to overflowing. "Wednesday night he made several attempts to commit suicide by hanging himself with a chain which he had wrenched from the door, but his heart failed him. He spent the night in cursing the sheriff and officers. Thursday night a guard was placed in his cell to prevent self-destruction. . . ."[14]

Friday morning he was still alive when they took him out of the jail, seated him on his own coffin in an ordinary farm wagon, and drove him off to the place of execution just north of town.

The old folk story is told over again about his last ride. Some cowboys went hurrying past him on their way to see the show, and he called out to them, "Don't hurry, boys! Nothing will happen till I get there."[15]

Since this was Hood County's first and last legal hanging, equipment had to be improvised. The wagon was driven up under a tree and the noose was tied to a strong limb. When everything was arranged, Sheriff Wright asked Mitchell if he had anything to say. He had. And only a few years ago people were still alive who heard that speech and wished they could forget it.[16]

He stood up in the wagon, a thin, dried-up old man with a long white beard and white hair hanging down to his shoulders, his body quivering with this last burst of feeling, and addressed the crowd. He told how he had tried to be honest (everybody agrees that he was, whatever other faults he may have had).[17] He gave his side of the crime of which he was accused. He talked about the death of young Jeff and what it meant to him—how proud he was that there was "not a drop of cowardly blood in that boy's body"[18]—and he accused the guards of knowing who it was when they fired. He called upon his son Bill, wherever he was, whatever he might be doing, and however long it might take, to hunt down his father's murderers.[19] Then, as the story is told today, he saw Jim Truitt out there in the great crowd of five thousand people and motioned with his hand for him to come nearer. Jim wouldn't do it, so Cooney addressed him across the heads of the crowd:

"Jim, when you didn't have nothing but one pony and a wagon, didn't I take you in and feed you? Didn't I?"

Jim said nothing.

"When you wanted to go to preaching, didn't I buy you the first suit of clothes you ever had?"

Jim said nothing.

"Didn't I buy you a Bible—a good Bible—to start you out?"

Still Jim said nothing. Sheriff Wright drove the wagon out from under the old man and left him hanging.[20]

When it was over, people began to wonder about that execution. The old man, so weak and scrawny but so bold and ready in his own justification, standing up there in the wagon with the rope around his neck, left a scar on the memory of every man who saw him that day. They wondered if justice had been overdone.

His own family never had the least doubt of it, but there was nothing they could do at the moment. They buried Cooney in sight of his own front porch. Then his family broke up and the widow left Mitchell's Bend. So did the Truitts. And for the next fourteen years in Hood County the Truitt-Mitchell business was just something for the men to talk about on Sunday afternoons while they whittled in the shade outside and the women washed the dinner dishes.

The currents of life carried Bill Mitchell and Jim Truitt far apart. Jim went on to become a dignified and respected minister of the gospel. Bill became a hunted fugitive—a man on the dodge whose only home was a bed roll somewhere on the cattle range and whose only hope of survival lay in always moving on. People who live in houses and carry fountain pens instead of guns can have no conception of what this means, or what it does to a man. It takes away the hope that keeps most of us human and sharpens the instincts that should belong to the wolf and the mountain lion. Unless the fugitive has something in the back of his mind to keep him going, his life is apt to be violent and short.

Bill Mitchell had something in the back of his mind which did keep him going. He had a job to do, a job which obsessed him day and night. He had had to let them hang his father. There was nothing to do but lie low while that was going on, or two Mitchells would have been hanging from that limb instead of one. But he had resolved that this would not be the end. Sometime—somewhere—somehow—the score would be evened. He would take all the time he needed. He would wait till his enemy had laid all fear aside. Then he would act.

During the twelve years that he waited, Bill lived in many places under many names. Eventually he settled down, after a fashion, in the neighborhood of Fort Stanton, New Mexico, right in the middle of Billy the Kid's feud with Murphy and Dolan. It was an ideal environment for a man on the dodge, so Bill stayed around for a spell, going under the name of John W. King and conducting a freighting business to El Paso and other points.

By 1883 he was back in Texas and had teamed up with a man named Nathan Becket. Becket's daughter Mary, a divorcee, had become Mrs. John Davis—Bill's new name.[21] We know no more of her than this, but she must have been about as indestructible as Bill himself, for she lived with him and her father in a primitive camp twenty miles out in the brush from Bracketville in lonesome country west of San Antonio. Her husband was hunting and trapping for a living.[22] The only possession they had of which they could be proud was a handsome claybank horse.[23]

That was Bill Mitchell's situation in the summer of 1886. The man he hated was living a much more normal and satisfying life. In 1874 James Truitt, still "on trial" as a minister, had been assigned to the Marlin Circuit, Waco District. In 1875, finally admitted to full con-

nection, he had a charge in Waco. From there he went on to Waxa-
hachie and to Centerville, and finally (in 1880) was transferred to
the East Texas Conference, serving at Henderson, at Marshall, and
finally at Timpson.

It was at Timpson in 1884 that he gave up full-time preaching. Assisted by his wife, who later made a considerable reputation as a writer
under the name of Julia Truitt Bishop, he became editor of the Timpson *Times*.[24] He was also county clerk for a while.

After all this it must have seemed to him that he had left the past
behind and that he could lay aside forever the fears that had marched
by his side for so many years. And he might actually have lived out
his life in peace if it had not been for a dark-skinned, strongly built
stranger in a white Stetson who rode a handsome claybank horse into
town from the west on July 20, 1886. Later that horse was to become
pretty well known. A family living a short distance from town ad-
mired him when his rider stopped to water him at their spring just
off the public road late that afternoon.

It was a little before eight when horse and rider entered the village,
and the lamps were being lighted here and there. The stranger spotted
a little Negro boy and asked him where the Reverend James Truitt
lived.

"Over that way," the boy said, and started to give directions.

"I'll give you fifteen cents to show me the place."

So the boy guided him to the door, got his money, and went away.
The man entered the house without knocking.

Mr. and Mrs. Truitt and their little daughter were sitting together
in their living room. As the story is often told, James Truitt was reading his Bible, getting ready for his sermon in the local Methodist
church next day. July 20, 1886, happened to be a Tuesday, however,
and the story may be classed as folklore.[25] Mrs. Truitt looked up first
and saw the grim, sunburnt stranger looking at them.

"Is this the Reverend James Truitt?" he asked.

"Yes it is," she answered. "What do you want with him?"

Without further words the stranger pulled out a forty-five and shot
Mr. Truitt through the head. Leaving him dying on the floor, he
walked leisurely out, mounted his horse, and rode away while Mrs.

Truitt's screams brought her startled neighbors running from every direction.[26]

It took Sheriff Sims several hours to come up from Center, the county seat. More precious time was wasted while he looked the situation over. Finally Sims sent off to Nacogdoches for Sheriff A. J. Spradley, a famous man hunter, but it was forty-eight hours after the murder before Spradley could get on the trail.

The killer had too much start. Spradley followed him for a hundred miles, until he crossed the Trinity River, identifying him by his fine horse and by a little coffee pot which he carried tied to his saddle. It was amazing how that coffee pot caught people's eyes. As plain as his traces were, however, he was traveling faster than Spradley could follow, and the Sheriff finally turned back.

By that time Truitt's friends in Timpson were beginning to remember that there was some sort of feud situation in the dead man's background, and Spradley thought this angle was worth investigating. As soon as he could get away, he took a trip to Granbury, where Old Man Mitchell had dropped off a wagon into eternity twelve years before. It took him hardly any time at all to find out that a man with a coffee pot had spent two days with Dan Mitchell, Bill's brother, just before the tragedy at Timpson. But where was the man now? Nobody knew.

In his old age Sheriff Spradley had his famous cases and selected portions of his life history written up, and in this autobiographical narrative he tells how he found out what he wanted to know. First he arrested Dan and took him off to Timpson, where he arranged for a fake mob to talk things over under Dan's cell window. This scared Dan so badly that he broke down and told all. Yes, Bill had been to see him. The last address he had for him was Fort Stanton, New Mexico.

So Spradley followed the scent out to New Mexico, but found his game gone. Mitchell, or King, had disappeared from those parts a long time before Truitt was killed. Spradley was stumped again—but not for long.

From a former justice of the peace he learned about John Davis down in the brush near Bracketville and was off on the trail again.

He fully expected that time and distance would have undermined Mitchell's vigilance at least a little. He soon found that Bill never let down his guard, even for an instant.

None of the local officials at Bracketville wanted to go into the brush with Spradley, so he hired a horse and rode in alone. He found the Becket camp without difficulty—it consisted of a tarpaulin thrown over some mesquite stumps—but Bill was not there. Pretending to be a cattleman, Spradley had breakfast with Mr. and Mrs. Becket, who were very grumpy about his visit, and then rode back empty-handed. He noted, however, that the Beckets were using a small coffee pot exactly like the one Jim Truitt's slayer had tied to his saddle. He noted also as he rode away that a man with a rifle across his knees was sitting on a rock on a nearby hillside watching him.

When he got back to Bracketville, he sent Becket a note stating that Dan Mitchell was about to be hanged for Bill's crime and asking if they were willing to let that happen. Becket turned the note over and wrote on the back, "Go to hell," before sending it back with Spradley's messenger.

As a last resort Spradley left word with a Ranger company that they might try their luck later, but when the Rangers showed up at the Becket camp, Bill had cleared out completely.[27]

H. W. Henslee of Granbury saw Mitchell later on in Kimble County, where he was going under the name of Russell, though Henslee did not realize until much later that it was Bill Mitchell he had talked to. Eventually he drifted back to the old stomping ground in New Mexico, where he was located in the spring of 1907.

Sheriff Swofford of Hood County was the man who ran him to earth. Swofford was supposed to have learned Bill's whereabouts "through the Indian Agency"—whatever that means.[28] At any rate he began to devise a trap which might deceive even the wariest outlaw. First he selected two of his deputies who were cautious as well as brave and sent them out to New Mexico to work as cowboys. Eventually they gained Bill's confidence and went to work for him. When this happened, Swofford got ready to spring his trap.

Taking one deputy with him, he too journeyed out to New Mexico, posing as a ranchman looking for some property to buy. Eventually he approached Mitchell, whom he found armed and vigilant as always. Swofford knew better than to hurry. He talked and looked and considered. At the right moment he decided that he ought to make an inspection of the outlying pastures he was getting ready to buy, and the three men rode out together. At noon they got down to fix lunch.

Up to that time there had not been one single opportunity for either of the officers to lay a hand on Mitchell without being killed, but now their luck changed. There was coffee with the meal, and as Bill raised a cup to his mouth, they saw their chance. Both of them came down on him like greased lightning and they fought all over the camp, Bill trying to get to his gun and the others trying to hold him down long enough to get handcuffs on him. Once they thought he was going to make it, but Swofford sprang back ready to shoot and Bill let them put the steel around his wrists.[29]

They took him back to Granbury, where the Grand Jury indicted him for the Truitt killings and he made bond. Then they drove him over to Center to answer for the death of James Truitt. Mrs. Truitt, by now Mrs. Julia Truitt Bishop, came down from Chicago to testify, and said at once that Bill was the man in the white hat. He was indicted again, in August, and the trial was set for a month later.[30]

For the next five years he became a familiar figure in Texas courtrooms. He had many friends, and they hired the smartest lawyers in the business for him with the result that he was able to take full advantage of "the law's delay." In September the jury failed to agree. The case was set for re-trial in the following March term, and Mitchell was turned loose under a $20,000 bond.[31] He used the time allowed him by going back to Granbury and standing his trial there. The case was called about the first of November.[32]

Bill's return caused a lot of excitement in that country town. Some loose ends still remained from the early days of the feud, and everybody wondered if he would be looking for further revenge. How would he feel, for instance, about George Wright, son of the old sheriff? George and a man named Selvage had been on guard the night Bill's brother Jeff had come over the bluff with a bottle of laudanum for Old Man Cooney three days before the hanging. George was a deputy sheriff now.

He was walking down the courthouse steps with a friend shortly after Bill's return and the friend asked, "Do you really think they've got Bill Mitchell? Did you recognize him?"

"Why yes," said George. "I'd know his shadow in Afriky. Of course I recognized the sonofabitch."

Sheriff Swofford heard him and remarked, "If I was you and that really is Bill Mitchell, I wouldn't talk thataway. Remember, what happened to Jeff Mitchell is between you and Selvage, and Selvage is dead." No more was heard from George after that.[33]

H. W. Henslee met Bill on the street and recognized the man Russell to whom he had delivered cattle over west in Kimble County years before. "How are you, Mr. Russell," he said.

Bill laughed. "That's all played out now," he answered. "I'm Bill Mitchell."

The jury decided that he was not guilty of the killing of Ike and Sam Truitt in 1874. W. J. Owens, who was with the Mitchells when it happened, was out of prison now and his presence turned the tide. He brought up the matter of "Little Isaac's" derringer which, according to the Mitchell party, had fired the first shot. The derringer had not been used as evidence at the first trial but now, after thirty-two years, it was dusted off and examined. One cartridge had been fired. It occurred to the spectators that Cooney Mitchell's life might have been saved by that empty shell.[34]

The verdict was hailed with joy by Mitchell's friends, of whom there were many, and with deep disappointment by the Truitt family and their sympathizers. Alfred Truitt, then a ranch manager in Starr County, was outraged. He wrote to Judge Tom Davis of Center, a family friend who had taken a deep interest in the case: "I was at the trial and those lawyers of his went back up there and told so many lies, and worked up so much sympathy that there was no chance to convict him."

Alfred was determined to get a conviction next time, however. "I have spent about 3 or 4 hundred dollars now," he said, "and am willing to spend all that I can get to convict him."[35]

Judge Davis wrote to Mrs. Bishop, at home in Chicago: "Mr. Spradley of Nacogdoches is willing to take the matter up if we can get together enough money to pay his expenses . . . he says they will amount to about $100."[36]

Spradley set off on a last sleuthing expedition, backed by Judge Davis, Mrs. Bishop, and the Truitt brothers, Alfred and Lee. He was out to prove the identity of John Davis of Bracketville and Bill Mitchell of Granbury; to show that the claybank horse was really the property of Nath Becket; and to establish the fact that Davis, or Mitchell, was absent from Kinney County at the time of the Truitt murder.

He came back with his evidence, and the case went to trial a second time. Again the jury hung, this time because one lone juror was obstinate. The venue was changed to Cherokee County, and Bill was out on bail again. He went back to New Mexico and did not reappear for two years. His case was continued four times, and once when the State was ready to go to trial (in January, 1909) affidavits were filed, sworn to before J. N. Broyles, notary public of Socorro, New Mexico, that Mitchell was unable to travel on account of bronchitis.[37]

According to Sheriff Spradley, when Mitchell was finally brought into court on December 23, 1910, he tried to prove an alibi by a woman who turned out to be his own sister. He was adjudged guilty in the courthouse at Rusk and given a life sentence which the Court of Criminal Appeals upheld two years later.[38] The papers were filed on March 16, 1912.

Thus, almost forty years after the first blood was shed, Bill Mitchell went to prison. He was sixty-four years old by that time, and the greater part of those sixty-four years he had spent in hiding and in flight. Most men, after a life as long and as hard as that would have been content to sit quietly for a little time in a peaceful prison cell. But not Bill Mitchell. At sixty-four he was still hard to hold. After serving a little over two years, he escaped.

Nobody seems to know quite how he managed it, but there was something queer going on. Probably Bill did not manage it alone, but who his friends were, and how they operated is something nobody will talk about—assuming that anybody knows.

Nobody knows what happened to him after his escape, either. He disappeared as completely as if he had taken a rocket to the moon. His old acquaintances think he went to Mexico and started life over under a new name. If he is still alive, he is 105 years old at this writing. And maybe he is still alive. He was always a hard man to kill.

10. *A Gentleman from Pecos*

In one respect Jim Miller of Pecos, Texas, was superior to all other bad men —he had the best manners. You would never have taken him for what he was. He was a well dressed, quiet, decent sort of fellow, moderately tall and a little on the bony side, who seemed (and maybe was) genuinely kind and friendly. Church members thought of him as a fine religious character. Ladies warmed to his deferential politeness. He never cursed. He did not smoke. He was no frequenter of saloons. He showed up at church on Sundays. In all ways but one he was a model citizen.

He differed from the rest of his fraternity also in his willingness to accept personal criticism. When anyone remonstrated with him for something he had done, he would reply gently, "Well, maybe you're right. We ought to think about that."

If there was anything suspicious about him it was the presence of a bony lump, almost as big as half an egg, behind each of his rather prominent ears. Amateur phrenologists of his day called such swellings "murder bumps" and expected the worst from a man who had them.[1]

When he became a citizen of the dry and dusty little village far out on the mesquite flats of West Texas in the year 1890,[2] not much was known about him. He was a brother-in-law of Mannen Clements, who was already a resident, and a cousin by marriage of the notorious John Wesley Hardin, but the mere fact of kinship with these illustrious pistol toters carried no stigma. Pecos was a frontier cow town where questions about a man's past were considered in bad taste, and where a newcomer made his reputation as he went along. Pecos accepted Miller at his own valuation. Its leading citizens became his friends. Sheriff Bud Frazer, in spite of warnings that there were some dark chapters in the man's history, made him his deputy.

All went smoothly for a while. Miller secured his position with the cattlemen by going after the numerous cattle thieves operating in the region. He and Frazer seemed to think a lot of each other and worked well as a team. Once the deputy killed a Mexican prisoner who had to be taken to Fort Stockton, explaining that the man had tried to escape. People were a little disturbed over that, but no other black marks showed up on his record.

Then, almost overnight, he fell out with Bud Frazer, his boss. Old residents of Pecos still wonder why. It was thought at the time that cattle stealing was at the bottom of it—that Frazer had stumbled upon evidence linking Miller with the ring that was running stolen cattle into Mexico. Miller supposedly found out that he was suspected and laid plans to do away with the Sheriff.

A man named Con Gibson came to Frazer and said that Miller and Mannen Clements had tried to persuade him to join them in this scheme.[3] The next thing people knew, Captain Hughes of the Rangers was in town, and Miller was in jail.[4]

Captain Hughes' biographer says that the charge against Miller and the three men arrested with him was conspiracy to murder the Sheriff. Perhaps it was fear for his life which was behind Frazer's unwillingness to turn Miller loose. He refused all proposals to let the man out on bail, thereby arousing some of the leading ranchers who thought Miller was all right.

Among these was Mr. E. O. Lochausen, who owned a big ranch eighteen miles out and operated a hardware store in town. When he heard what had happened, he went into action at once. "I'll bet he'll have to allow the kind of bail I'll offer him," he said, and saddled up for the trip to town.

Lochausen made his point. Miller was allowed bail, and when he came to trial in El Paso, he won an easy acquittal. It was typical of Miller that he got two fine lawyers, A. M. Walthall and W. W.

Turney, to appear for the defense.[5] Walthall later became a District Judge and Turney a State Senator.

Gibson, the informer, knew what his actions might lead to, and hastened to leave the country. He stopped at Eddy (now Carlsbad), New Mexico, where one of his fellow townsmen happened to be John Denston, a cousin of Miller's wife. Before long Denston and Gibson quarreled in the most natural way imaginable, with the result that Gibson was buried.

People said it was a revenge killing and that it was done in cold blood, but there wasn't much chance of pinning anything on Denston. He had friends who "swore him out of it"[6] and Miller was not even implicated. It would have been hard, anyway, to blame the gentle and kindly Mr. Miller for acts done by his over-conscientious relatives, and his friends still stood by him. Bud Frazer was the only one who seemed to harbor bitterness against him.

By now Miller was operating a hotel in Pecos and was often on the streets near his place of business. One morning he stepped outside and fell into conversation with a rancher friend who was sitting on the spring seat of a wagon. The horses were standing quietly, shaking an ear at an occasional fly. Miller, completely relaxed and at ease, had one foot on the hub of a front wheel and seemed immersed in talk about cow business. His back was toward the street. If he was expecting trouble, he made no sign.

Bud Frazer walked past, but Miller did not notice. In a little while Frazer walked past again, but still Miller saw, or pretended to see, nothing. The man on the spring seat was more alert, however, and said, half to himself, "I wonder why Bud Frazer keeps walking by that way. Every time he does it he looks at your back."

"Well, I don't know," Miller answered, and turned around just as Frazer passed them again. In an instant the two men were shooting at each other. Frazer's first shot hit Miller in the right shoulder, disabling his gun arm. He reached around behind himself with his left hand, got hold of his pistol, and started blazing away. Left-handed shooting was not his specialty, however. Frazer got away unhit.[7]

Miller was a long time getting well. He went off to a ranch some distance from town where he could be with his own people. Mrs.

Lochausen saw him there. She was a refined and gentle lady but she had a substratum of granite in her makeup and wasn't afraid of anybody.

"Why don't you pack up and get out of the country?" she asked him. "You'll just get into more trouble if you stay here, and maybe get some of the rest of us in trouble, too."

"No," Miller answered—and his bright blue eyes turned cold—"I am going to kill Frazer if I have to crawl twenty miles on my knees to do it."

Mrs. Lochausen turned to Mrs. Miller and asked her the same question. She flared up at once. "I guess we've got as good a right to live in this county as anybody else. Nobody is going to run us off."

Mrs. Lochausen retreated.

Before Miller was well enough to risk another argument, Frazer left town. There had been another election in which he had lost out. He relaxed after the campaign by going out to Lordsburg, New Mexico, for a visit with relatives. When he got ready, he came back—and he must have known that he was asking for trouble.

Sure enough, shortly after his return (on April 12, 1894), the men met again. Frazer was armed with a Winchester and Miller with a shotgun, and when the lead stopped whistling, Miller was disabled again with bullets in an arm and a leg. He kept on coming at Frazer, however, in spite of his wounds.[8] There can be no doubt that the man had plenty of cold nerve.

He was carried to Mrs. Lochausen's house in Pecos, and for a while his hostess had a combination fort and hospital on her hands. One night the new sheriff came in and said they would have to guard the place because there was danger that Miller might be mobbed. Guards were posted, and the wounded man laid out plenty of cartridges on his bed. He was a good shot and a cool head in an emergency, and would have given a good account of himself if the expected visitors had arrived. But nobody came.

After that there was a feud in Pecos which threatened to take in the entire population. Both men had relatives who were pretty positive characters and had got up a good deal of steam over the quarrel. In addition many of the best citizens took sides. They stood up for

Miller because they liked him and because they thought he was being persecuted.

Before long the church members were drawn in. Miller had been "converted" at a revival meeting shortly after the second round with Frazer, and some of the deacons and preachers were passionately for him. There could have been the worst kind of trouble in the months that followed. What saved the situation was a growing conviction that something was wrong about Miller himself.

The talk went round that when he was only eighteen years old he had killed his own brother-in-law, John Coop, as he lay sleeping on his front porch one hot night in 1884. To make it worse, Miller had slipped out of a camp meeting just long enough to get on a fast horse, ride three miles to commit the crime, and return before the end of the sermon. The case was a famous one in the country near Gatesville. Miller had been convicted, but managed to get a new trial in which he fared better.[9] Later he had drifted to San Saba County, where he ran with some very hard characters and was almost shot by a young deputy sheriff.[10]

These stories did Miller no good with the people who had befriended him, especially since he kept on trying to get Frazer and never seemed to worry about implicating innocent men and women.

Once when Mr. and Mrs. Lochausen were setting out onions and radishes in their garden in town, they saw somebody coming.

"That looks like Jim Miller," Mrs. Lochausen observed. "I suppose he wants something out of us. You'll have to quit playing with that crowd or they'll get you into trouble one of these times."

It was Miller, and he wanted to borrow "Old Hawk" for the night. Hawk was a fine horse which Mr. Lochausen kept saddled all the time for emergencies. Many people had borrowed him. Lochausen hesitated for a minute but finally said, "I guess so, Jim."

"You shouldn't have done it," Mrs. Lochausen protested as soon as horse and man were gone. "He's probably on his way to kill Frazer, and if he does, and it comes out that he used our horse, we'll be in a fine fix."

"That's right," her husband agreed. "We'd better be more careful."

Later they found out that Miller had actually tried to waylay

Frazer on this trip, but his friends had tipped him off as usual. Mrs. Lochausen taxed Jim with it in very blunt terms. "Now tell me the truth," she said, looking him in the eye. "You were trying to kill Frazer when you borrowed that horse, weren't you?"

"That's really my business, isn't it, Mrs. Lochausen?" Miller replied, irritation showing through the veneer of politeness.

"No, it isn't. You'd have had us in plenty of trouble if you had killed Frazer."

Miller wanted to keep the good people with him and did his best to placate the Lochausens by being friendly and deferential, but they let him alone as much as possible after that.

Meanwhile the mills of the Law ground slowly on, and Frazer had to answer in court for shooting Miller in their second encounter—when Bud had no sheriff's badge to give him authority. The case was set for November, 1895, and Texas took note. Among those interested was another gentlemanly outlaw named John Wesley Hardin, a cousin of Miller's wife, who had recently been let out of the State Penitentiary at Huntsville. During his retirement Hardin had served as superintendent of the Prison Sunday School and had studied law so assiduously that he had been admitted to the bar. After dabbling unsuccessfully in politics at Gonzales, he had decided to come West and see what he could do for Cousin Jim Miller during the trial at El Paso. It was assumed that he was now a reformed character.

His journey westward was a leisurely and in some ways a triumphal progress. Everywhere he stopped people wanted to see him, and he was graciously willing to be seen. In the spring of 1895 he finally reached Pecos.

Edith Lochausen had her sixth birthday while he was there, and her parents gave a big party for her. She remembers that Miller and Hardin appeared late, after most of the guests had gone, and consumed a quantity of homemade ice cream—a great rarity in that iceless country. Hardin was a handsome man, and as elegant in his manners as Miller. Probably never before had so much ruthlessness and so much refinement been seen together.

As it turned out, Hardin was not able to do much for Cousin Jim. He reached El Paso without trouble, but on August 19 Uncle John

Selman shot him in the back of the head.[11] He retired to Concordia Cemetery and was unable to assist with the prosecution in November.

There was not much to the trial, anyway. Frazer's lawyers asked for and got a change of venue. He stood his trial at Colorado City, and on May 20, 1896, was acquitted.[12]

Miller was disgusted, of course, and determined to end this sort of thing once and for all. He had to lie low while Frazer loitered around El Paso and then moved over to Eddy, New Mexico, but after four months of waiting the game came to his hand. The grapevine brought him word that Frazer had appeared in the little town of Toyah, eighteen miles from Pecos, where he was visiting his sisters and helping a friend organize a political campaign.

Frazer thought he was safe, for he was kept informed of Miller's smallest movement, but this time his luck had run out.

It is supposed, but not proved, that Bill Earhart of La Luz, New Mexico, helped Jim do the deed. Earhart got two horses out of Pecos on the night of September 13, 1896, and held them at the outskirts while Miller walked out of town. Somebody would have spotted him if he had ridden out. Together they rode to Toyah, where Earhart had reserved a front room at the hotel. They slipped in the back way, and Miller began to watch the saloon directly across the street, where Frazer spent much of his time.

In the morning the victim entered the place as usual. Earhart moseyed across to see if the time was ripe, and signaled Miller that it was. Miller came down with his shotgun in hand, looked up and down the street, walked rapidly across, pushed open the swinging door with his gun barrel and blasted the life from the unsuspecting Frazer as he sat with his friends playing a game of seven-up. His job finished, Miller got his horse and rode back to Pecos.[13]

The news got there almost as soon as he did. Frazer's mother and sister confronted Miller in great grief and anger. It is said by the old-timers that the sister, in her desperation, came with a pistol. Miller said to her, "If you're going to take a man's place, you're going to have to take a man's medicine. If you just raise that gun, I'll give you what your brother got. I'll shoot you right in the face."

The girl did not raise the gun, but she gave Miller a tongue lashing which neither he nor the bystanders ever forgot.[14]

It was Frazer's brother-in-law Barney Riggs who took up the quarrel. Riggs was a famous character in West Texas—a hold-over from frontier times. He was a brave and determined man who worked as a peace officer around Pecos and Fort Stockton for many years until he was killed in a family quarrel. It is thought by local sages that he came to Pecos, after getting out of some difficulty in Arizona, expressly to help Frazer in his trouble.[15] Now Frazer was gone, but Riggs was still to be disposed of, and it was no small chore.

The same sort of plotting and sparring went on as the two men tried to catch each other at a disadvantage. Once, for instance, the Miller supporters used a performance of Barnum and Bailey's Circus to cover up their plans. John Denston and Bill Earhart came down from Eddy to attend—and to look for an opportunity. They caught Riggs alone, pinchhitting for a bartender in a Pecos saloon, and went after him. Riggs had a pistol thrust into the waistband of his pants. He got Earhart through the head, and Denston ran, but not fast enough. Riggs got him too.[16]

His trial was held in El Paso. The jury which brought in a verdict of not guilty on May 18, 1897, remained out only long enough to write the two words down.[17]

Meanwhile Miller was being prosecuted for killing Frazer, and the case was transferred to the "post-oak" town of Eastland, not far from Fort Worth. To make sure that all possible precautions were taken, Miller moved to Eastland well in advance of the trial, went into business as a hotel operator, transferred his church membership, and set about making a good impression. He succeeded. At his trial his friends gave him a good character, but somebody had made sure of the outcome by other means. One lone juror held out for acquittal and refused to give in.[18] When the case was called again, Miller was acquitted.[19]

After that the streets of Pecos knew Jim Miller no more, except for one brief visit when his former friends treated him so coldly that he had no temptation to return. He moved to Memphis, Texas, where he kept a saloon and worked as a Texas Ranger. Then he went to

Gainesville and to Monahans, where he is said to have had an appointment as a Deputy United States Marshal.[20] Eventually he settled in Fort Worth.

By now the worm in him which had lain so long concealed had gnawed its way to the surface. Miller no longer cared to hide his nature under the cloak of politeness. He bragged of his crimes and "sometimes predicted them."[21] In these casual discussions he made no bones of letting his listeners know that betrayal meant death. "You see, boys," he said of one such killing, "Joe Earp turned State's evidence on me, and you know that no man can do that and live."[22]

Judge Charles R. Brice was living at Memphis during Miller's sojourn there, and heard all about it from Miller himself. "I have killed eleven men that I know about," he said with evident pride. "I have lost my notch stick on the Mexicans I killed out on the border."[23]

The truth was that Jim Miller had no more scruples about taking human life than he did about killing coyotes. He killed for revenge and he killed for money. Not afraid to stand up and shoot it out, he preferred to stand behind a bush or a barn and annihilate his victims with buckshot. Through it all he was unusually clever or unusually lucky, for he was always able to prove an alibi, get his cases postponed, or intimidate a witness. Perhaps his success was his undoing, for it began to look as if he was invincible and he developed what might be described as delusions of grandeur.

Perhaps his most sensational exploit was the killing of Pat Garrett. In February, 1908, Garrett was shot to death, supposedly by a tenant on his ranch property near Las Cruces, New Mexico. It was noted and publicly discussed that Miller had been in Las Cruces and El Paso just before the murder, and that a man and horse had been concealed in the brush not far from the scene of the shooting. Old-time peace officers, as well as the arm-chair detectives, still believe there was some connection.[24] Dee Harkey says Miller rode one of his horses to death getting away from the excitement which followed.[25]

In the spring of the next year it was all over for Jim Miller. He was mixed up in some very shady business in Oklahoma. He hired out once more to do a killing job, and succeeded; but he bungled it by hiring a seventeen-year-old boy to point out the man he was to murder. He was caught near Fort Worth and brought back to Ada, where the citizens were much aroused. They knew how slippery Miller was and were afraid he would weasel out somehow. So they took the law into their own hands.

At two o'clock in the morning, April 19, 1909, a group of vigilantes cut off the electric current, leaving the town in darkness. They subdued the jailers and led out four men, including Miller. In an unused livery stable near the jail they hanged all four of them.[26]

Characteristically this brave but bad man was the only one who met his fate calmly. While the others begged or fought he stood quietly by. Just before they swung him up he took a diamond from his shirt front and asked that it be sent to his wife. A diamond scarf pin he handed over with the request that it be given to a guard named McCarthy who had been kind to him.[27] When that was attended to, he reminded the lynchers politely that they had a job to do and that they had best get on with it.

His death tied up several loose ends of the feud. His cousin and ex-partner Mannen Clements had been killed in an El Paso saloon not long before these events, and Miller had announced that he planned to even that score next. There was likewise the Riggs matter. Barroom arguments had been going on for years over who would win when the inevitable happened and Riggs and Miller came face to face. Miller's demise put this interesting question into the realm of the Great Unsolved.

Even after such a horrible finale, it was amazing how many people still wanted to believe the best of Jim Miller. "He was popular among the best class of citizens here," said a Fort Worth dispatch. "Most of his victims were either cattle thieves or men whom he shot in self defense."[28]

"Thousands . . . called at the undertaking parlors," said a later news story.[29]

"He was just a killer—the worst man I ever knew,"[30] said Judge Charles Brice almost forty years later. But it was hard to convince people that Jim Miller was really bad. Even in the murder business, it seems, good manners are an asset.

Epilogue

**TEXANS
WILL FIGHT
ABOUT ANYTHING**

You see how it is: when times are bad and people are desperate, anything can happen. In the early days of Texas the times could not have been worse, and people were desperate all too often. They did not feud for pleasure, however, and the best men among them hated to see bloodshed taken for granted.

This is the way a DeWitt County schoolmaster reported a multiple killing in 1867:

" 'Hit seems John Bell and Walt Edwards had words up on Sandies, and Bell sent Edwards word not to come stock hunting on his range. Well, they met out on Lower Hog Eye, hit's a branch of the Cabasas over in the edge of Karnes, and who begun it and shot first he couldn't ondertake to say, but hit was a very good fight and only four in it, there was old man Edwards and Walt agin John Bell and Charley Thee, two and two aside and a very good fight. Walt Edwards and Charley Thee was shot down directly, but Charley kept a shootin' at old man Edwards long as he could raise his weepin—it was a very good fight and John Bell emptied his six-shooter and never missed only one shot, Walt Edwards and Charley Thee fell in thar tracks and was killed on the ground, and old man Edwards is dead since, of a wound through his shoulder, and John Bell was the only one not hurted and hit was a very good fight.' Was there no one to interfere and stop it? 'Well, the boys was all round; they was on a stock hunt, and nigh the pen, but it come on suddint, and was all over in half a minute; only four in it; two and two aside, but it was very good fight; the best he had heerd on since the war.' So much from the gentleman from Lower Hogeye, and nothing more—'*a very good fight.*' Three immortal souls gone to their account, a few families desolate, a few women heart broken, and a few children orphaned; but nevertheless, indisputably a 'very good fight!' "[1]

"So that's what it is like in Texas!" your grandfather said when such stories were snatched up and retailed to Eastern readers. "What a horrible place!"

There was much evidence to justify your grandfather in his revulsion. In Texas all sorts of unlikely people were continually getting into hot water. Teachers, preachers, and women were just as apt as anybody else to find themselves in difficulties. Doctors, dentists and lawyers kept guns in their offices and sometimes took pot shots out of the window.

But it is enough to say that these people had their reasons, and very good ones, too. Dr. J. B. Cranfill, a famous Baptist leader in Texas, tells how it was with him:

"During all these years at Gatesville, the pall of mob murder hung about us. We were in hourly dread of the visitation of the Coryell County assassins. So strong was this solicitude upon us that we never at any time, winter or summer, lighted a lamp in our house until all the curtains were drawn. We felt sure that if any assassin could slip upon us and shoot us from the open window, this would be done. My wife suffered more in fear, dread, and terror than I did, but never once did she wince. . . .

"The Northern and Eastern reader will wonder how a man could be a Sunday School teacher and at the same time carry a 45 Colt revolver in his hip pocket. The fact was that I put my revolver in my pocket every morning when I put on my trousers. Indeed, I would have felt much more comfortable going up the street without trousers than I would without a gun."[2]

Men like Cranfill were not looking for trouble, but they wouldn't run, either. Consequently the Texas legend grew until your grandfather believed that the only peaceful citizens of the state were the dead ones.

It wasn't true at all. The bad men were always a very small minor-

ity, and Texas eliminated them as fast as possible. It was just unfortunate that the peaceful people got so little publicity and the pugnacious ones got so much.

Even the pugnacious ones were capable of settling their differences
when they had a chance, or there would have been a thousand feud
situations in Texas instead of a mere hundred or so. Look, for instance,
at the Butler-Allen broil in 1872.

Green Butler, who lived on Clear Creek, had some cow trouble with
Old Man Sam Allen whose range was near Houston. Two of Allen's
cowboys, with or without encouragement from their boss, decided to
get rid of Butler and shot him down at his own front gate.[3] Jeff Black
and Andrew Walker were arrested for the crime and rotted in jail
until 1878 while the lawyers postponed their cases and waited for
the law's delay to give them a better chance.

In April of that year Bob Stafford, Sam Allen, and others raised
$10,000 bail for Black, who was a sick man after his long confine-
ment.[4] Allen took him home to his ranch to recuperate. On the first
of July, as Black lay in his bed, a person or persons unknown tried
to shoot him through the window. He absorbed ten buckshot, which
did not hurt him particularly, while Sam Allen got down his gun
and made a battle of it.[5]

In September Black and Allen went on trial at Wallisville. As their
party went up the steps of the courthouse, Sam Wright, sitting on
his horse, cut loose with a shotgun and Black would have passed in
his checks then and there if he had not stumbled over a step just as
the shot was fired. He said he "felt the wind of it."

A friend of his named Autry took the matter up at this point,
walked over to a brother of Green Butler, and asked him if that was
the way he wanted it settled—if so he could go and get his gun. Butler
said that was all right with him, and both sides went after their arms.
In a few minutes the street was full of angry men just waiting for
a reason to begin shooting.

Then something almost incredible happened. There they were,
lined up and ready, when "one of the Butler party came running
down the street, stopped within ten feet of the foe, threw his hat up
in the air, caught it on his left heel, kicked it into the air again and

caught it on his head, turned a back double somersault, fell full face to the enemy, and, with drawn pistols announced himself ready. This act so amused both parties that they closed all hostile demonstrations and put away their arms."[6]

A good laugh had stopped that feud for good.

There were not many such cases. Too often the only way to end bad blood was by bloodletting. But if Texans seemed to be willing to fight about anything in the early days, there is still this to be said for them:

Most of the time they fought because they had to; and when they could, they stopped.

NOTES and BIBLIOGRAPHIES

*There are so many customs connected with every histori-
cal event that to know folk habits is almost to know human
history, the written and, still more, the unwritten. Our own
American history is written much more in the changing customs than hundreds of years of writing can ever record it.
When more historians realize . . . that folk movements are
the basis of our formal history, then a true history can be
written.*

Gordon Wilson,
Passing Institutions.

Notes and Bibliographies

The people and events described in this book are still subjects for controversy. In the notes which follow I have tried to account for every statement which might be questioned, and for a good many others as well. The men and women who helped me put these stories together are mentioned individually in appropriate places, but I should like to thank them collectively here. I know no finer people and have no better friends than these Texans.

I feel deep gratitude also to a number of organizations and executives who helped me get on with the job:

The Texas State Historical Association arranged a grant-in-aid from the Rockefeller Foundation in the summer of 1944.

The late Mr. G. B. Dealey, Mr. Stuart McGregor, and Mrs. Marie Peterson of the Dallas *News* placed their unique file of the Galveston *News* at my disposal.

Libraries and librarians have done more for me than I can ever acknowledge. I owe a special debt to Miss Harriet Smither and the staff of the Texas State Library—to Miss Winnie Allen, University of Texas archivist—to Mrs. Marcelle Hamer, formerly of the Texas Collection at the University of Texas—to the late Mrs. Maude L. Sullivan and her successor Mrs. Helen Farrington Kister, of the El Paso Public Library—to Mr. Baxter Polk and Miss Frances Clayton, librarians at Texas Western College—and to several dozen cheerful assistants whose names I do not know in big and little libraries all over the state.

Friends who have been willing to talk feuds with me include Dr. Eugene Porter and Dr. Rex Strickland of Texas Western College; Dr. H. Bailey Carroll and Dr. Mody C. Boatright of the University of Texas; Mr. C. Stanley Banks of San Antonio and Mr. Chris Emmett of Houston. Mrs. Erlwood von Clausewitz provided expert help with the manuscript.

Among the documentary sources the most useful are Texas newspaper files and the reports of the Texas Rangers to the Adjutant General. The Ranger papers are preserved in the Adjutant General's files in the State Library, Austin, and are referred to hereafter by the letters AGF.

The following newspapers are quoted:

The Augusta (Ga.) *Chronicle and Sentinel*
The *Weekly Austin Republican*
The Austin *Daily Statesman*
The Austin *Weekly Statesman*
The Bastrop *Advertiser*
The Clarksville *Northern Standard*
The Hempstead *News*
The Houston *Daily Post*
The Houston *Telegraph and Texas Register*
Flake's Daily Bulletin (Houston)
Flake's Semi-Weekly Bulletin
The Mesilla *Independent*
The Nacogdoches *Weekly Sentinel*
Niles' National Register
The Dallas *Daily Herald*
The Dallas *Weekly Herald*
The El Paso *Times*
The Galveston *Civilian*
The Galveston *Daily News*
The Mississippi Free Trader and Natchez Daily Gazette
The San Antonio *Daily Express*
The San Antonio *Daily Herald*
The Redlander (San Augustine)
The Western Chronicle (Sutherland Springs)
The Timpson *Daily Times*

Two books of special value to students of Texas material are H. Bailey Carroll's *Texas County Histories,* Texas State Historical Association, Austin, 1943; and Ike Moore's *Texas Newspapers, 1813-1939,* issued by the Historical Records Survey Program, Division of Professional and Service Projects, Works Projects Administration of Texas, and published by the San Jacinto Museum of History Association, Houston, 1934.

PROLOGUE TO TROUBLE

1. William Seagle, *The Quest for Law,* Alfred A. Knopf, New York, 1941, Chapter III ("Up from the Blood Feud"), p. 30 ff. For a fuller discussion of this and following points see C. L. Sonnichsen, *I'll Die Before I'll Run,* Harper

and Brothers, New York, 1951, "The Theory and Practice of Feuding" (Introduction).

2. William A. Robson, *Civilization and the Growth of Law,* The Macmillan Company, New York, 1935, pp. 97-106; Sir Frederick Pollock and Frederic William Maitland, *The History of English Law before the Time of Edward II,* Cambridge University Press, 1895, vol. II, pp. 238-240, 458-459.

3. Sir Frederick Pollock, "The King's Peace in the Middle Ages," *Harvard Law Review,* vol. 13, 1899-1900, Nov., 1899; William Seagle, *The Quest for Law,* p. 36.

4. John Maxcy Zane, *The Story of Law,* Garden City Publishing Company, Garden City, New York, 1927, p. 26.

5. Wayne Gard, *Frontier Justice,* The University of Oklahoma Press, Norman, 1949, ch. 10, "Prairie Necktie Parties," pp. 189-213. For further discussion see Arthur F. Raper, *The Tragedy of Lynching,* The University of North Carolina Press, Chapel Hill, 1933; James C. Leyburn, *Frontier Folkways,* Yale University Press, New Haven, 1935; J. E. Cutler, *Lynch Law,* Longmans, Green, New York, 1905, p. 42.

6. Charles S. Sydnor, "The Southerner and the Law," *Journal of Southern History,* Feb., 1940, vol. VI, pp. 2-23.

7. Sonnichsen, *I'll Die Before I'll Run,* "Old Southern Style."

8. Austin *Weekly Statesman,* March 2, 1876.

9. Galveston *News,* Dec. 16, 1866.

10. Austin *Weekly Statesman,* July 18, 1874.

1. WAR OF THE REGULATORS AND MODERATORS

A. W. Arrington (Charles Summerfield, pseud.), *The Rangers and Regulators of the Tanaha: or, Life among the Lawless. A Tale of the Republic of Texas.* Robert M. Dewitt, publisher, New York, 1856.

Dr. Levi Ashcroft, *Thrilling Scenes in Texas, Comprising the History of Regulators and Moderators of Shelby County, Texas, etc.* MS copy from the library of John Wright of Dallas. No date (presumably written in the early 1850's).

Robert M. Coates, *The Outlaw Years.* The Macaulay Co., New York, 1930.

Rev. George W. Crocket, *Two Centuries in East Texas.* The Southwest Press, Dallas, 1932.

George W. Crocket, *Manuscript Notes,* left by the Rev. George W. Crocket, Archives, State Capitol, Austin.

Eph M. Daggett, *Recollections of the War of the Moderators and Regulators.* MS copy of the original, destroyed by fire, in the Asbury Collection, University of Texas Archives.

J. H. Green, *The Secret Band of Brothers or the American Outlaws*. G. B. Zieber & Co., Philadelphia, 1847.

Samuel A. Hammett (Philip Paxton, pseud.), *A Stray Yankee in Texas*. Redfield, New York, 1859 (entered in 1853).

William Ransom Hogan, *A Social and Economic History of the Republic of Texas*. Ph.D. dissertation, U. of Texas, 1942.

Alexander Horton, "The Shelby War." San Augustine *Weekly News,* Aug. 16, 1888. (Clipped from a series called "History of San Augustine Reminiscences of an Old Time Resident"; obtained from the Rev. G. W. Crocket by Samuel Asbury and deposited in the Asbury Collection, U. of Texas Archives.)

Emerson Hough, *The Story of the Outlaw*. Copyright, 1907. In *The Frontier Omnibus,* Grosset and Dunlap, New York, n.d.

L. W. Kemp, "Gallows Ends East Texas Reign of Terror." *Frontier Times,* Nov., 1929, pp. 79-82.

Mary Daggett Lake, "Helen Daggett Famous in Texas History." *Frontier Times,* March, 1930, pp. 270-273.

J. W. Lockhart, "Reminiscences." Galveston *News,* April 29, 1900.

John W. Middleton, *History of the Regulators and Moderators and the Shelby County War in 1841 and 1842, etc.* Loving Publishing Co., Fort Worth, 1883.

J. M. Morphis, "Descriptions of Nacogdoches, San Augustine, Sabine, Shelby, Panola, and Harrison Counties," etc. Austin *Daily Democratic Statesman,* April 19, 1874.

Oran M. Roberts, "The Shelby War, or the 'Regulators and Moderators.'" *The Texas Magazine,* Aug., 1897, vol. iii, pp. 49-57.

Kate Mason Rowland, "General John Thomas Mason." *Texas State Historical Association Quarterly,* Jan., 1908, vol. xi, pp. 163-198.

Noah Smithwick, *The Evolution of a State*. The Steck Company, Austin, 1935 (reprint of the first edition of c. 1900).

Ben C. Stuart, "Texas Civil War." Galveston *News,* July 28, 1907. (Digest of an article by "the late Hamilton Stuart" published in the *Cherokee Standard* at Rusk "some twenty years ago.")

C. W. Webber, *Tales of the Southern Border*. Lippincott, Grambo, & Co., Philadelphia, 1855 (first copyright, 1852).

D. W. [Dudley Wooten?], "Observations on the Sabine River." Galveston *News,* May 14, 1899.

H. Yoakum, *History of Texas*. The Steck Company, Austin, 1935. Facsimile reproduction of the original.

The Shelby warriors are long dead and their feud has to be written up from documentary sources. Of the three most important accounts only one (Middleton's) is in print. It is a rough-hewn but indispensable pamphlet by a sturdy Texan who had some narrow squeaks in brushes with the Moderators. The fullest and most important history is by Dr. Ashcroft, who came to Shelby County in 1838 and wrote his story in the early fifties. Somehow he was disappointed in his plans for publishing this well-written and spirited account and it has to be read in typed copies in the hands of a few Texas collectors. Ashcroft tried to be non-partisan, but he leaned toward the Moderators. The third important source is Eph Daggett's manuscript, giving the Regulator side. One of the few copies available is in the Asbury Collection, University of Texas Archives. Crocket's *Two Centuries in East Texas,* the only recent book giving much space to the subject, is an excellent though condensed study.

Newspaper material is scattering and not easy to find. Some of the most out-of-the-way citations used here were run down by William R. Hogan for his fine doctoral dissertation listed above.

Much valuable material, not all of it used or mentioned here, has been assembled by Mr. Samuel Asbury of the staff of Texas A. and M. College, one of the country's best historical detectives, and placed in the collection named for him in the University Archives.

ROGUE'S PARADISE

1. The Jackson-Goodbread trouble is from Daggett, p. 10 ff. Middleton, p. 15, merely says "Goodbread had been waylaying Jackson."

2. Kemp, pp. 79-82, tells of early settlement; see also Roberts, pp. 49-51.

3. Daggett, p. 18; Middleton, pp. 8, 27.

4. The Murrell break-up and the clean-up in Southern cities: Coates, p. 272 ff.; Hough, pp. 47-73. Hammett ("Introduction," p. xiv) goes into the spread of Murrell's men into Texas; see also Ben C. Stuart's article. Green's *Secret Band of Brothers* describes the band's ceremonies, secret language, and extension, possibly with the help of the imagination. For an earlier organization of this kind see Cutler, *Lynch Law,* p. 52.

5. Hammett, pp. 322, 355, 357.

6. Ashcroft, ch. 1-5. Daggett adds some details.

7. Smithwick, p. 87.

8. The land racket: Smithwick, pp. 90-92; Yoakum, vol. ii, p. 438; Ashcroft, ch. v; the articles by Barker and Rowland.

9. More on the Yoakums: Smithwick, p. 92; Hammett, pp. 382-383; "The Journal of Lewis Birdsall Harris," *Southwestern Historical Quarterly,* Oct., 1921, vol. xxv, pp. 141-142.

THE BIRTH OF THE REGULATORS

10. Jackson's pre-Texas experiences: Daggett, p. 6 ff.; Ashcroft, ch. vi.

11. Jackson and the Ring: Yoakum, vol. ii, p. 438; Daggett, p. 9; J. M. Morphis's article in the *Statesman.*

12. Ashcroft, ch. vi.

13. In the Asbury Collection is an "Affidavit of Peter Tumlinson" from the Real Estate Records of San Augustine County, Book J3, pp. 718-719, containing information about the Humphreys family. The quotation is from Ben C. Stuart.

14. Daggett and Ashcroft differ in their accounts of this affair. I follow Daggett, p. 11. Cutler, *Lynch Law*, p. 121, summarizes a story which appeared in the *American Whig Review* for February, 1845, called "Jack Long; or Lynch-Law and Vengeance." It is about a whipping case in Shelby County—obviously the Humphreys case.

ONE BAD TURN . . .

15. The trial: Daggett, p. 21.

16. *The Redlander,* July 22, 1841.

17. Daggett, p. 22 ff.

18. Ashcroft, ch. vi; Roberts, p. 51.

19. "Halifax Law," etc.: Cutler, *Lynch Law,* p. 8, pp. 20-136; Hammett, p. 315 ff. *The Dictionary of American History* discusses Regulators but the writer as usual has apparently never heard of Texas.

20. Daggett, p. 12.

21. *Ibid.,* pp. 5-6; Middleton, p. 15.

22. Jackson's death: Ashcroft, ch. vii; Daggett, p. 12. Middleton says there were three "stands" of ambushers. The first stand let Jackson pass because of Lauer. The second got both men.

WATT MOORMAN TAKES CHARGE

23. Kemp, p. 79.

24. Moorman's early life and personal characteristics: Ashcroft, ch. vii; Daggett, pp. 13, 23; Roberts, p. 52.

25. Ashcroft, ch. vii, Daggett, p. 12, Roberts, p. 52, and Middleton, pp. 17-19, tell very different stories of the pursuit and capture of the McFaddins. I follow Middleton, who led the posse and tells the best story.

26. Daggett, pp. 13-14.

27. The execution: Dagget, p. 13; Middleton, p. 19.

28. Daggett, p. 15.

29. What happened to Tiger Jim? Daggett, pp. 16-18, talks as if he came back and hid in the canebrakes after the Jackson killing, but says he eventually "got his brains blown out." H. W. K. Myrick, a Regulator leader, speaks of him as being dead in *The Redlander,* Nov. 10, 1842.

30. Ashcroft, ch. vii. Boatwright's death was written up in *The Mississippi Free Trader and Natchez Daily Gazette,* Oct. 26, 1841.

31. Ashcroft, chs. vii, viii.

32. Houston *Telegraph and Texas Register,* Feb. 9, 1842.

33. Middleton, p. 19; Daggett, pp. 41-42.

34. Lockhart, Galveston *News,* April 29, 1900.

35. Houston *Telegraph and Texas Register,* Feb. 9, 1842.

HEAVY SKIRMISHING

36. Ashcroft, chs. viii, ix.

37. Ashcroft, chs. x, xi; Daggett, p. 36.

38. Daggett, p. 39; Ashcroft, ch. xi.

39. Ashcroft, ch. xi; Horton, p. 10; Crocket, *Two Centuries,* p. 198.

40. Roberts, p. 54.

41. Bradley's letter was located by Miss Harriet Smither, State Library.

42. Daggett, pp. 39-40; Ashcroft, ch. xi.

43. Daggett, pp. 35-36.

44. Ashcroft, ch. xi.

45. *Ibid.*

46. *Ibid.,* ch. xiii.

47. *Ibid.*

A WEDDING AND A MURDER

48. Mary Daggett Lake to Samuel Asbury, March 17, 1933, Asbury Collection.

49. Daggett, p. 36.

50. Mrs. Lake has the articles of agreement. A copy is in the Asbury Collection through her kindness.

51. Ashcroft, ch. xiv.

52. Accounts of Bradley's death are contradictory. Ashcroft thinks he was unarmed and unsuspecting. Daggett, pp. 24-26, says he was armed and ready.

THE STORM BREAKS

53. Lindsey's arrest: Ashcroft, ch. xiv.

54. Ashcroft, chs. xv, xvi.

55. *Ibid.,* ch. xvi.

56. Daggett, p. 27.

57. Ashcroft, ch. xvi.

58. Daggett, pp. 27-28.

59. Ashcroft, ch. xvii.

60. Daggett, pp. 29-30.

61. *Ibid.,* p. 30; Middleton, p. 23.

62. Daggett, p. 31, barely mentions his sister's stratagem, but does so with approval. Ashcroft, ch. xviii, tells the whole tale. Middleton, p. 23, says "We had ladies out all the time acting as spies for us," and names three more.

63. Horton, p. 9.
64. Ashcroft, ch. xix.
65. *Ibid.*

THE SHOUTING DIES

66. Roberts (pp. 55-56) was on the woodpile.
67. Ashcroft, ch. xx.
68. Crocket Manuscript Notes.
69. Daggett, p. 34.
70. Crocket Manuscript Notes.
71. Daggett, p. 34; Ashcroft, ch. xx.
72. *Two Centuries,* p. 201. Ben C. Stuart gives more details.
73. Ashcroft, ch. xxi.
74. *Ibid.*
75. *Niles National Register,* May 22, June 5, 1847; Augusta (Ga.) *Chronicle and Sentinel,* June 14, 1847; notes by Samuel Asbury in the Asbury Collection.
76. Ashcroft, ch. xxii.
77. Ashcroft, ch. xxiii, has a long and scandalous explanation for the enmity between Moorman and Dr. Burns. In the Asbury Collection is an unsigned, undated letter from the Clerk of Court at Mansfield, Louisiana, describing the killing and prosecution. The case was called on May 24, 1850, and resulted in acquittal for Dr. Burns.

AFTERMATH

78. Daggett, p. 15.
79. Lake, pp. 272-273.
80. Roberts, p. 56; Lake, p. 272; Galveston *News,* May 14, 1899.

2. OLD ROSE AND SENATOR POTTER

Harriet A. Ames, *The History of Harriet A. Ames during the Early Days of Texas. Written by Herself at the Age of Eighty-three.* Unpublished manuscript. My copy from a typescript in the library of John Wright of Dallas.

A. W. Arrington (Charles Summerfield, pseud.), *Duelists and Dueling in the Southwest.* W. H. Graham, H. Long and Brother, New York; Zeiber & Co., Philadelphia, 1847.

John Henry Brown, *History of Texas from 1685 to 1892.* L. E. Daniell, St. Louis, 1893. 2 vol.

James Blount Cheshire, *Nonnulla,* The University of North Carolina Press, Chapel Hill, 1930.

Charles Dickens, *American Notes (Works,* vol. 20). P. F. Collier and Son, New York, n.d.

L. W. Kemp, *The Career of Robert Potter.* Manuscript in the Asbury Collection, University of Texas Archives.

Rev. John H. McLean, *Reminiscences.* Smith and Lamar, Nashville, Tenn., 1918.

Macum Phelan, *A History of Early Methodism in Texas.* Cokesbury Press, Nashville, Tenn., 1924.

V. M. Rose, *Some Historical Facts in Regard to the Settlement of Victoria, Texas; its Progress and Present Status.*

Robert Watson Winston, "Robert Potter: Tar Heel and Texan." *South Atlantic Quarterly,* April, 1930. Vol. xxix, no. 2.

Much good work has been done on the Rose-Potter case. Winston's article tells the story in sprightly style, emphasizing the Carolina background. Bishop Cheshire devotes a chapter to Potter. Arrington includes a highly colored and inaccurate version in his *Duelists,* etc. Very interesting and informative is Harriet Ames's manuscript. It is freshly and charmingly written and has persuaded more than one student of Texas history that Harriet was an abused woman. All these sources make Old Rose out to be a very bad man. The tale is told in his favor by his son Victor M. Rose, by the Rev. John H. McLean, and by Macum Phelan, following McLean's lead. L. W. Kemp has collected the material available in court records and newspapers about Rose's appearances in court for the Potter killing. This, with other material on Potter, is available in the Asbury Collection, University of Texas Archives.

Records are available also of a final unhappy chapter in the life of Harriet Ames. Just before his death Potter deeded his farm at Potter's Point to a woman he was attached to in Austin. Eventually the heirs of this woman pressed their claim, the case went to the Supreme Court of Texas, and Governor O. M. Roberts, then Chief Justice, handed down a decision that deprived Harriet of her home. The account of the proceedings occupies several hundred pages in the court records.

I have to thank Miss Fannie Ratchford of Austin, the late Mrs. Laura Ratchford Fromme of Elgin, and Mrs. Thomas O'Connor of Victoria, descendants of William Pinckney Rose, for talking over family traditions with me.

1. Best on Potter's early career is Winston's article.

2. Cheshire, pp. 68-71, describes *The Head of Medusa.*

3. Potter's provocation against his wife is doubtful. Harriet Ames heard that he was in love with a woman in Washington and took this means of getting rid of his wife. Arrington, p. 15, says Taylor was "the young husband's uncle." For "Potterizing" see Winston, p. 152; Cheshire, pp. 75-76.

4. Arrington, ch. iii, describes Potter. Harriet agrees with him.

5. See Winston, Cheshire, and John Henry Brown (vol. ii, p. 186) for Potter's political career in Texas.

6. Harriet describes his courtship in a way which indicates more finesse than honesty. She says he went through a contract ceremony with her. She found out about his past life later on.

7. Rose's appearance: Arrington, p. 16—misquoted by McLean, p. 22.

8. McLean, pp. 9-10, gives Rose's family background.

9. Harriet Ames, ch. vii.

10. Kemp says the men fell out about land and politics. McLean thinks Potter was rejected as a suitor by the Rose family but does not explain how such a thing could be.

11. McLean, pp. 16-20.

12. *Ibid.*

13. Houston *Telegraph,* July 13, 1842; *Niles National Register,* April 9, 1842.

14. Harriet's account of her attempts to bring Rose to justice is the most moving part of her book. She accuses him of fiendish cruelty and cunning in handling the case. The Clarksville *Northern Standard* for Oct. 22, 1842, tells about Rose's trial, application for bail, transfer to Nacogdoches, etc. Kemp uses this article as a basis for his account of the legal proceedings. See Kemp also for a good account of the legal maneuverings which gave Potter's estate to the Mayfield heirs in 1875.

15. Dickens' extract, *American Notes,* p. 259, seems to come from a metropolitan newspaper quoting from the *Caddo Gazette.*

3. BLOOD IN BELL COUNTY

1. Edith M. Ross, *Irregular Warfare During the Civil War.* Unpublished M.A. thesis, The University of Texas, 1934, pp. 22-23.

2. "Lest We Forget the Heroes of the Alamo," University of Texas Archives.

3. W. A. Craddock, interview (Austin, Texas, July 5, 1944).

4. George W. Tyler, *History of Bell County* (ed. Charles W. Ramsdell). The Naylor Company, San Antonio, 1936, p. 251.

5. W. A. Craddock, interview.

6. *Ibid.*

7. Tyler, p. 250.

8. Galveston *News,* March 29, 1870, notes the deaths of Hasley and his wife.

9. Charles W. Ramsdell, *Reconstruction in Texas.* Columbia University Press, New York, 1910, pp. 40, 55 ff., comments on lawlessness.

10. Galveston *News,* August 4, 1868, talks of "associations organized in other states with a view of coming to Texas to engage in armed robbery as a business."

11. W. A. Craddock, interview.

12. Galveston *News*, April 15, 1866.

13. Galveston *News*, June 28, 1866.

14. Tyler, p. 254.

15. The Committee on Lawlessness of the Constitutional Convention of 1868 mentioned the Christian murder "by a band of rebels" (Galveston *News*, July 10, 1868).

16. Tyler, p. 252.

17. Ramsdell, pp. 131-132, notes some of the sins of the elder Lindley.

18. Tyler, p. 251.

19. Galveston *News*, July 25, 1866.

20. *Ibid.*, July 31, 1866.

21. *Ibid.*, August 25, 1866.

22. *Ibid.*, December 12, 16, 19, 1866; April 7, 1867.

23. The Dallas *Weekly Herald*, September 4, 1869, describes the killing of McRae and the events leading up to it, copied from the Belton *Journal*. Galveston *News*, August 12, 1869, covers the same ground. The issues of August 5, 6, 7, and 12, retail rumors of terrible deeds in Bell County as they filtered out to the nearby towns.

24. Dallas *Weekly Herald*, September 4, 1869.

25. *Ibid.*

26. Quoted in the Dallas *Weekly Herald*, September 4, 1869.

27. Galveston *News*, August 31, 1869.

28. *Ibid.*, October 6, 1869.

29. *Ibid.*, March 2, 1870.

4. THE FRANKS CASE

1. Green Peyton, *City in the Sun*, Whittlesey House, New York, 1946, p. 36; Charles A. Herff, San Antonio *Express*, Jan. 22, 1928, and *Frontier Times*, Feb., 1929.

2. R. H. Williams' book *With the Border Ruffians* (ed. E. W. Williams, John Murray, London, 1907) is not completely reliable, but it comes closest to telling the Franks story in full. He calls Franks *French*, Mitchell *Minshull*, etc. The quotation is from p. 199. J. Frank Dobie in *A Vaquero of the Brush Country*, Little Brown, Boston, 1943, pp. 79-81, tells the story giving Mitchell his right name, but he calls Franks *French*, as Williams does.

3. See J. Marvin Hunter and George W. Saunders, *The Trail Drivers of Texas*. Cokesbury Press, Nashville, Tenn., 2nd ed., 1925, pp. 274 ff., 387-388, for material on the Franks family.

4. Taylor Thompson ("Some Early Day Outlaws," *Frontier Times*, May, 1924) saw the Franks hanging.

5. R. R. Smith to C. L. Sonnichsen, Oct. 1, 1943.

6. *Flake's Semi-Weekly Bulletin*, Nov. 25, 1871; San Antonio *Herald*, Nov. 24, 1871.

7. San Antonio *Express*, Dec. 30, 1871, April 4, 1872; San Antonio *Herald*, April 3, 1872; *Flake's Semi-Weekly Bulletin*, April 10, 1872.

5. THE HOODOO WAR

Margaret Bierschwale, "Mason County, Texas, 1845-1870." *Southwestern Historical Quarterly*, April, 1944.

Don Biggers, *History of Mason County*. Unpublished MS in the possession of Miss Margaret Bierschwale, Mason, Texas.

Kathryn Burford Eilers, *A History of Mason County, Texas*. Unpublished M.A. thesis, The University of Texas, 1939.

Claude Elliott, "Union Sentiment in Texas." *Southwestern Historical Quarterly*, April, 1947.

Thomas W. Gamel, *The Life of Thomas W. Gamel*. Privately printed, Mason, Texas, n.d.

Beatrice Grady Gay, *Into the Setting Sun: A History of Coleman County*. Privately printed, 1936.

James B. Gillett, *Six Years with the Texas Rangers*. Von Boeckmann-Jones Co., Austin, Texas, 1921.

Mrs. Henry M. Holmes, unpublished diary, in the possession of Miss Margaret Bierschwale and used by her permission.

J. Marvin Hunter, "Brief History of Early Days in Mason County." *Frontier Times*, November, 1928, March, 1929.

Captain Dan W. Roberts, *Rangers and Sovereignty*. Wood Printing and Engraving Co., San Antonio, Texas, 1914.

Mrs. D. W. Roberts, *A Woman's Reminiscences of Six Years in Camp with the Texas Rangers*. Von Boeckmann-Jones Co., Austin, Texas, n.d.

C. L. Sonnichsen, *Billy King's Tombstone*. The Caxton Printers, Caldwell, Idaho, 1942.

Walter Prescott Webb, *The Texas Rangers*. Houghton Mifflin Co., Boston, 1935.

Kurt Zesch, An article read before a "recent meeting of the Grossville community club." *Mason County News*, Feb. 23, 1939.

The best known of these sources is Gillett's *Six Years with the Texas Rangers*. Gillett came to Mason with the Rangers in September, 1875, and had personal knowledge of the last stages of the feud, but his account of earlier developments needs to be corrected. Tom Gamel includes more material than anybody else, but is not always reliable.

Three correspondents sent in valuable accounts of the feud to the newspapers. Major Henry M. Holmes, an "American," wrote to the San Antonio *Herald* on August 17 (published August 30) and on September 14 (published September 20), 1875. An anonymous writer who signed himself "Peter" contributed a good brief account of the trouble, dated October 8, to the *Daily Statesman* of October 17, 1875, and another, dated November 12, to the issue of November 18. Peter thought conditions were pretty bad and played up the race issue. Exception was taken to his views by a contributor calling himself "Dreux" who also wrote two letters to the Austin papers. His first, dated October 28, appeared in the *Daily Statesman* on November 14, 1875; his second, dated October 28 also, appeared in the *Weekly Statesman* for November 18.

Not many men are left who have personal recollections of the feud. I learned a great deal from Henry Doell and Ernest Lemburg, who were there when it happened. Roscoe Runge and Margaret Bierschwale of the younger generation helped with introductions, documents, and sympathetic interest.

1. Ernest Lemburg, interview, Mason, Texas, July 12, 1944.

2. Letter from Major Henry M. Holmes, San Antonio *Herald*, Aug. 30, 1875; Gamel, pp. 20-21.

3. Captain Dan W. Roberts, pp. 87-90. Additional facts from the recollections of Ernest Lemburg and Henry Doell.

4. "Peter" in the Austin *Daily Statesman*, Nov. 18, 1875.

5. Galveston *News*, Jan. 23, 1879.

6. Diary of Mrs. Henry M. Holmes, MS.

7. Hunter, pp. 226-229.

8. Kurt Zesch in Mason County *News*, Feb. 23, 1939.

9. Bierschwale, p. 380.

10. Elliott, pp. 402-406.

11. Webb, pp. 312-313.

12. Henry Doell, interview, Mason, Texas, July 12, 1944.

13. Biggers, p. 18 ff.

14. "Dreux" in the Austin *Daily Statesman*, Nov. 18, 1875.

15. *Ibid.*

16. Gamel, pp. 18-20. Mrs. Holmes also mentions the arrest.

17. San Antonio *Herald*, Aug. 30, 1875.

18. Gamel, p. 23.

19. Gillett, p. 74; Gay, p. 109.

20. Henry Doell, interview.

21. Austin *Daily Statesman*, July 19, 1874.

22. Gay, p. 109.

23. Henry Doell, interview.

24. Gamel, pp. 25, 31.

25. Henry Doell, interview. Bader's part in the Williamson murder has never been mentioned in printed sources.

26. Mrs. D. W. Roberts, pp. 8-9.

27. Major Holmes in the San Antonio *Herald,* Aug. 30, 1875.

28. Dan W. Roberts, p. 90; Gamel, pp. 21-22.

29. Henry Doell, interview; Austin *Daily Statesman,* July 31, 1875; San Antonio *Herald,* Aug. 30, 1875.

30. Gamel, p. 24.

31. San Antonio *Herald,* Aug. 17, 1874, translated from the Fredericksburg *Freie Presse* for Aug. 16, 1874.

32. Gillett, p. 79.

33. Gamel, pp. 25-26.

34. *Ibid.,* p. 26.

35. *Ibid.,* pp. 25-26; San Antonio *Herald,* Sept. 20, 1875; Austin *Daily Statesman,* Oct. 17, 1875.

36. AGF, Jones to Steele, Oct. 28, 1875; Austin *Daily Statesman,* Oct. 17, 1875; San Antonio *Express,* Oct. 6, 1875.

37. Gamel, p. 27.

38. *Ibid.*

39. This engagement is described by Gamel, pp. 27-30—also Dan W. Roberts, p. 91; San Antonio *Herald,* Oct. 11, 1875, Austin *Daily Statesman,* Oct. 17, 1875; Henry Doell.

40. AGF, Jones to Steele, Sept. 28, 1875.

41. *Ibid.,* Jones to Steele, Sept. 30, 1875.

42. Dan W. Roberts, p. 93.

43. Gillett, pp. 77-78.

44. AGF, Jones to Steele, Oct. 20, 1875.

45. Peter Bader's death notice, San Antonio *Herald,* Jan. 20, 1876, mentions the death of his brother "about two months ago."

46. Austin *Weekly Statesman,* Jan. 6, Nov. 9, 1876; Dallas *Weekly Herald,* Jan. 8, 1876.

47. Austin *Weekly Statesman,* Jan. 6, 1876.

48. *Ibid.,* June 8, 1876.

49. Gamel, p. 31; AGF, Long to Jones, Jan. 15, 1876.

50. These resolutions are in the AGF.

51. Austin *Weekly Statesman,* June 8, 16, 1876.

52. Henry Doell, and others.

53. Gillett, p. 80.

54. Gamel, p. 31.

55. Austin *Weekly Statesman,* Nov. 9, Dec. 7, 1876.

56. Sonnichsen, pp. 30-32.

57. Austin *Weekly Statesman,* Dec. 14, 1870.

58. Henry Doell, interview.
59. Austin *Weekly Statesman,* Feb. 1, 1877.

6. THE EL PASO SALT WAR

Annual Report of the Secretary of War for the Year 1878. Government Printing Office, Washington, 1878.

El Paso Troubles in Texas. House Executive Document No. 93, 45th Congress, Second Session (indicated by the initials E.P.T. in the notes).

Annie E. Hughes, *The Beginning of Spanish Settlement in the El Paso District.* University of California Press, Berkeley, 1914.

Grace Long, *The Anglo-American Occupation of the El Paso District.* Unpublished M.A. thesis, The University of Texas, 1931.

Esther Darbyshire MacCallum, *The History of St. Clement's Church, El Paso, Texas, 1870-1925.* The McMath Company, El Paso, 1925.

W. W. Mills, *Forty Years at El Paso 1858-1898.* Privately printed, 1901.

W. W. Mills, *El Paso. A Glance at Its Men and Contests for the Last Few Years.* The Republican Office, Austin, 1871.

Report of the Adjutant General of the State of Texas for the Fiscal Year Ending August 31, 1878. Book and Job Office of the Galveston *News,* Galveston, 1878.

J. Fred Rippy, *The United States and Mexico, 1821-1924.* Alfred A. Knopf, New York, 1931 (Revised Edition).

M. H. Thomlinson, *The Garrison of Fort Bliss, 1849-1916.* Hertzog and Resler, El Paso, Texas, 1945.

Ralph Emerson Twitchell, *The Leading Facts of New Mexican History.* 5 vol., The Torch Press, Cedar Rapids, Iowa, 1911-1917.

Charles Francis Ward, *The Salt War of San Elizario (1877).* Unpublished M.A. thesis, The University of Texas, 1932.

Owen P. White, *Out of the Desert. The Historical Romance of El Paso.* The McMath Company, El Paso, 1924.

I began studying the Salt War in 1933 when it was still possible to talk to men who had lived through it. I had their own stories from Jesus Montes of San Elizario; Francisco Gonzalez, Clemente Candelaria, Refugio and Jesus Rodela of Ysleta; Mrs. Isabel Kelly Fineau and her sister Mrs. Joe Silva who grew up in San Elizario. Miss Grace Long, Mr. G. N. Phillips, and Mr. Cleofas Calleros, specialists in El Paso history, helped in many ways. Miss Josefina Escajeda, a native of San Elizario, shared her knowledge of the background and interviewed several old timers on special points—especially Jesus Montes and J. D. Ponder. W. H. Burges and Major Richard Burges opened their libraries and their store of information. Mr. J. J. Fountain of Los Angeles lent me his unique file of the Mesilla *Independent* for 1877-1878. Mrs. Lillian Hague Corcoran of El Paso helped with time, encouragement, and an intimate personal acquaintance with early El Paso.

Several of these men and women are no longer with us, but I shall always feel a living sense of gratitude to them for their help and counsel.

The most useful source for the study of the Salt War will always be House Executive Document No. 93, 45th Congress, *El Paso Troubles in Texas* (E.P.T. in the notes), which contains depositions and correspondence from everybody the investigating committee could get to testify. Intelligent and thorough use of this material, with a great deal more, has been made by Charles F. Ward. What I have been able to add is talks with the old men of the El Paso region and investigation of newspaper sources—particularly a hitherto unavailable file of the only newspaper published in the Valley in 1877—the Mesilla *Independent*.

MAN FROM MISSOURI

1. Ward has put together Howard's biography before he came to Texas, p. 32 ff.

2. Galveston *News,* Oct. 16, 1877.

3. E.P.T., p. 65 (Stine).

4. *Ibid.,* p. 59.

5. *Ibid.,* p. 125.

6. Ward, p. 35, assembles family legends about Howard's marksmanship; Galveston *News,* Oct. 16, 1877, adds details.

7. E.P.T., pp. 52-53; Thomlinson, pp. 21-22.

8. Rippy, pp. 296-310.

9. The Valley, its people, and its history: E.P.T., pp. 50 (Hague to Hatch), 125 (Blacker), 3 (Dunn); Ward, pp. 1-18; Hughes, pp. 315-323.

10. E.P.T., p. 68.

11. *Ibid.,* p. 54.

12. For Mexican democracy see E.P.T., p. 70 (Blanchard on the *junta*), p. 100 (Agaton Porras, "the people are the law"), p. 122 (Allen Blacker on the "right to rise").

SALT TROUBLE

13. Discovery, development, and effect of the salt: E.P.T., pp. 65 (Ortiz), 105 (Miller), 127-129 (Fountain), 69-70 (Blanchard), 100 (Aranda). Fountain's account is the fullest. He thought the lakes were discovered in 1862. In his newspaper (The Mesilla *Independent*) he often recurs to the question (e.g., Oct. 6, 1877).

14. Facts about Cardis: E.P.T., pp. 52 (Zabriskie to Hatch), 65 (E. Stine— an adverse judgment); Austin *Weekly Statesman,* July 20, 1876 (Legislative Directory, Representatives); Galveston *News,* Oct. 16, 1877 (personal descrip-

tion); and Mills, *Forty Years,* p. 142.

15. Twitchell, vol. 2, p. 495, has a sketch of Fountain.

16. G. N. Phillips, Cleofas Calleros, Jesus Montes, and Josefina Escajeda told me about Father Borrajo.

17. The Fountain-Mills trouble: *Forty Years,* pp. 111-116; Austin *Weekly Republican,* June 15, Sept. 29, 1869; *Flake's Semi-Weekly Bulletin,* Aug. 9, Oct. 11, 1871 (plots against Mills); *Weekly Republican,* Dec. 1, 1869 (bitter attack on Fountain); *El Paso. A Glance at Its Men and Contests* (Mills' pamphlet attacking Fountain); *Weekly Republican,* July 20, 1870 (Fountain's acquittal); *Semi-Weekly Bulletin,* Dec. 20, 1871; *Flake's Daily Bulletin,* March 13, 30, 1872; San Antonio *Express,* Jan. 17, 30, May 30, 1872.

18. E.P.T., pp. 127-129.

RISING TEMPERATURES

19. San Antonio *Herald,* Nov. 19, 1872.

20. *Ibid.,* Dec. 17, 1872.

21. Mesilla *Independent,* Nov. 3, 1877.

22. Austin *Daily Statesman,* Dec. 9, 1874.

23. Dallas Weekly *Herald,* April 8, 1874.

24. Long, p. 115.

25. Ward, pp. 34-35.

26. Austin *Weekly Statesman,* June 28, 1877.

27. E.P.T., p. 65 (E. Stine) mentions the beginning of the breach.

28. Mesilla *Independent,* Oct. 6, 1877.

29. Austin *Daily Statesman,* March 28, 1874.

30. E.P.T., pp. 122-123 (Allen Blacker).

31. Austin *Weekly Statesman,* April 6, 1876.

32. E.P.T., p. 65 (E. Stine); Ward, p. 36.

33. E.P.T., pp. 120-121 (B. S. Dowell and Miguel Garcia), p. 96. (J. N. Garcia testifies that he was offered inducements to kill Howard).

34. Interview with Clemente Candelaria, Jesus Rodela and Refugio Rodela, July 21, 1934. Refugio was eighty years old at this time.

35. E.P.T., pp. 67-68.

ACTION AT SAN ELIZARIO

36. Mesilla *Independent,* Dec. 29, 1877.

37. Mrs. I. K. Fineau and Mrs. Joe Silva told me about the old residents.

38. Atkinson's political activities: Mills, *Forty Years,* pp. 117-118 (he was Mills' bitter enemy); *Flake's Semi-Weekly Bulletin,* Aug. 9, 1871; E.P.T., p. 66 (Stine on his disposition).

39. Mesilla *Independent,* Nov. 3, 1877.

40. Interview with Jesus Montes, son of Telesforo, July 21, 1934; E.P.T., p. 66

(E. Stine), p. 70 (Blanchard), p. 77 (Kerber); *Report of the Secretary of War for 1878,* p. 53.

41. E.P.T., pp. 98-99 (Father Bourgade's account), p. 66 (E. Stine); Letter from Corporal Matthews to the Mesilla *Independent,* Feb. 2, 1872.

42. E.P.T., pp. 120-121 (B. S. Dowell), pp. 69-70 (Blanchard), p. 71 (Clark).

43. E.P.T., p. 106 (G. N. Garcia), p. 118 (Kerber and Blanchard); Mesilla *Independent,* Oct. 6, 1877 ("Howard's Statement").

44. Not to be confused with Captain Gregorio Garcia, who appears later, or with County Commissioner J. N. Garcia.

45. E.P.T., p. 106 (G. N. Garcia), p. 151 (Kerber to Steele), pp. 71-72 (Cobos).

46. *Ibid.,* p. 54.

47. *Ibid.,* p. 59 (Wesley Owens).

48. Mesilla *Independent,* Oct. 6, 1877 ("Howard's Statement").

49. E.P.T., p. 151.

50. *Ibid.,* p. 107 (G. N. Garcia).

51. Mesilla *Independent,* Oct. 6, 1877.

52. E.P.T., p. 99 (Bourgade), p. 107 (Garcia).

53. *Ibid.,* p. 152 (Kerber to Steele).

54. Ward, pp. 52-53, quotes the telegram. The line was extended to El Paso about this time. See the *Independent,* Nov. 10, 1877.

55. E.P.T., pp. 141-142 (Blacker to Hubbard).

56. *Ibid.,* p. 142 (Steele to Hubbard).

57. AGF, Cardis to Hubbard.

58. Mesilla *Independent,* Oct. 6, 1877.

DEATH OF A CHIEFTAIN

59. E.P.T., p. 113 (G. W. Wahl).

60. *Ibid.,* p. 62.

61. *Ibid.,* p. 59.

62. Depositions describing the killing are in E.P.T., pp. 59-64.

63. Oct. 13, 1877. The file belongs to Jack Fountain of Los Angeles, son of Col. Fountain, the publisher.

64. E.P.T., pp. 59-64 (H. H. Harvey).

65. *Ibid.,* p. 62.

66. *Ibid.,* p. 56.

67. *Ibid.,* p. 64.

A JOB FOR THE RANGERS

68. E.P.T., p. 14 ("Final Report"), pp. 55, 58 (Blair), p. 145 (Atkinson).

69. *Ibid.,* p. 143; Austin *Daily Statesman,* Nov. 4, 1877.

70. E.P.T., pp. 100, 102, 154.

71. Atkinson's letter is in the AGF, quoted by Ward, pp. 65-66.

72. Jones at San Elizario: E.P.T., p. 155 (telegram, Jones to Hubbard), pp. 99-100 (Bourgade), p. 26 (Jones' "Minority Report"); Galveston *News,* Dec. 20, 1877.

73. E.P.T., p. 155 (telegrams, Jones to Steele).

74. For Tays see E.P.T., pp. 139-140 (testimony of citizens); MacCallum, pp. 32-33, 41; Galveston *News,* Dec. 20, 1877.

75. Ward, p. 74; AGF, Howard to Jones.

76. E.P.T., p. 80 (Magoffin).

77. AGF, Tays to Jones.

SHOWDOWN

78. The raid on the salt: E.P.T., p. 73 (V. Garcia), pp. 130-131 (Magoffin), p. 126 (Blacker).

79. Quoted by permission of Judge Hague's daughter, Mrs. Lillian H. Corcoran.

80. AGF, Bourgade to Jones; Ward, p. 85.

81. E.P.T., pp. 55, 108 (Tays).

82. *Ibid.,* pp. 78-79, 144, 149.

83. *Ibid.,* p. 54 (Dowell).

84. Father Bourgade (E.P.T., p. 100, tells about events at San Elizario).

85. Francisco Gonzalez, interview; E.P.T., p. 98 (J. N. Garcia). Jesus Montes told me about Angela.

86. E.P.T., p. 109.

87. Blair's conduct: E.P.T., pp. 55-57 (his own statement), pp. 101-102 (opinions of various citizens); *Report of the Secretary of War for 1878,* p. 52.

NOW IS THE TIME

88. Ellis's fate: E.P.T., p. 66 (E. Stine on his enemies), pp. 80-81 (Tays), pp. 97-98 (J. N. Garcia's letter to the *Independent*). Sergeant Matthews, *Independent,* Jan. 5, 1878, says they caught Ellis listening. The issue of Dec. 12 tells "How They Died."

89. Jesus Montes knew about Carrasco.

90. E.P.T., pp. 31-32 (J. N. Garcia, Tays, and Ball).

91. Mrs. I. K. Fineau and Mrs. Joe Silva knew Salcido.

92. E.P.T., p. 81 (Tays).

93. J. D. Ponder, interview with Josefina Escajeda.

94. E.P.T., p. 81 (Tays).

95. *Ibid.,* p. 81; Mesilla *Independent,* Jan. 5, 1878.

96. Captain Blair (E.P.T., p. 57) estimates the casualties.

97. Mrs. Marsh and Loomis: E.P.T., pp. 81, 114-115.

98. E.P.T., p. 58 (Blair), p. 81 (Tays).

99. Mesilla *Independent,* Jan. 5, 1878. Other details of the surrender: E.P.T., p. 82 (Atkinson's part), pp. 102-103 (J. K. Ball's story), p. 73 (Vidal Garcia's).

100. E.P.T., p. 98 (J. N. Garcia).

101. After the surrender: Mesilla *Independent,* Jan. 5, 1878 (Matthews' account); E.P.T., p. 57 (Blair).

SUDDEN DEATH

102. The executions: Mesilla *Independent,* Jan. 12, 1878 (J. N. Garcia); E.P.T., p. 74 (Mary Antonia Cooper), pp. 97-98.

103. E.P.T., pp. 30, 74, 78-79, 98. Major Jones estimated the loss.

104. Issue of Jan. 5, 1878.

105. Release of the Rangers: E.P.T., pp. 82, 113, 158; AGF, Tays to Jones, quoted by Ward, p. 118.

106. Troop movements: E.P.T., p. 148 (telegrams), p. 28 (Jones's "Minority Report"), pp. 146-150 (official communications); *Independent,* Dec. 22, 1877.

107. E.P.T., pp. 78-79, 83-95, 113-117, 145, 149.

108. Mesilla *Independent,* Jan. 5, 1878.

109. *Report of the Secretary of War for the Year 1878,* p. 51.

110. E.P.T., pp. 86, 94, 102-103, 112.

111. Proceedings of the Board: E.P.T., pp. 1-33.

112. Feeble attempts of U. S. officials to recover property and to punish the thieves: E.P.T., pp. 29-30, 124-125, 132-138.

113. Ward, p. 145, has collected facts about indictments and rewards.

7. BOOTS AND SANDALS

The Laredo riot caused considerable excitement and was covered in great detail by the newspapers, particularly the San Antonio *Express* (April 8, 9, 10, 11, 13, 1886) and the Galveston *News* (April 2, 8, 9, 10, 13, 15, 16). A fine study of the whole affair has been made by Seb S. Wilcox of Laredo for the *Southwestern Historical Quarterly* ("The Laredo Election Riot"), July, 1941. Mr. Wilcox used the San Antonio and Galveston papers, the Laredo *Times,* transcripts of testimony from the Webb County records, and his own expert knowledge of the background. This chapter could not have been written without his essay. The part played by the Army is sketched in Don Russell's *One Hundred and Three Fights and Skirmishes The Story of General Reuben F. Bernard,* reprinted from the Cavalry Journal, Washington: U.S. Cavalry Association, 1936.

1. Wilcox, p. 8.
2. *Ibid.,* p. 4: The population of Laredo had passed 8000 by 1886, four-fifths being of Latin origin.
3. Judge Harbert Davenport, interview, Brownsville, Aug. 13, 1944.
4. Galveston *News,* April 15, 1886.
5. Wilcox, p. 6.
6. Galveston *News,* April 15, 1886.
7. *Ibid.,* April 2, 1886.
8. Wilcox, p. 8.
9. Galveston *News,* April 15, 1886.
10. *Ibid.*
11. *Ibid.*
12. Wilcox, p. 10.
13. See Wilcox, p. 10, for a reproduction of the funeral notice and the translation quoted here.
14. Galveston *News,* April 8, 15, 1886.
15. *Ibid.,* April 8, 1886.
16. Wilcox, p. 12.
17. *Ibid.,* p. 14.
18. Galveston *News,* April 15, 1886.
19. San Antonio *Express,* April 11, 1886; Wilcox, pp. 16-17.
20. Wilcox, p. 15.
21. Galveston *News,* April 9, 1886.
22. Wilcox, p. 20.
23. AGF.

8. A FEUD FOR MISS SUE PINCKNEY

Elizabeth Brooks, *Prominent Women of Texas.* The Werner Company, Akron, Ohio, 1896 (Biographical sketch of Miss Sue Pinckney).

Glynn Austin Brooks, *A Political Survey of the Prohibition Movement in Texas.* Unpublished M.A. thesis, The University of Texas, 1920.

F. B. Chilton, compiler and publisher, *Unveiling and Dedication of Monument to Hood's Texas Brigade on the Capitol Grounds at Austin, Texas, Thursday, October Twenty-seven Nineteen Hundred and Ten.* Privately published, Houston, 1911. (Material on John Pinckney and Groce Lawrence.)

John McPherson Pinckney Memorial Addresses, Fifty-Ninth Congress, First Session, House of Representatives, April 29, 1906. Government Printing Office, 1907.

Susan Shubrick Pinckney (Miss McPherson), *Douglas: Tender and True.* The Nixon-Jones Company, St. Louis, 1892.

—. *In the Southland* (containing "Disinherited," and "White Violets"). The Neale Publishing Company, New York and Washington, 1906.

—. *Darcy Pinckney*. The Neale Publishing Company, New York and Washington, 1906.

C. L. Sonnichsen, "Miss Sue Pinckney and Her Private World." *Southwest Review*, vol. xxix, No. 1, Autumn, 1943, pp. 80-92.

Frank Edd White, *A History of the Territory that Now Constitutes Waller County Texas, from 1821 to 1884*. Unpublished M.A. thesis, The University of Texas, 1936.

Mrs. George Scott of Houston, Miss Sue's niece, has her scrapbooks and other unpublished material (much was destroyed at her death), which has been graciously placed at my disposal. The Adjutant General's files in the State Library at Austin contain some pertinent matter.

"We have lived all that down now," says "Miss Matt" (Mrs. J. J.) Crook about the Hempstead troubles, but she doesn't mind talking ancient history with anyone interested. To her and to Miss Barbara Groce I am grateful for hospitality and friendship. I owe much also to Mrs. R. E. Tompkins, the late Mr. John C. Amsler, and Mr. J. L. Foster of Hempstead; to Mr. Wally Ward of Dallas, Mrs. Loula Dixon and Mrs. Nellie Mahan of El Paso (all former residents of Hempstead), and to Mr. and Mrs. George Scott of Houston.

1. Mrs. R. E. Tompkins, interview, Hempstead, Texas, June 30, 1943. Mr. Tompkins told the story to her as they too started for the courthouse.

2. For more on this subject see C. L. Sonnichsen, "Miss Sue Pinckney and Her Private World."

3. Information about Miss Sue comes from Mr. and Mrs. George Scott (interview, July 2, 1943); Mrs. M. T. Crook, Miss Barbara Groce and others (June 29, 30, and later interviews); Elizabeth Brooks, "Miss Sue Pinckney."

4. *In the Southland* and *Darcy Pinckney*.

5. *Darcy Pinckney*, pp. 146, 246.

6. *Douglas: Tender and True*, p. 203.

7. *In the Southland*, p. 54.

8. *Darcy Pinckney*, p. 133.

9. *Ibid.*, p. 112.

10. Miss Sue's scrapbooks, in the possession of Mrs. George Scott, contain a full account of this episode written by Thomas S. Pinckney himself.

11. Mr. and Mrs. George Scott, interview.

12. *Douglas*, p. 144; *Darcy Pinckney*, p. 378.

13. *Darcy Pinckney*, p. 154.

14. Mr. and Mrs. George Scott, interview.

15. *Darcy Pinckney*, p. 291; *Douglas*, p. 118; *In the Southland*, p. 139. There

is some question about who turned Lee's horse back. See F. B. Chilton, p. 175; *Pinckney Memorial Resolutions* (Address of John N. Garner), p. 44.

16. Mr. and Mrs. George Scott, interview.

17. "Stories of Pinckney," Galveston *News,* April 26, 1905.

18. *Pinckney Memorial Resolutions,* p. 32.

19. Wally Ward, interview, Dallas, Texas, June 11, 1944.

20. An account of one of Dick Pinckney's adventures during a Negro riot appeared in the Bastrop *Advertiser,* May 17, 23, 1884.

21. Hempstead's early history is fully covered by White.

22. White, p. 120 ff.

23. Galveston *News,* July 6, 1888; Mrs. M. T. Crook, interview.

24. Galveston *News,* Sept. 4, 7, 8, 11, 1888 (trials of McDade and Springfield); interviews with Mrs. M. T. Crook, Wally Ward, and J. C. Amsler.

25. Galveston *News,* Nov. 27, 28, 30; Dec. 2, 1888.

26. Wally Ward, J. C. Amsler, Mrs. M. T. Crook, interviews.

27. Mr. and Mrs. George Scott, interview.

28. *Pinckney Resolutions,* p. 40 (Mr. Beall of Texas).

29. Mrs. R. E. Tompkins, interview. Mrs. Tompkins went along on this trip, as did Miss Sue's nephew, Tom Scott.

30. Galveston *News,* April 12, 13, 15, 1904.

31. White, p. 120. Since the passage of the Terrell Election Law in 1903, "the negro vote in Waller County has not been a controlling factor."

32. Hempstead *News,* Jan. 27, 1905

33. Mr. and Mrs. George Scott, interview.

34. Especially in "White Violets" (*In the Southland,* p. 86).

35. For the background of the Prohibition Movement in Texas see Glynn Austin Brooks. Galveston *News,* April 25, 1905, covers happening in Hempstead.

36. Hempstead *News,* March 31, April 7, 14, 21; Mrs. M. T. Crook, interview.

37. The case against J. H. Lipscomb, who became sheriff, took two years to decide. It went to the State Supreme Court, which finally ruled in favor of Lipscomb's opponent, Perry (Hempstead *News,* Oct. 26, Nov. 9, 23, 1906).

38. Assisting Mrs. Zehner was Rev. Granville Jones. Cyclone Davis and a colored lecturer, Mrs. Peterson, also appeared (Hempstead *News,* April 21, 1905).

39. John C. Amsler, interview.

40. Galveston *News,* April 26, 1905; Houston *Post,* April 25, 1905; Hempstead *News,* April 26, 1905.

41. The Houston *Post* scored a beat on the Hempstead story and gave it front-page display on April 25 and 26, 1905.

42. Mr. and Mrs. George Scott, among many others, are convinced that there was somebody in the jury boxes.

43. Hempstead *News,* April 28, 1905.
44. *Ibid.,* April 28, 1905; Galveston *News,* April 27, 1905.
45. Mr. and Mrs. George Scott, interview.

9. THE FEUD AT MITCHELL'S BEND

The important documents for the study of the Truitt-Mitchell affair include only two books—Thos. T. Ewell, *A History of Hood County,* The Granbury *News,* Granbury, Texas, 1895; and Henry C. Fuller, *A Texas Sheriff,* Baker Printing Co., Nacogdoches, Texas, 1931. More of the story can be learned from court records, especially 'from the criminal files of Shelby County at Center and of Cherokee County at Rusk. The Rusk papers contain a very illuminating correspondence between Judge Tom Davis, A. J. Spradley, A. L. Truitt, Julia Truitt Bishop, and others. Methodist Conference records in the School of Theology at Southern Methodist University are also useful. Unfortunately for history, the Hood County Courthouse burned in 1875, destroying all official papers which would have thrown light on the beginning of this feud. As a result the first part of the tale had to come from the old men.

In the summer of 1944 I browsed around Granbury and Timpson, where stories of the feud are still alive. I talked to D. C. Cogdell, ninety-five years old at that time but clear in his memory, to H. W. Henslee, a friend of the Mitchells, and to Ashley Crockett (only surviving grandson of the immortal David), who knew both sides—all three long-time residents of Granbury. Suggestions came also from Ernest (Bull) Adams of Glen Rose and from C. H. Rhodes of El Paso, an old Hood County boy.

In Timpson I have pleasant memories of an afternoon with Mr. W. H. Whitton (ninety-eight years old with recollections of Sam Houston) and his daughters Miss Hazel Whitton and Mrs. Lela Haggerty. Messrs. Molloy and Winfree, publishers of the Timpson *Daily Times,* kindly allowed me to search their old files. Thanks go also to Mr. Giles Haltom of Nacogdoches, who once employed Julia Truitt Bishop and knew Jim Truitt; to the Rev. Charles F. Smith of Houston and Mrs. John H. Warnick (Librarian of the S.M.U. School of Theology) for help in locating the Methodist Conference Records; and to Herbert Morgan for trusting me with his copy of Ewell's *History of Hood County.*

1. Austin *Daily Statesman,* Oct. 31, 1874 (quoting from the Granbury *Vidette*): "There has been a continuous stream of immigrants passing through town all week. . . . It would seem as if the entire population of the United States was moving to Texas."
2. H. W. Henslee, interview, July 19, 1934.

3. Mr. Henslee says a brother older than Bill had already left home. Jim was twenty-three years old in 1874. Bill was twenty-four.

4. Background on the Truitts and the Mitchells is from Mr. Henslee and Mr. Crockett, interviews, July 19, 20, 1944.

5. Conference Records in the Library of the Theological School, Southern Methodist University, Dallas.

6. Dallas *Weekly Herald,* March 20, 1875.

7. *Ibid.,* April 7, 1874; Ewell, p. 132.

8. Austin *Weekly Statesman,* April 7, 1874.

9. Dallas *Weekly Herald,* April 11, 1874.

10. Henslee and Crockett give the Mitchell version of the fight.

11. Austin *Daily Statesman,* Dec. 16, 1874; Dallas *Weekly Herald,* Dec. 12, 1874.

12. San Antonio *Herald,* Oct. 16, 1875.

13. Ashley Crockett, interview.

14. San Antonio *Herald,* Oct. 16, 1875.

15. Ashley Crockett, interview.

16. D. C. Cogdell (interview, Granbury, July 19, 1944) saw the hanging and hoped he might never see another.

17. Ewell, p. 132.

18. Ashley Crockett, interview.

19. *A Texas Sheriff,* p. 25.

20. H. W. Henslee, interview.

21. Spradley to T. C. Davis, Feb. 29, 1908, filed with papers in Criminal Case 3558, District Clerk's Office, Rusk, Texas.

22. *A Texas Sheriff,* p. 28.

23. Spradley to Davis, Jan. 5, 1908.

24. Giles Haltom of Nacogdoches knew Mrs. Truitt and both her husbands. She once wrote for Brann's *Iconoclast* and had a long career in newspaper work before her death in New Orleans.

25. *A Texas Sheriff,* p. 19.

26. Galveston *News,* July 22, 24, 1886.

27. *A Texas Sheriff,* p. 28, and correspondence in the Cherokee County courthouse at Rusk, especially T. C. Davis to the Sheriff of Kinney County, Feb. 8, 1908, and Spradley to T. C. Davis, Feb. 29, 1908.

28. Timpson *Times,* April 1, 1907.

29. *A Texas Sheriff,* p. 32; Timpson *Times,* April 1, 1907.

30. Timpson *Times,* Aug. 15, 1907.

31. *Ibid.,* Sept. 12, 13, 1907.

32. *Ibid.,* Nov. 4, 1907.

33. H. W. Henslee, interview.

34. *Ibid.*

35. Alfred Truitt's letter, dated Nov. 15, 1907, is in the files at Rusk, Case 3558.

36. Letter dated Jan. 13, 1908, in the file at Rusk. Davis tried unsuccessfully to get Spradley a commission as a Special Ranger for the sake of the expense money (Davis to A. L. Truitt, Nov. 20, 1907; Davis to Spradley, Nov. 20, 1907, Jan. 13, 1908). Davis sent instructions to Spradley on Jan. 28, 1908.

37. Case 3558, Rusk County. The affidavit about Bill's bronchitis is there also.

38. *Ibid.*

10. A GENTLEMAN FROM PECOS

1. The late Mrs. E. O. Lochausen lived in Pecos for many years and had vivid recollections of Miller, as has her daughter, Mrs. R. B. Kimbrough, of Anthony, New Mexico.

2. El Paso *Times,* July 17, 1910.

3. *Ibid.*

4. Jack Martin, *Border Boss* (The Naylor Company, San Antonio, Texas, 1942, pp. 150-154), tells a good deal about Miller, including Captain Hughes' part in his arrest. Dee Harkey in his book *Mean as Hell* (The University of New Mexico Press, Albuquerque, 1948) says the charge was stealing a pair of mules.

5. El Paso *Times,* July 17, 1910.

6. *Ibid.*

7. Recollections of Mrs. Lochausen.

8. *Mean as Hell,* p. 176; El Paso *Times,* April 13, 1894.

9. William A. Keleher, *The Fabulous Frontier,* The Rydal Press, Santa Fe, New Mexico, 1942, p. 79, quoting eighteen *Texas Appeals Reports,* p. 232.

10. *Mean as Hell,* pp. 17-18.

11. El Paso *Times,* Aug. 20, 1895.

12. *Ibid.,* Oct. 2, 1895; District Court Minutes, El Paso County, vol. 8, p. 425, Case 1789; District Court Minutes, Mitchell County, vol. 1, p. 305, Case 1110 (courtesy of H. A. Pond).

13. Galveston *News,* Sept. 15, 1896; El Paso *Times,* July 17, 1910; recollections of Mrs. E. O. Lochausen.

14. Reminiscences of Mrs. Lochausen.

15. *Mean as Hell,* p. 175.

16. *Ibid.,* p. 104.

17. El Paso *Times,* May 19, 1897, July 17, 1910.

18. *Mean as Hell,* p. 177.

19. Eastland County records show that Miller was indicted in March, 1897, tried for the first time in June, 1897, and last in January, 1899.

20. *The Fabulous Frontier*, p. 80.

21. *Ibid.*

22. *Mean as Hell*, p. 178.

23. *Ibid.*, pp. xi, 175.

24. *Border Boss*, p. 150; *Mean as Hell*, p. 180; Charles A. Siringo, *Riata and Spurs*, Houghton Mifflin Company, Boston, 1931, pp. 215-218; *The Fabulous Frontier*, p. 78.

25. *Mean as Hell*, p. 180.

26. Texas and Oklahoma papers for March 1 and April 10, 1909, cover the last chapter of Miller's life. See also *Mean as Hell*, pp. 181-182.

27. Galveston *News*, April 20, 1909.

28. *Ibid.*

29. *Ibid.*, April 21, 1909.

30. *Mean as Hell*, p. xi.

EPILOGUE:

TEXANS WILL FIGHT ABOUT ANYTHING

1. Galveston *News*, Oct. 11, 1867. The author, who signed himself "Lunar Caustic," dated his contributions from Concrete College, a pioneer educational institution which has long since disappeared.

2. J. B. Cranfill, *Dr. J. B. Cranfill's Chronicle. A Story of Life in Texas Written by Himself about Himself.* Fleming H. Revell Co., New York, 1916, p. 314.

3. Galveston *Civilian*, May 20, 22, 1872.

4. *The Western Chronicle* (Sutherland Springs), April 12, 1878.

5. Galveston *News*, July 3, 1878.

6. *Ibid.*, Sept. 10, 1878. Black was acquitted at Wallisville, and Walker's case, set at San Antonio in March, 1879, is said never to have been called. The minutes of the 37th District Court, Case of Andrew Walker, No. 16208, indicates that the trial was scheduled, but the papers are not available.